D1126631

Modern Linguistics

Modern Linguistics

The Results of Chomsky's Revolution

Neil Smith and Deirdre Wilson

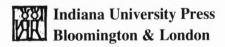 Indiana University Press
Bloomington & London

Copyright © 1979 by Neil Smith and Deirdre Wilson

All rights reserved

No part of this book may be reproduced or utilized in any form
or by any means, electronic or mechanical, including photocopying
and recording, or by any information storage and retrieval system,
without permission in writing from the publisher. The Association
of American University Presses' Resolution on Permissions constitutes
the only exception to this prohibition.

Manufactured in the United States of America

Library of Congress Cataloging in Publication Data

Smith, Neil.
    Modern linguistics.

    Bibliography: p.
    Includes index.
        1. Linguistics.   2. Language and languages.
    3. Chomsky, Noam.   I. Wilson, Deirdre, joint author.
    II. Title.
    P121.S58   410   78-20405
    ISBN 0-253-19457-1 (previously published by Penguin
    Books under ISBN 0-14-02.2069-0)

P
121
S58
C.1

To Saras Smith and Theodore Zeldin

734801

Contents

8   Contents

Introduction

The publication of Noam Chomsky's *Syntactic Structures*, in 1957, marked the start of a revolution in linguistics. The effects of that revolution are still being worked out. One immediate result was that linguistics began to be of interest to philosophers, psychologists and logicians; this was largely because Chomsky was proposing to draw conclusions from the nature of language to the nature of the human language-user – conclusions which directly contradicted assumptions currently being made in philosophy and psychology, and which seemed to warrant serious consideration by philosophers and psychologists. Our main purpose in writing this book has been to give our own account of these conclusions.

Chomsky was not the first to set up links between linguistics and human psychology. However, he was probably the first to provide detailed arguments from the nature of language to the nature of mind, rather than vice versa. Before Chomsky, assumptions about psychology had often influenced assumptions about language: since Chomsky, the influence has been largely in the other direction, with arguments about the form of language being used to justify conclusions about human psychology. We might here contrast Chomsky directly with John Locke, whose account of linguistic knowledge was a special case of his account of knowledge in general; or with Leonard Bloomfield, the major figure of the American structuralist school which preceded Chomsky's, who allowed then current psychological dogma to influence his account of linguistic knowledge and language use. This reversal of the relationships between linguistics, psychology and philosophy has been one of Chomsky's main contributions to the field.

In writing this book, we had to make two choices. First, how much attention should we give to Chomsky's immediate precursors and his present rivals: should this be a book based on historical comparisons? Second, how much should we try to give a historical treatment of the development of Chomsky's own thought? In particular, there have been substantial changes in Chomsky's technical analyses of individual points of grammar over the past twenty years, and we could have spent a lot of time criticizing each individual argument in his overall framework and tracing its development. In both cases, we have deliberately decided to avoid historical and comparative treatment as much as possible. The reason for this is that we believe Chomsky's main contribution has been as a system-builder, who has constructed a complete picture of the nature of language and of the language-user. It is the consistency and power of his overall framework, rather than the individual arguments which make it up, that we feel makes Chomsky's work revolutionary. Many other linguists have equalled Chomsky in particular technical insights. Many philosophers and psychologists have put forward coherent views on the nature of human beings. However, no other thinker has managed to combine the two in such a way that his views on human beings can be used to reinforce his views on language, and his views on language in turn support his theory of psychology. It is some idea of this total framework that we have tried to present here.

Because Chomsky's thought is constantly developing, there is no one place to which the reader can be referred for his definitive views on language. We should emphasize that this book is not designed as a definitive summary of Chomsky's views. What we have tried to do is present a picture of language as *we* see it, largely under Chomsky's influence. For this reason, we have felt free to depart from some of Chomsky's published views in cases where we disagreed with them, or to suggest innovations which we felt would improve the overall theory. We have also used or adapted many arguments and examples due to colleagues in the field: in general, we have not directly attributed these arguments in the text, but have mentioned their sources in the further reading for each chapter, given at the end of the book.

It should also be emphasized that we have not tried to provide a detailed linguistic analysis of English. We have given a large number of illustrations from all levels of language, but we do not intend our descriptions to be exhaustive or definitive. The examples used are meant to show what sort of facts the theory accounts for. It should be possible in principle to extend such examples to cover a wider and deeper area, but we have concentrated on the conclusions we can draw from our examples, rather than on the data *per se*.

We would also like to point out that the analyses and examples we have provided are crucial to the understanding of the book, and the theory, as a whole. They are not meant to be skipped over: by thinking over them carefully, the reader should be able to reconstruct for himself the conclusions that we have drawn from them, and, in certain cases, to provide further evidence that would either support or refute these conclusions. To make reading as easy as possible, we have defined each technical term as it is introduced, and provided a glossary at the end of the book, in which these definitions are summarized.

We would like to express our thanks and appreciation to all those who have helped to make this book possible. Our greatest intellectual debt is obviously to Noam Chomsky. Although we have not set out to write a work of straightforward exegesis, what we have written would not have been possible without him. Many friends and colleagues have read some or all of the manuscript at varying stages of its production, or have discussed with us problems arising from it. We are particularly grateful to John Lyons, who made detailed comments on an earlier draft, and to Geoff Pullum: both of them saved us from numerous infelicities, mistakes and oversimplifications. We would also like to thank Janina Giejgo, Dick Hudson, Yamuna Kachru, Ruth Kempson, Judy Klavans-Rekosh, Dan Sperber, Julia Vellacott and Theodore Zeldin for their comments, help and advice. We are afraid to say that we have not always followed the suggestions made, and any mistakes that remain are our responsibility alone.

1. What is a Language?

At different times, different features of language have struck people as particularly significant, typical or worthy of attention. Any system as complex as a human language is bound to lend itself to a variety of independent approaches. For example, languages are used to communicate; one obvious line of research would be to compare human languages with other systems of communication, whether human or not: gestures, railway signals, traffic lights, or the languages of ants and bees. Languages are also used by social groups; another line of research would be to compare languages with other social systems, whether communicative or not: economic, political or religious, for example. Again, languages change through time: comparison of languages with other evolutionary systems, organic and inorganic, might also be pursued. While all of these approaches have undoubted appeal, there is an obvious logical point to be made: one must be able to describe a language, at least in part, before going on to compare it with other systems.

It seems to us that there is no way of describing or defining a given language without invoking the notion of a linguistic rule. If this is true, it is clearly important, since by investigating the nature and variety of linguistic rules we may be able to provide quite detailed evidence about points of comparison between human languages and other systems. It is for this reason that we have chosen to spend our first chapter justifying the claim that a language is definable in terms of a set of rules, arguing against some alternative conceptions of language, and examining the nature and status of linguistic rules.

Linguistic Rules

Within modern linguistic theory, to claim that a language is rule-governed is to claim that it can be described in terms of a grammar. A grammar is conceived of as a set of rules which have two main tasks. They separate grammatical from ungrammatical sentences, thus making explicit claims about what is 'in the language' and what is not. They also provide a description of each of the grammatical sentences, stating how it should be pronounced and what it means. In other words, linguistic rules are not just the isolated and scattered maxims we memorized at school ('Prepositions are things you shouldn't end sentences with'); they combine with each other to form a system – a grammar – which gives an explicit and exhaustive description of every sentence which goes to make up a language. Throughout the book, we shall use 'grammar' to mean a set of rules with this dual function.

It is easy to see that speakers of a language often behave as if their language were rule-governed. Fluent speakers may nonetheless make mistakes in speaking, and when they do, they have no hesitation in correcting themselves. Utterances like (1) and (2), for example, are commonplace:

(1) The thought of those poor children were really . . . WAS really . . . bothering me.
(2) Even though they told me to, I didn't sit down and be quiet . . . WAS quiet . . . I mean I didn't sit down and I wasn't quiet.

Such examples give clear evidence that speakers have some means of distinguishing grammatical from ungrammatical sentences, and are prepared to correct their mistakes even when no threat to communication is involved.

It is also possible for a speaker to feel that others around him are making mistakes – although his willingness to correct them will, in many cases, be tempered by considerations of politeness at least. An English speaker who hears (3), for example, will probably agree with the message it conveys, regardless of whether he interprets it as (4a) or (4b):

(3) Ze pound are worthless.
(4) a. The pound is worthless.
   b. The pound is worth less.

However, he will simultaneously recognize that the pronunciation of *the* is incorrect, and that *are* should have been *is*. In other words, he knows not just *that* a mistake has been made, but also *what* the mistake is.

When speakers of two different dialects of English meet, each is likely to feel that the other is making some mistakes. Readiness to correct what sounds like a mistake is affected here, not just by considerations of politeness, but also by the fact that certain dialects are generally considered superior to others, so that speakers of standard dialects will be more likely to correct those of nonstandard dialects than vice versa. In any case, the speaker of standard British English who hears (5a) and (5b) is likely to feel that they are incorrect:

(5) a. Mr Zed's done gone mental.
   b. Lord God, I done made a mess.

In most cases, he could also supply the standard equivalents (6a) and (6b):

(6) a. Mr Zed has gone mental (mad).
   b. Lord God, I've made a mess.

Similarly, speakers of the dialect which permits (5a) and (5b) would regard (6a) and (6b) as needing some correction. This case seems to show, not just that speakers of a language possess a set of rules, but that not all speakers of a language possess the same set of rules. In fact, as we shall show in the next section, it is probably quite fair to say that no two speakers of a language possess exactly the same set of rules: in other words, the rules which adequately describe a language are not the simple, prescriptive maxims of the classroom, but a far more complex and subtle set of constructs.

The speaker who is willing to correct himself and others gives evidence that there is, for him, a right and a wrong way of saying things. However, it does not necessarily follow that in making these corrections he is applying a set of linguistic rules. He might, for example, be following a set of linguistic conventions, or habits, or customs, which he dislikes seeing disrupted. In claiming that a language is rule-governed, we are also claiming that languages are not definable in terms of linguistic habits, conventions or customs; to see why, it is necessary to look a little more closely at what linguistic rules, embodied in grammars, actually do.

So far, we may have seemed to imply that a grammar simply provides a means of registering and correcting mistakes. This copy-editing function is an important one; however, grammars are also concerned with the description of sentences which contain no mistakes at all. As mentioned earlier, a grammar must provide a means of associating each sentence of a language with its correct pronunciation and meaning. Now speakers of a language are capable of pronouncing and understanding sentences which they have never heard before. For example, many readers of this book will be encountering at least one of the following for the first time:

(7) a. I can see a robin pecking around the ashes of the bonfire.
　　b. Would you let us have poached egg for elevenses please, Mummy?
　　c. If you tell that joke again I shall divorce you.

However, none of these sentences is likely to present the slightest difficulty of understanding. It follows that one's ability to understand a sentence does not depend on custom, convention or habit, all of which would imply that repeated encounters with a sentence would be necessary before its correct interpretation could be established. Neither the ability to recognize a sentence as grammatical, nor the ability to produce or understand it, seems to depend on prior encounters in this way.

Conventions are social constructs: it takes at least two people to establish and operate a system of conventions. Rule-systems, on the other hand, could easily be constructed and operated by a single individual. There exist two main types of case where single individuals do seem to operate their own private linguistic rules: the case of children learning their first language, and the case of adults with idiosyncratic speech patterns. Both provide arguments against linguistic conventions, and in favour of linguistic rules.

Children learning their first language seem to construct rules for themselves – but they often get them wrong: they produce utterances which are ungrammatical from the adult point of view. The sentences in (8), produced by a three-year-old, are examples; the adult equivalent is given on the right:

(8) a. What that was? [What was that?]
   b. Where it is? [Where is it?]
   c. Where Amahl can write?[1] [Where can Amahl write?]

That many children pass through a similar phase is not surprising, since they will have heard adult sequences exactly parallel to their own, as in (9), for example:

(9) a. I don't know *what that was*.
   b. Tell me *where it is*.
   c. I think that is *where Amahl can write*.

However, the fact remains that the child who says one of the sentences in (8) is using a different grammatical rule from those of the adults around him, and which he seems to have made up for himself.

Another case where the child's system may differ from the adult's is when the child has learned a linguistic rule, but has not yet learned that it has exceptions. On the analogy of (10), for example, children regularly produce forms such as those in (11):

(10) a. I talked, he danced, she moved, they waited, etc.
    b. One car, two cars; an elephant, lots of elephants, etc.

1. *Amahl* is the name of the child speaking.

(11) a. I comed, John runned, they singed, she teached me, etc.
    b. Two sheeps, lots of tooths, some mouses, etc.

In other words, the child has overgeneralized the rules for regular past-tense and plural formation to cases where in the adult system they do not apply. This again indicates that the child makes up rules of his own, which only he actually follows.

The number of verbs with an irregular past tense, and of nouns with exceptional plurals, is rather small: the resulting overgeneralizations are hardly surprising. However, children seem able to construct generalizations, make up rules, on the basis of extremely limited data. For example, *in newen times* for *nowadays* has been found on the sole analogy of *in olden times*, and *twoth* and *threeth*, with the sense of *second* and *third*, have been recorded from a child who could only count up to four. Moreover, examples of this kind are not limited to word-formation. On the analogy of such regular adult examples as (12), children will frequently supply the missing fourth item in (13):

(12) a. Pick the book up.
    b. Pick it up.
    c. Pick up the book.
(13)   Pick up it.

(13) is, of course, ungrammatical from the adult point of view, and the child is most unlikely ever to have heard it. Other examples of the creative use of language by children provide further evidence of their ability to control regularities: the following pairs were all taken from children aged between two and three:

(14) a. Pick me up. (and when the adult obliges)
    b. Pick me down.
(15) a. Plug the light in.
    b. Plug the light out.
(16) a. Amahl wakened up. (raising his head from the pillow)
    b. Amahl wakened down again. (putting his head back on the pillow)

Perhaps the clearest example, and the one most frequently commented on, is provided by the two-year-old who on seeing his uncle for the first time asked his mother:

(17) *What*'s that, Mummy?,

using *what* as a cover term for both humans and things. Two days later he was addressing his uncle as 'Mummy'.

As a last example of how children construct rules for themselves, consider the following solution to the problem of how to pronounce long words with an unstressed initial syllable, taken by one three-year-old. Observing that many such words were complex, consisting of a prefix *re-* and a stem, he generalized this pattern to all of them, with the result that while *recorder* and *remember*, for instance, were pronounced correctly, the following forms – which he clearly could not have imitated from those around him – also occurred:

(18) attack –   pronounced *retack*
     disturb –   pronounced *resterve*
     elastic –   pronounced *relastic*
     enjoy –   pronounced *rejoy*
     guitar –   pronounced *retar*
     conductor – pronounced *reductor* etc.

On this occasion, as on many others, the child's hypothesis is wildly out, but the regularity with which the forms appear shows that he is constructing rules. That they are the wrong ones merely makes it more obvious that linguistic rules are not always shared rules, and that the child can operate a rule-system which diverges markedly from the systems of those around him.

Divergencies between rule-systems are not just found in the case of children who are still learning their language. Perfectly fluent adults may find idiosyncrasies in their own speech. The most common of these are in pronunciation and vocabulary. It seems clear that no two adults possess exactly the same set of vocabulary items, pronounced in exactly the same way. This is true of syntactic rules too. A very few readers may find that they regularly produce sentences like (19b), on the analogy of (19a) (as does one of the authors):

(19) a. He is happy, isn't he?
     b. I am happy, amn't I?

Others will find themselves reluctant to produce (19c), on the same analogy:

(19) c. He may leave, mayn't he?

Similar differences of opinion may arise over sentences like the following:

(20) a. What did you go out and do?
     b. What did you go out without doing?
     c. What did you go out before doing?
     d. What did you go out before you did?

Most people will find at least one of these sentences ungrammatical, but there may be disagreement about just how many should be rejected. These differences in rule systems do not appear to be geographically based, but they are nonetheless real. They indicate that languages are not entirely social constructs, possessed in the same form by all members of a social group, but that it is perfectly possible for an individual to possess a set of rules that he shares in its entirety with no one else.

A more extreme instance of adult idiosyncrasy is seen in the speech of people who have had a stroke, or have otherwise suffered damage to the brain, with resultant speech loss or aphasia. In fact the best defining criterion of aphasia is that the rules normally characteristic of speech have broken down, leading the patient to produce utterances which, depending on the severity of his case and the number and type of rules involved, may be complete nonsense (jargon), or merely inappropriate, e.g.:

(21) a. I was working with the shop is in the other room, dear.
     b. Have you got a match, I can't light my guitar. [=cigar]

In the case of (21b), we can recognize what should have been said, but in the case of (21a) it is clear that something has gone very seriously awry in the set of rules characterizing the linguistic system of the speaker.

What we have tried to show in this section is that a language is best described in terms of a grammar, or system of rules. For each speaker, there is a right and a wrong way of constructing and understanding sentences. This cannot be explained solely in terms of habit or custom, because of the case of novel utterances, which are produced and understood without having been heard before. It cannot be explained solely in terms of convention or social agreement, because each speaker has certain methods of construction and understanding which he shares with no one else. For the same reason, it cannot be seen as a prescriptive system, handed down by authority and imposed on each speaker from the outside. The only unitary way of describing the linguistic system of a speaker is to see it as governed by a set of rules which he may share, in part, with other speakers, but which he must ultimately have constructed for himself. We turn now to a closer examination of the nature and status of such rules.

The Psychological Reality of Rules

We have so far been assuming that speakers of a language actually know the grammars which they use in producing and understanding sentences, correcting mistakes, and so on. This assumption that speakers know grammars – usually expressed as a claim that grammars are *psychologically real* – pervades the whole of modern linguistic theory. Learning a language, as we have already seen, is equated with learning a grammar; knowing a language is equated with knowing a grammar. Linguistic differences between speakers are analysed as differences in their grammars. Linguistic change is analysed as the alteration of grammars through time. And a language itself is defined as the set of sentences described by a given grammar. Most of these definitions rest on the assumption that speakers actually know the grammar which describes their language: without this assumption, the postulation of grammars would contribute nothing to explaining linguistic behaviour.

Clearly, the knowledge that speakers have of their own grammars is not conscious knowledge. This is obvious enough in the case of adults, but even more so in the case of children, who are normally completely unaware of the way in which they form relative clauses, for example, or the conditions under which they would use the word *come* rather than *go*. The linguistic knowledge that speakers have is unfortunately unconscious knowledge: the job of the linguist is to attempt an explicit, conscious formulation of the grammatical rules that speakers know. Linguistics conceived of this way is concerned with one aspect of the human mind, and is therefore correctly classed as a branch of psychology.

Many people – most notably the philosopher Locke – feel unhappy about the idea of unconscious knowledge. These people have difficulty in explaining how speakers are able to produce, understand and form judgements about utterances that they have never heard before. The idea of a grammar which embodies the principles of sentence-formation and interpretation plays a crucial role in explaining how novel utterances are produced, understood and judged grammatical or ungrammatical. Someone who understands the principles of sentence-formation will be able to apply them to any sentence at all – even one he has never heard before. Someone who has no knowledge of such principles should not be able – as humans clearly are – to deal with utterances in this way. Moreover, those who believe that there is no such thing as unconscious knowledge have difficulty in explaining what goes on when an act of memory is performed. Memory is the classic case of unconscious knowledge: to remember something is to bring to consciousness an item of unconscious, stored knowledge. Thus it seems that, however repugnant the notion of unconscious knowledge may be, it is necessarily involved, both in linguistic and non-linguistic behaviour.

Sometimes those who object to the idea of unconscious knowledge and the notion of linguistic rules argue that novel utterances are produced and understood 'by analogy' to sentences one has already heard and understood. This does not, of course, solve the problem of how these latter sentences themselves were produced and understood; but it also raises the much more serious question of how speakers know which is the correct analogy to draw. The following sentences, for example, are both grammatical and similar in meaning:

(22) a. It is likely that John will leave.
    b. It is probable that John will leave.

By any normal notion of analogy, then, one might expect that (23a) and (23b) should also both be grammatical:

(23) a. John is likely to leave.
    b. *John is probable to leave.[2]

But of course (23b) is ungrammatical. This raises the whole question of how the *correct* analogy is determined; now the notion of 'correct analogy' seems itself to presuppose the existence of a set of rules distinguishing the correct from the incorrect analogies, returning us, by a slightly different route, to the idea of a grammar as a set of rules or principles for correct sentence-formation.

In looking at a set of linguistic facts, it is often fairly easy to find a pattern in them. For example, consider the following set of words from French:

une balle –	tennis ball
un ballon –	football
une bille –	billiard ball
une boule –	croquet ball
un boulet –	cannonball
une boulette –	meatball

It is tempting to see the striking regularity of the appearance of *b* and *l* in these words as indication of some fixed relation between the sound and meaning of French words for *ball*. This might in

2. From now on we shall follow the convention of indicating with an asterisk those sentences which we are judging ungrammatical.

turn have a natural historical explanation: for example if all the words evolved from a common root. However, if the job of the linguist is to reconstruct the grammar which speakers of a language actually know, it will be important for him to discover whether the patterns he finds are psychologically valid for speakers of the language, or whether they are there merely by accident or coincidence. The distinction between rule-governed regularities and fortuitous patterns in the language is usually treated in terms of a distinction between *accidental generalizations* and *significant generalizations*. The significant generalizations are those produced by the operation of rules; the accidental generalizations are the result of chance, or the effects of rules which applied at an earlier stage of the language, or of causes external to the language – anything except the operation of currently valid linguistic rules. Thus the search for linguistic rules has two aspects: first the search for patterns, and second, the rejection of those patterns which are judged accidental.

For example, there is a clear pattern in the occurrence of reflexive pronouns (*myself, herself*, etc.) in (24a–e):

(24) a. We washed ourselves.   *Ourselves washed us.
     b. John hurt himself.   *Himself hurt John.
     c. They surprised themselves.   *Themselves surprised them.
     d. Your argument refutes itself.   *Itself refutes your argument.
     e. You behaved yourself.   *Yourself behaved you.

The pattern might be expressed as follows: a reflexive pronoun is the direct object of a verb, and agrees in number, person and gender with the subject noun-phrase of the same verb.[3] The

3. In English, *number* involves a distinction between singular and plural: e.g. *I* versus *we*; *person* involves a distinction between speaker, hearer and a third party: e.g. *I* versus *you* versus *he*; *gender* involves a distinction between masculine, feminine and neuter: e.g. *he, she, it*. A *noun-phrase* is a group of words which contains a noun: e.g. *the little man*; the *subject* noun-phrase is normally the one which precedes the verb, and the direct object noun-phrase is normally the one which immediately follows it.

resulting generalization relates subjects, verbs and reflexive direct objects. Is this a significant generalization about English? A little consideration shows that it is an accident of the limited data considered in (24), and that a more adequate formulation would contain no reference to subjects and direct objects. For example, in (25) the reflexive pronoun is not a direct object:

(25) I talked to Mary about myself.

In (26), the reflexive pronoun does not agree with the subject:

(26) I talked to Mary about herself.

By considering (24)–(26), one might propose the following alternative generalization: a reflexive pronoun must agree in person, number and gender with *some* preceding noun-phrase. While this generalization is more adequate, consideration of still further data might show that it too was incorrect. For example, in (27a) the reflexive pronoun agrees with a preceding noun-phrase, but the result is ungrammatical; and in (27b) the reflexive pronoun agrees not with a preceding but with a following noun-phrase, and the result is nonetheless grammatical:

(27) a. *John said that himself was leaving.
   b. The story about himself that John told Mary was a pack of lies.

Gradual expansion of the data considered leads to successive rejection of accidental, incorrect generalizations and formulation of successively more adequate ones.

Cases like the above tend to show that it is easier to refute a proposed generalization than to show conclusively that it is correct. By the same token, it is easier to show that a proposed rule of grammar *cannot* be psychologically real than to show that it *must* be. Even when a proposed rule is consistent with all the data so far considered, there may be some further data not yet incorporated into the grammar which would either support it or conclusively refute it. One of the problems in writing grammars is thus to have some clear idea about the possible range of data which would have a bearing on the formulation of linguistic rules. The claim that rules of grammar are psychologically real extends the range of relevant data in important ways. For example, if rules are psychologically real, a consideration of how children learn them becomes relevant to decisions about their final form. If language change can be traced back to change in rules of grammar, then historical change in language may provide vital evidence about the form of rules before and after change. If dialect study is the study of similarity among grammars, then dialect comparison may provide valuable insights into the form of the grammars being compared; and finally if, as we shall argue, all languages are similar in certain respects, then even facts from totally unrelated languages may become relevant to the formulation of rules in a given language. Hence, although the claim that the rules of grammar are psychologically real is a strong, and seemingly unprovable one, it does allow for a considerable expansion in the range and type of data that become relevant to their formulation. We shall make use of this fact in later chapters.

In this section we have tried to show how the assumption that speakers of a language possess psychologically real grammars can be used to explain their command of language. The grammar that a speaker actually possesses will depend, at least in part, on the utterances he has heard in the past – mainly as a child learning his language for the first time. Since each speaker will have heard a different set of utterances, it is not surprising that he comes to possess a slightly different grammar from those of people around him. Strictly speaking, then, we cannot talk of *the* grammar of English, but only of the grammars of individual speakers of English.

However, what *is* surprising is how much agreement there is among the adult speakers of a language. We were able to assume, for example, that most of our readers would agree with our judgements about the grammaticality of the sentences in (24)–(27). In spite of the diversity of the utterances to which speakers are exposed in learning their language, there seems to be a remarkable similarity in the grammars which result from the learning process. Having emphasized the individual and idiosyncratic aspects of grammar, we now turn to its universal, common features.

Innateness and Universals

The work of Noam Chomsky, which provides one of the most coherent overall frameworks for the study of language ever seen, first came to the attention of the general public because, as part of that framework, he claimed that human beings were innately disposed to learn certain types of language. In other words, the languages that actually exist are the ones that children are predisposed to learn. This claim is supported by two further facts: first, that human languages do exhibit remarkable similarities; second, that children follow remarkably similar routes to learning the languages they learn. Both these facts would be explained on the assumption that children are innately equipped to learn only certain types of language, and that the form their linguistic development takes is genetically determined.

As an example of the similarities among languages, one might cite the two main strategies used in forming relative clauses. Certain languages, like English and French, use relative clause constructions like those italicized below:

(28) a. The man *that I saw* was your brother.
   b. I read the book *that you read.*
(29) a. L'homme *que j'ai vu* était ton frère.
   b. J'ai lu le livre *que tu as lu.*

Other languages, for example Hebrew, use relative clauses which contain an extra pronoun: translated into English, these sentences would look as follows:

(30) a. *The man *that I saw him* was your brother.
   b. *I read the book *that you read it.*

The fact that most languages tend to adopt one of these two

strategies for forming relative clauses is itself quite striking: logically speaking, there are thousands of alternative possibilities. What is even more striking is that languages which have opted for the same strategy as English and French usually turn out, on closer investigation, to possess traces of the Hebrew strategy too. So, for example, though standard French forms its relative clauses as in (29), many regional dialects of French adopt the Hebrew strategy. In these dialects, sentences like the following are perfectly grammatical:

(30) a. L'homme *que je l'ai vu* était ton frère.
   b. J'ai lu le livre *que tu l'as lu.*

Moreover, although so far as we know there are no regional dialects of English which adopt this same strategy, there are certain complicated (and strictly ungrammatical) sentences of English in which it sounds fairly natural: for example, the following:

(31) a. *That's the kind of answer *that, when you come to think about it, you find you've forgotten it.*
   b. *This is the sort of book *that, having once read it, you feel you want to give it to all your friends.*

To see that these sentences are indeed ungrammatical, one simply has to omit the parenthetical clauses:

(32) a. *That's the kind of answer *that you find you've forgotten it.*
   b. *This is the sort of book *that you feel you want to give it to all your friends.*

Clearly (32a) and (32b) are ungrammatical, and we would not want to incorporate into English grammar the principles of relative clause formation that they share with (31). However, it seems that this strategy of forming relative clauses by leaving in an extra pronoun is so powerful that even those languages, like English and French, which do not explicitly adopt it, nonetheless show traces of it in certain ways: in regional dialects of French, and in long and complex constructions of English. In other words, relative clauses seem to be formed on broadly similar lines in many entirely unrelated languages. The assumption that human beings are predisposed to construct relative clauses along these lines would explain this striking similarity among languages.

The evidence that all children learning a language pass through similar stages is also compelling. For example, children learning English pass through a stage of producing two-word utterances like the following:

(33) a. Daddy gone.
    b. Susie shoe.
    c. Mummy play.

In their earliest attempts to form negative sentences, they merely put a *no* or a *not* in front of a sentence:

(34) a. No Daddy come.
    b. Not Susie shoe.
    c. No Mummy play.

Later, they incorporate the *not* into a sentence before a verb:

(35) a. Daddy not come.
    b. Mummy not play.

Finally, the full complexity of the English verbal system is grasped, leading to the correct adult forms:

(36) a. Daddy didn't come; Daddy hasn't come; Daddy won't come.
    b. Mummy didn't play; Mummy isn't playing; Mummy mustn't play; etc.

As with many other cases of language learning that we have seen, the sentences in (33)–(35) could not have been directly imitated from anything the children had heard around them, since they are ungrammatical in adult English. The assumption that the child's linguistic development is predetermined from birth to follow certain patterns would provide an attractive account of the clearly parallel linguistic development shown by all normal children.[4]

The assumption that all languages are cut to the same pattern – that is, that there are *linguistic universals* – places an extra constraint on the search for linguistic rules. We have already argued for a distinction between accidental and significant generalizations, the latter being those that are psychologically real. We have also suggested that it is much easier to show that a proposed generalization is *not* significant than to show that it is. If there are linguistic universals, however, the domain of data that can be considered in formulating rules becomes much wider. First, a linguistic theory which incorporated explicit claims about the universal features of language would automatically disallow certain proposed rules as inconsistent with the known properties of language. Second, and more important, it would permit certain facts from other languages to have a bearing on – say – the formulation of the rule of relative clause formation in English, in the following way. Even though more than one possible generalization might be consistent with the facts of English, when relative clauses in other languages were considered, it might turn out that only one possible generalization was consistent with *all* the facts. If such a generalization could be found, and if it was of a type permitted or favoured by the theory of linguistic universals, then, within the framework we are considering, we would be justified in concluding that it was correct for English too. This is not, of course, to say that languages, like humans, do not have their own linguistic idiosyncrasies. However, it does say that even these idiosyncrasies will fall into universal patterns: languages do not vary without limit.

Those who have heard about the famous 'language-using' chimpanzees Washoe and Sarah sometimes feel that these animals pose some threat to the claim that humans are innately endowed with linguistic abilities. Although Washoe and Sarah do not speak, they have been taught to manipulate sign systems, and

4. For further discussion of how negatives are learned, and of the relevance of linguistic development to the theory of language, see Chapter 10.

use them to communicate with humans in a limited way. This is sometimes felt as a threat to man's linguistic uniqueness. In fact, the uniqueness issue, unlike the innateness issue, seems to us to be entirely trivial. From the fact that human beings can be taught to construct bird's-nests, it may follow logically that bird's-nesting is no longer unique to birds; and from the fact that chimpanzees can be taught to communicate with a humanly constructed linguistic system, it may follow that human language is not unique to man. We do not see these conclusions as particularly exciting, either for bird-fanciers or for linguists. However, from the fact that humans can be taught to build bird's-nests, it does *not* follow that birds are not innately programmed to build them; and from the fact that chimpanzees can be taught to talk, it does *not* follow that human beings are not innately programmed to learn and use languages. It is the genetic issue which seems to us to be interesting, and we return to it in our next chapter. On the subject of talking chimpanzees we shall have nothing more to say.

In this chapter, we have tried to give the following picture of a human language. It is a rule-governed system, definable in terms of a grammar which separates grammatical from ungrammatical sentences, assigning a pronunciation and a meaning to each grammatical sentence. This grammar is, in a minor sense, a construct of the linguist, in that linguists do attempt to construct grammars. However, in a much more important sense it is the construct of the child who has learned it, and the adult who knows it. We have expressed this as the claim that grammars are psychologically real. Each person has his own grammar – which is likely to change through time, and to differ in certain respects from the grammars of other speakers of the language. However, every grammar will have certain things in common with every other grammar, as a result of genetic constraints on the ability of human beings to learn languages. We have expressed this as the claim that all languages have an innately determined and universal structure. In the next chapter, we look a little more closely at what knowledge of language actually involves.

2. Knowledge of Language

In the last chapter, the crucial connection we attempted to establish was between knowing a language and knowing a grammar. In this chapter we attempt to clarify the relation between knowledge and language from two quite different directions. First, we want to distinguish between two types of knowledge, linguistic and non-linguistic (and hence between two types of rules, linguistic and non-linguistic); second, we want to distinguish between knowledge of rules and the exercise of that knowledge (and hence, between knowing a language and speaking or understanding it). Our main purpose is to give a general idea of the range and type of facts which fall within the domain of a grammar: of the facts that can be handled by linguistic rule, and those that cannot.

Linguistic and Non-linguistic Knowledge

Granted that a human being can have knowledge at all, it seems obvious that this knowledge can be classified in various ways. One such classification would involve separating linguistic from non-linguistic knowledge. Following Chomsky, we want to argue that such a classification is not only possible but correct: that it is not just imposed by the analyst, but has a basis in human mental organization. In other words, language, though only one among many cognitive systems, has its own principles and rules, which are different in kind from those governing other cognitive systems, and for this reason must be studied separately.

This is one of the claims which most sharply distinguishes Chomsky from others who have thought seriously about the nature of language. While it is a commonplace to say that language is specific to humans, part of the human essence, what crucially distinguishes man from beast, most linguistic theorists have been extremely cautious about concluding from this that humans must have a specific genetic endowment for language-learning. They attempt instead to explain the acquisition of language in terms of whatever general learning theory they espouse. If they believe that knowledge in general is acquired by observation and generalization, then they will claim the same for language. If they believe that knowledge is generally acquired by some form of conditioning, then they will claim the same for language. If they think that knowledge is best analysed as a disposition to behave in certain ways, then they will claim that knowledge of language is best analysed as a disposition to behave linguistically in certain ways. Language will thus be seen as acquired in the course of general intellectual development, and no language-specific endowment, apart from general intelligence and the ability to learn, will be needed for its acquisition. It is clear, though, that there is an alternative to this position. Language may be *sui generis*, different in kind from other cognitive systems, requiring different learning strategies and different genetic programming. The two claims reinforce each other: if linguistic knowledge is different in kind from non-linguistic knowledge, then it is more likely that we need special programming to learn it; and if we have such special programming, then it is more likely that the result of language-learning *will* be different in kind from other systems not so programmed.

There are a number of rather obvious points that support the special-programming view of language acquisition, and disconfirm the general-intellectual-ability approach. If we measure general intellectual development in terms of logical, mathematical and abstract-reasoning powers, these powers are still increasing at puberty, when the ability to acquire native fluency in a language is decreasing rapidly. A child of eight who can beat an eighteen-year-old at chess is something of a prodigy; if an eighteen-year-old acquires native fluency in a language as quickly as an eight-year-old, simply by being exposed to it, and without any formal training, it is the eighteen-year-old, not the eight-year-old, who is the prodigy. If it is thought unfair to compare linguistic skills with powers of abstract reasoning in this way, the point has already been granted: there is a difference between mathematical and linguistic abilities: linguistic knowledge can be distinguished from other types of knowledge, which depend on different intellectual endowments, and are acquired at different rates.

Particularly striking evidence for this mismatch between linguistic and general cognitive abilities comes from the case of the American girl Genie. Genie was discovered in Los Angeles in 1970, at the age of thirteen; she had been kept locked up in conditions of severe sensory deprivation from infancy. In particular, she had heard virtually no speech throughout the period in which children normally learn their first language. Despite this horrifying background, Genie's intelligence turned out to be within normal limits in essential respects, and thus her progress with language learning provides a useful basis for comparison with the language acquisition of more ordinary children. Her early language acquisition was typical of all children in that it passed through stages of one-word, two-word, three-word and then four-word utterances; however, Genie's three- and four-word utterances typically displayed a cognitive complexity not found in the early speech of normal children, and her vocabulary was much larger than that of children at the same stage of syntactic development. In general, her ability to store *lists* of words is very good, but her ability to learn and manipulate rules has been minimal. This is reflected in the fact that whereas the 'two-word' stage lasts for about two to six weeks with normal children, with Genie it lasted over five months:

e.g. Doctor hurt.
　　Like mirror.

Moreover, the kind of early negative structures which most two-to-three-year-old children use for a few weeks, where the negative element is initial in the sentence, still persisted with

Genie some one and a half *years* after she had first learned to use negatives:

> e.g. No more ear hurt.
> No stay hospital.
> Not have orange record.

Indeed, no syntactic rule which is normally taken to involve the *movement* of a word or phrase from one point in a sentence to another (cf. Chapter 4 for examples) has been consistently mastered by Genie as yet. But in contrast with this slow and partial linguistic progress, Genie's intellectual development appears to be progressing extremely rapidly, and to be approaching the normal for her age.

It seems, then, that language-learning abilities are not only different in kind from other intellectual abilities, but that they also become considerably impaired at a time when other intellectual abilities are still increasing. People who retain these language-learning abilities after puberty are as rare as infant mathematical prodigies. One reason for being interested in linguistic knowledge is thus for the light it might shed on human linguistic programming. If it is reasonable to suspect that such programming exists, then one obvious way of investigating it would be to examine the result of language acquisition – linguistic knowledge – and work out what principles would be needed to acquire it. And since the argument works two ways, someone who is not convinced that any linguistic programming exists might become convinced of its necessity simply by examining the contents of linguistic knowledge and asking himself how they could have been arrived at: could they have been acquired by 'general intellectual reasoning' or all-purpose learning strategies?

One common objection to this programme is that it is not always obvious where the line between linguistic and non-linguistic knowledge should be drawn. In fact some people would want to argue that no such line exists: that all knowledge involves both linguistic and non-linguistic aspects. For example, in order to know that children enjoy games – clearly not the sort of knowledge we would want to record in a grammar – one might nevertheless have to know the meanings of the words *children*, *enjoy* and *games*, and how to combine them into a meaningful sentence. On the other hand, in order to know that *giraffe* is a noun – clearly an item of knowledge that we would want to record in a grammar – one might nevertheless have to have some exposure to the use of English in general; and it is not, practically speaking, possible to acquire such knowledge without having some knowledge of the outside world. Hence, the argument goes, there is no clear-cut division between linguistic and non-linguistic knowledge, or between knowledge of a grammar and knowledge of the world.

This argument is not really sound. It is perfectly possible to distinguish the contents of knowledge from the preconditions for acquiring it. Thus, in order to know the laws of physics, one must be able to breathe: it does not follow that physics cannot be distinguished from human biology. There may be linguistic preconditions for acquiring knowledge of the world, and non-linguistic preconditions for learning a language: this in no way shows that knowledge of language cannot be distinguished from knowledge of the world.

In fact the notion of linguistic knowledge that we shall adopt is a quite narrow and exclusive one, in the sense that not even all knowledge about language is to count as linguistic knowledge. The principle behind this decision is as follows: knowledge about language which is merely a special case of some wider generalization about human beings does not count as linguistic knowledge. Knowledge about language which does *not* emerge as a special case of some wider generalization about human beings is the only knowledge that we are prepared to call linguistic. This of course makes the theoretical distinction between linguistic and non-linguistic knowledge – the claim that language is *sui generis* – true by definition; however, it still leaves open the empirical question of whether anything actually satisfies our definition of linguistic knowledge.

As an example of knowledge about language which does not count as linguistic knowledge in our sense, consider the following.

Most linguists have a stock of odd items of knowledge about various languages: that Japanese has the verb in sentence-final position, that Turkish exhibits vowel-harmony, that Latin has no definite article, and so on. This knowledge seems rather clearly to be encyclopedic, of the same type as knowledge that France is a republic, that the capital of Italy is Rome, and that elephants are found in India. Given the capacity to acquire the latter type of knowledge, one should automatically be able to acquire the former; no special abilities would be required.

Similar remarks apply to certain types of knowledge that native speakers have about their own language. For example, most native speakers of English can recognize the social or regional origins of others on the basis of linguistic cues such as accent, intonation, choice of words and syntactic constructions. They can also recognize such things as colloquial, formal, deferential and authoritarian styles of speech, they can tell whether a particular remark is socially or factually appropriate, literally, sarcastically, humorously or otherwise figuratively intended. Although there are certainly rules and principles which make such judgements possible, and which deserve investigation in their own right, we do not want to say that these judgements are evidence of linguistic knowledge, in our sense. The reason for this is that each such principle seems to be a special case of a more general principle which applies to human non-linguistic behaviour too. For example, one can often tell someone's national, regional or social origins by the way he walks, or his gestures, or his clothes, or his facial expressions, as well as by the way he speaks. There are formal, deferential and authoritarian styles of behaviour as well as speech – and like language they vary from culture to culture. There are constraints of appropriateness, sincerity, politeness, clownishness and so on on behaviour, as well as speech. In general, then, we would expect the principles behind all these aspects of language-use to fall together with other human social and behavioural principles, and to be in no way *sui generis*.

Strictly linguistic knowledge, then, will reduce to knowledge of those principles of sentence-construction and interpretation which do not fall together with wider generalizations about human non-linguistic behaviour. Consider, for example, the claim already mentioned, that children pass through regular stages in learning a language. This would be explained on the assumption – which is not specific to language-learning – that there are degrees of complexity in the material to be learned, and that the simplest material is learned first. What *is* specifically linguistic is not the assumption that the learning process passes through successively more complex stages: it is the definition of linguistic complexity itself. Thus there is no generally observable reason why *Not Johnny go* is simpler than *Johnny not go*. The fact that children tend to learn the former before the latter indicates quite strongly that there is a notion of linguistic complexity which does not follow from general cognitive principles – which is specific to language alone and therefore part of linguistic knowledge as we are defining it. The remainder of this chapter, and indeed of this book, is devoted to giving further examples of strictly linguistic knowledge, and to discussing techniques for studying it.

Intuitions

A native speaker of English has at his disposal a vast amount of fairly uncontroversially linguistic knowledge. For example, he knows when two words rhyme; he knows when two sentences are paraphrases; when a single sentence has two different meanings; when a change in word order results in a change of meaning, and when it merely results in ungrammaticality. We have argued that the aim of writing grammars is to give a full account of all these facets of linguistic knowledge. How do we go about doing this?

Because, as we have already seen, linguistic knowledge lies well below the level of consciousness, direct questioning of speakers of a language is likely to yield little reliable information about their linguistic knowledge. If we approach a native speaker of

English and ask him whether (1) and (2) have the same syntactic structure, there is not the slightest chance of predicting what he will say:

(1) I'm leaving, for he makes me nervous.
(2) I'm leaving, because he makes me nervous.

He may have his own consciously worked out grammatical theory, or he may have no conscious idea of syntactic structure at all. In either case, there is no particular reason for believing the answer that he actually gives us, and his knowledge of language will have to be investigated by rather more indirect means.

Whatever their conscious views on grammatical theory, most native speakers will be able to provide us with evidence of the following kind: they will be able to tell us that each of the following sentence pairs has one grammatical member and one ungrammatical one:

(3) a. It was because he was nervous that he left.
    b. *It was for he was nervous that he left.
(4) a. Because he makes me nervous, I'm leaving.
    b. *For he makes me nervous, I'm leaving.
(5) a. Did you leave because he made you nervous?
    b. *Did you leave for he made you nervous?
(6) a. I left, because I was nervous and because I wanted to go.
    b. *I left, for I was nervous and for I wanted to go.
(7) a. Maria, who left because I made her nervous, is returning today.
    b. *Maria, who left for I made her nervous, is returning today.

The native speaker of English clearly has some linguistic knowledge which enables him to distinguish *for*-clauses from *because*-clauses, in spite of their similarity in meaning. An adequate grammar must provide some way of replicating this linguistic knowledge. For our present purposes it is not the actual rules which explain the speaker's linguistic judgements that are of interest. What *is* interesting is that such judgements give us good ground for imputing a particular type of linguistic knowledge to the speaker: in this case, knowledge of syntactic structure.[1]

What we have just been suggesting is that one good way of investigating linguistic knowledge is to ask the native speaker for judgements about the sentences of his language: not directly, by asking 'Which of these is a subordinate clause construction?', but indirectly, by eliciting a range of judgements about, say, grammaticality, ungrammaticality, paraphrase and ambiguity, and then constructing a set of rules which will account for these judgements. The relevant judgements are generally called *intuitions*. It is often felt, by both philosophers and linguists, that reliance on native-speaker intuitions is an extremely suspect part of Chomskyan theory: intuitions are 'unscientific', not amenable to direct observation, variable and untrustworthy. It seems to us that this is not a valid theoretical objection: discovering linguistic rules seems to us exactly analogous to discovering the rules of an invented, uncodified children's game by asking the children concerned whether certain moves are permissible or not, good moves or not, dangerous or not, and so on. How else would one go about discovering unwritten rules?

This is not to say that there are not considerable practical difficulties in deciding how much reliance should be placed on native-speaker intuitions on any given occasion. Consider, for example, a fairly uncomplicated sentence with more than one meaning:

(8) I like Indians without reservations.

A speaker presented with a questionnaire in which he sees (8) divorced from any context, and given a limited amount of time to decide how many meanings it has, might well be unable to produce more than the following two:

1. In fact, the relevant distinction seems to be that between subordinate and co-ordinate clauses. *For, and* and *but* all link co-ordinate clauses, of roughly equal importance. *Because, although* and *when* introduce subordinate clauses which are in some sense dependent on the main clause which precedes or follows them. It is the fact that co-ordinate clauses have very limited freedom of movement, compared with subordinate clauses, which explains the differential patterns in (3)–(7).

(9) a. I have no reservations in my liking for Indians.
   b. I like Indians who don't live on reservations.

Given more time, and perhaps some contextual guidance, he might have noticed that there is a further possible interpretation along the following lines:

(9) c. I like Indians without reservations (about appearing in cowboy films).

Or he might have noticed another alternative:

(9) d. I like Indians without reservations (for seats on the first scheduled flight to the moon).

And there may be still more possibilities. While this indicates that any judgement that (8) has only two interpretations must certainly be set aside, it does not indicate the total unreliability of intuitions. When shown the interpretations in (9a–d), most speakers of English would indeed agree that each was a possible interpretation of (8), and given a suitable context of utterance, most speakers would probably arrive at these interpretations for themselves. In other words, these examples merely indicate that the use of questionnaires is not likely to be a very reliable method of studying linguistic knowledge.

In a similar way, initial judgements about grammaticality, or about the literal interpretation of unambiguous sentences, may well have to be set aside in the light of further investigation. For example, quite often a sentence like (10) will be either judged ungrammatical or wrongly interpreted when heard out of context, even by perfectly competent speakers of English:

(10) The train left at midnight crashed.

Where it is wrongly interpreted, it will be taken to mean the same as (11) or (12):

(11) The train which left at midnight crashed.
(12) The train left at midnight and crashed.

A little thought or prompting, however, should lead to a re-evaluation. First, (10) is perfectly grammatical. Second, it means not (11) or (12) but (13):

(13) The train which was left at midnight crashed.

An exactly parallel structure which presents no difficulties of interpretation would be (14):

(14) The baby abandoned at midnight cried.

We would thus, on consideration, not want to write a grammar which would disallow (10), or interpret it as (11) or (12), even though we can elicit speakers' judgements which would initially support this treatment.

Examples like (10) seem to show that the relation between knowing the grammar of a language and actually producing or understanding utterances may be rather indirect. The grammar of the language, and the speaker of the language on mature consideration, associate (10) with the meaning in (13). However, the speaker's first reaction when presented with (10) out of context, is to associate it with the meaning in (11) or (12). This seems to indicate that the speaker who misunderstands (10) has used something other than the rules of his grammar in arriving at his interpretation. Again, as long as he can be brought to see the correct interpretation, there is no reason why this sort of case should lead to scepticism about the validity of intuitions as a guide to linguistic knowledge: but it does emphasize that intuitions do not give us direct insight into the form of linguistic knowledge, and should be treated with corresponding caution.

The reason why (10) causes difficulties of interpretation, while (14) does not, seems to be that in (10) the sequence *the train left at midnight* could itself stand as a complete (and plausible) sentence, and is initially perceived and interpreted accordingly, with wrong results. The corresponding sequence in (14), *the baby abandoned at midnight*, could not itself be a complete sentence, so that (14) is not misleading in the same way. In other words, speakers of English seem to use the following strategy for analysing complex sentences: 'Take the first sequence of words which sounds like a complete (and plausible) sentence, and interpret it *as* a complete sentence.' This strategy leads, as we have seen, to a misanalysis of (10). Now though this strategy seems to play a genuine part in the interpretation of utterances, we would not want to call it a rule of grammar, since it can so clearly lead to wrong results. What this suggests is that speakers invent short-cuts to the analysis of utterances, by-passing the rules of grammar which they also know, gaining speed but occasionally losing accuracy as a result. Such short cuts are occasionally referred to as *perceptual strategies*: strategies used in the perception (understanding) of utterances; we shall have more to say about them in the next section.

The well-known and deceptively innocent reviewer's comment in (15) is another case where the English speaker's initial interpretation turns out, on closer examination, to be incorrect:

(15) This is a book you must not fail to miss.

At first sight, one is tempted to equate it with (16):

(16) This is a book you must not fail to read.

It is only on closer inspection that it turns out to mean (17):

(17) This is a book you must on no account read.

The problem here seems to be not syntactic, as with (10), but rather semantic or logical: sentences containing a combination of semantically 'negative' items are notoriously difficult to understand, and (15) contains *not, fail* and *miss*, in the space of four words. It is arguable that people who hear sentences like (15) and (16) do not give them a serious linguistic analysis at all: they simply guess what the speaker would be most likely to want to say, and interpret accordingly. In the absence of clues to the speaker's intentions, the process of working out what has actually been said is an exceedingly laborious one, often involving paper and pencil analysis, as the reader of (18) may check for himself:

(18) Common courtesy is a virtue that few people would fail to forget unless not specifically forbidden to do otherwise.

Again, this argues for caution in dealing with initial interpretations of certain types of sentence, and for a distinction between the speaker's perceptual or understanding abilities and his actual knowledge of the language. It is to this latter distinction between knowledge of a language and the exercise of that knowledge that we turn in the next section.

Competence and Performance

Many of the examples we have used in these first two chapters have required assessment on two quite different levels. First, do they conform to the principles for correct sentence-formation in standard English: are they *grammatical*? Second, on an actual occasion of utterance, how appropriate, felicitous or comprehensible would they be: are they *acceptable*? The first level of assessment is a purely linguistic one: the second involves knowledge and abilities that go well beyond the purely linguistic. Within Chomskyan theory, the first is called the level of *competence*, the speaker's knowledge of language, and the second is called the level of *performance*, the speaker's use of language. The study of competence, then, is the study of grammars which are psychologically real, and which contain all the linguistic knowledge, whether innate or acquired, possessed by a given speaker of the language. Such grammars are often referred to as *competence models*. The study of performance, by contrast, is concerned with the principles which govern language use: here such dimensions as appropriateness to context, ease of comprehension, sincerity, truth and stylistic euphony all play a part. Moreover, a *performance model* would have to include, as a competence model would not, some account of the principles by which sentences are actually produced and understood – and hence occasionally misproduced or misunderstood. Like the notion of intuition, the competence–performance distinction seems to us a theoretically valid one, although like the notion of intuition, it raises certain practical difficulties which we shall continue to illustrate in the course of this book.

Up till now, we have been able to refer indifferently to the objects of linguistic investigation as either *sentences* or *utterances*. In fact, along with the distinction between competence and performance, grammaticality and acceptability, comes a parallel distinction between sentence and utterance. Sentences fall within the domain of competence models; utterances within the domain of performance models. Sentences are abstract objects which are not tied to a particular context, speaker or time of utterance. Utterances, on the other hand, are datable events, tied to a particular speaker, occasion and context. By contrast, sentences are tied to particular grammars, in the sense that a sentence is not grammatical in the absolute, but only with respect to the rules of a certain grammar; utterances, however, may cross the bounds of particular grammars and incorporate words or constructions from many different languages, or from no language at all. Given a bilingual English-French speaker and hearer, (19) might be a perfectly acceptable utterance, although it could never be a grammatical sentence:

(19) [*]John's being a real idiot – I suppose cela va sans dire.

In other words, acceptable utterances need not be the realization of fully grammatical sentences.

There are also grammatical sentences which can never be realized as fully acceptable utterances. This may be because of their semantic, syntactic or phonological content. Thus (20) would be unacceptable in most contexts because it would patently label its speaker as insincere:

(20) Your hat's on fire, though I don't believe it.

It is perfectly easy to see what this sentence is claiming: it is not even claiming anything contradictory, since it is perfectly possible for people to make assertions which they do not in fact believe. What is not legitimate, as a matter of human behaviour, is to behave insincerely while explicitly drawing one's audience's attention to the fact. In other words, the oddity in (20) is a performance matter rather than a fact of language. (21) would also be unacceptable in most contexts, this time because of its extreme syntactic complexity:

> (21) If because when Mary came in John left Harry cried, I'd be surprised.

It is possible, on closer examination, to see that (21) is quite regularly formed according to standard principles of English.[2] However, its syntactic complexity is such that normal speakers would have some difficulty in unravelling its message. Again, this indicates that the oddity in (21) is a performance matter, traceable to whatever principles hearers use in utterance comprehension, rather than a matter of linguistic competence. Finally, (22) would also be unacceptable to many hearers, this time for phonological reasons:

> (22) We finally sent an Edinburgh man, for for four Forfar men to go would have seemed like favouritism.

There is nothing wrong with the syntax or semantics of (22): it is just that the accidental accumulation of *for* sounds makes it seem like a joke or a play on words, and diverts attention from the intended message.

To say that there is a distinction between competence and performance is not to deny that there is an intimate connection between the two. Perceptual strategies are often based on rules of grammar, and, if they are used often enough, may themselves actually *become* rules of grammar. For example, the perceptual strategy mentioned in the last section: 'Treat the first string of words that *could* be interpreted as a sentence, as being a sentence, and interpret accordingly', is ultimately based on the organization of English grammar. English has a number of ways of showing the start of a subordinate clause: the relative pronouns *who* and *which*, and the complementizer *that*, are the most common.

---

2. The structure of (21) is as follows: If A happened, I'd be surprised. A = Because B happened, Harry cried. B = When Mary came in, John left.

Where these devices are used, the perceptual strategy just mentioned will be inoperative, as in (23):

(23) The train which left at midnight crashed.

Thus, when the subordinating devices are omitted, the hearer has a certain right to assume that no subordinate clause is involved: hence the existence of the perceptual strategy. As we have seen, the principles of English grammar are such that this perceptual strategy will occasionally lead to a misinterpretation; nonetheless it is the principles of English grammar which originally gave rise to the perceptual strategy itself.

Conversely, what started out as a perceptual strategy may become so entrenched in the use of language that it gives rise to a rule of grammar. For example, the complementizer *that* which marks the start of a subordinate clause may optionally be omitted in a great many cases, as shown in (24) and (25):

(24) a. I believe that John left.
     b. I believe John left.
(25) a. I told Mary that Bill was sorry.
     b. I told Mary Bill was sorry.

One of the few places where it may never be omitted is when it introduces a subordinate clause at the very beginning of a sentence: compare (26a) and (26b):

(26) a. That John should have left upset me.
     b. *John should have left upset me.

There seems to be no doubt that (26b) is actually ungrammatical, and that English therefore contains a rule of grammar which forbids deletion of a sentence-initial *that*. Returning now to our perceptual strategy, notice that it would invariably lead to a misanalysis of (26b), since the string of words *John should have left* can stand as a sentence on its own, and would thus be taken as the main clause of (26b). Forbidding the deletion of the *that* in (26a) thus guarantees that there will be no wrong application of the perceptual strategy in this case: *That John should have left* cannot stand as a sentence on its own, and hence cannot be treated by the perceptual strategy mentioned. In this case, the rule of grammar is based on the existence of the perceptual strategy, and is designed to prevent its misapplication. Thus there is a clear interaction between rules of grammar and perceptual strategies, either one being capable of giving rise to the other.

Given that there is such a close connection between rules of competence and perceptual strategies, there have been those who are prepared to argue that any clear-cut distinction between the two is impossible to draw. For example, it might be possible to argue that there is not a distinction between competence models and performance models, but merely between more and less abstract rules of performance, each of which has its part to play in the full production and understanding of utterances. And in general, it might be possible to argue that the difference between linguistic and other principles, or linguistic and other rules, is not one of kind, but merely one of degree.

While this is a perfectly reasonable alternative to the view of language that we have been, and shall be, presenting, it is not one we shall pursue ourselves. Our main reason for this is that we have never seen a fully coherent outline of a theory based on a single notion of performance, which could account in an adequate way for the facts which can be accounted for in terms of the competence–performance distinction. Returning to an example used in the previous chapter, we have argued that, however easy it is to produce and understand, (27) is actually ungrammatical: it is not formed according to established principles of English grammar:

(27) *This is the sort of book that, having once read it, you feel you want to give it to all your friends.

If we incorporated the principles used to form (27) into English grammar, they would immediately give rise to the clear ungrammaticality of (28):

(28) *This is a book which I gave it to my friend.

In other words, whatever it is that makes (27) sound natural, it is not, and cannot be, a linguistic rule. It seems to us important that linguistic theory should be able to make this sort of distinction, and we see no way of drawing it without making use of a distinction between competence and performance, language knowledge and language use.

What we have tried to do in this chapter is present a particular view of how knowledge of linguistic rules interacts, on the one hand, with other types of knowledge, and on the other hand with principles of utterance-production and comprehension. The picture that emerges is complex. Firstly, presented with a particular item of knowledge, we must be prepared to argue about how it should be classified, and we have outlined some arguments which might be used. Where the knowledge can be classified as linguistic, then we claim that it forms part of a grammar – a competence grammar – which incorporates linguistic rules. Secondly, presented with a set of judgements about a sentence – how it should be interpreted, how it relates to other sentences, how it is pronounced – we must be prepared to argue about whether these judgements give direct insight into the competence grammar, or whether the judgements themselves must be set aside, or treated as evidence about performance models rather than grammar. Again, we have outlined some arguments which might be used. Where the judgements do not give direct insight into the competence grammar, we may find that they give us clues to the sort of principles used in utterance-comprehension, which are themselves valid objects of study. However, in general it seems to be both correct and interesting to regard the rules of language as separate from those of other cognitive systems, and to regard knowledge of these rules as only indirectly reflected in linguistic behaviour.

In the next chapter, we take a closer look at the types of linguistic knowledge which the competence grammar is designed to describe, bearing in mind that our ultimate interest is in justifying the claim that such knowledge is different in kind from other types of knowledge available to humans.

3. Types of Linguistic Knowledge

In the first two chapters, we have argued that a language is a set of sentences described by the rules of a competence grammar, and that knowing a language is, essentially, knowing these rules. In fact, a complete description of linguistic knowledge must invoke a number of different types of rule, corresponding to the different types of linguistic knowledge that speakers control. In this chapter, we look more closely at these different types of knowledge, and at how they interact.

Just as the speaker's ability to detect and correct mistakes indicates the existence of linguistic rules, so his reactions to mistakes of different kinds indicates the existence of different types of linguistic rule. Consider the following examples:

(1) a. Melanie's clarinet is tarnished.
    b. ?Melanie's clarinet is not a clarinet.[1]
    c. *Melanie's clarinet does be a B*b* one.
    d. *Melanie's ctarinel is defective.
    e. ?Melanie's clarinet is made of cottage cheese.

Whereas (1a) is fully acceptable in every respect, all of (1b)–(1e) are odd in some way. (1b) is contradictory and makes no consistent assertion, although it is perfectly well-formed in all other respects. (1c) is meaningful, but is syntactically ill-formed, since it contains a sequence of words, *does be*, which does not occur in standard English. (1d) is defective in neither of these

---

1. In future we shall indicate with a question-mark those sentences which, if uttered, would be unacceptable for either semantic or pragmatic reasons. Our use of the question-mark thus cross-cuts the linguistic–non-linguistic distinction.

ways, but includes a word *ctarinel* which, because it begins with a sequence of consonants pronounced *kt*, is impossible in English. (1e), while admittedly peculiar, is not in the same category as any of the three preceding examples. It appears to be grammatically well-formed, and unless we stipulate arbitrarily that a defining criterion for clarinets is that they not be made of cottage cheese, it displays no oddity of meaning either. In this case the apparent deviance is not linguistic at all, but is due solely to knowledge of the world. Thus we can imagine situations where (1e) would cease to be odd at all, for instance in a fairy story, or in a community with an advanced technology for hardening cottage cheese.

The intuitive differences among these sentences are reflected in the typical reactions to them of native speakers. (1b) is likely to be met by a blank and baffled 'what?'; (1c) is likely to be corrected to (2):

(2) Melanie's clarinet *is* a Bb one.

(1d) is likely to evoke a request for the repetition of the offending (non-) word; and (1e) will probably be greeted with incredulity.

The various examples given here indicate that we probably need to make separate statements of well-formedness reflecting knowledge of meaning, or *semantics*, knowledge of pronunciation, or *phonology*, and knowledge of what is traditionally referred to as grammar, or *syntax*. Despite this separation of linguistic knowledge into different types, there is one domain in which all of them converge: the *lexicon* or dictionary. While a language cannot be considered simply as a set of words, but must also contain principles of sentence-formation and interpretation, it is obvious that knowledge of a language includes knowledge of its vocabulary. Accordingly we look first at the kind of information the lexicon needs to contain if it is to reproduce correctly the speaker's linguistic knowledge about the words of his language.

The Lexicon

If we restrict our attention to a single word, say *flaw*, and consider what native speakers of English know about it, we can distinguish knowledge of each of the three types mentioned above.

First, pronunciation. Clearly, knowledge of how a word is correctly pronounced is involved in full mastery of the vocabulary, and we must have available some method of representing facts about pronunciation in the grammar. This is not a trivial matter. Consider *flaw* and *floor*, for example. For many speakers of British English, these two words are generally pronounced the same, as in (3):

(3) a. That is a real flaw.
    b. That is a real floor.

However, many speakers also distinguish the two, when they occur before a vowel, by pronouncing the final *r* in *floor*. For such people (4a) and (4b) are easily distinguishable:

(4) a. There is no flaw in that building.
    b. There is no floor in that building.

An adequate analysis of these two words, therefore, must be able to account for the fact that they are indistinguishable in certain contexts, but distinguishable by the presence or absence of *r* in others.

Second, meaning. Our knowledge of the word *flaw* includes not only its pronunciation but also, for example, the fact that it may convey the same meaning as *defect* or *blemish*: the pairs of sentences in (5) and (6) are roughly synonymous:

(5) a. We found but one blemish on her otherwise flawless complexion.
    b. We found but one flaw on her otherwise unblemished complexion.

(6) a. There is a flaw in your argument.
   b. There is a defect in your argument.

Again, finding just the right analysis of *flaw* is no easy matter: while taking account of the synonymy in (5) and (6), it must also account for the differences in (7) and (8), where the (b) sentences are infelicitous to the point of being unacceptable:

(7) a. I think there is a flaw in your reasoning.
   b. ?I think there is a blemish in your reasoning.
(8) a. John's major defect is his inability to take criticism.
   b. ?John's major flaw is his inability to take criticism.

Third, syntax. Full knowledge of the sound and meaning of a word is not itself enough to ensure that it will always be used correctly in sentences. What is also needed is the knowledge that *flaw* is a noun or a verb, and so may occur in either of the positions typical of those categories. As a noun, it may be preceded by a definite or indefinite article, by the numerals *one*, *two*, etc., and by adjectives such as *serious* or *dangerous*. Moreover as it is an *abstract* noun it is referred to by the pronominal forms *it* and *which* rather than *him*, *her* or *who*. As a verb, it can be marked for the difference between present and past tense – *flaw* as opposed to *flawed* – and be preceded by adverbs rather than adjectives as in (9a) as opposed to (9b).

(9) a. His theory is fatally flawed.
   b. *His theory is fatal flawed.

Mastery of all three types of rule given here is involved in linguistic knowledge, and a grammar designed to give a full account of linguistic knowledge will simply have to list in the lexicon for each word of the language the sum total of its syntactic, semantic and phonological properties.

So far this information appears to be closely parallel to that found in any dictionary. The lexicon as we see it, however, differs considerably from dictionaries of a more traditional kind. In the first place, it will contain only the vocabulary known to the speaker whose grammar we are attempting to describe: there will be none of the historical and pan-dialectal comprehensiveness of the O.E.D. Since it is highly probable that no two speakers of English know exactly the same set of words, it is also extremely likely that no two English speakers will have identical lexicons. In the second place, there will generally be no room for the sort of etymological information given in good traditional dictionaries: for example, that *flaw* comes from the Old Norse *flaga*, 'slab', or that *lens*, 'curved glass', comes from the Latin *lens, lentis*, 'lentil'. This is not the sort of information that is normally acquired in the course of becoming a native speaker of English, and hence does not form part of linguistic knowledge as we have defined it. Such etymological information, if acquired, would be entered in the mental encyclopedia – the storehouse for non-linguistic knowledge – rather than in the lexicon.

Although these constraints would seem to ensure that the lexicon was much smaller than a standard dictionary, it will also contain some information that a standard dictionary would not normally contain. For example, it will record the native speaker's knowledge not only of the actual words of his language, but also of rules of word formation. As native speakers we know that *slip* is a word of English and that *slib* is not. Similarly we know that *spill* is a word of English and that *sbill* is not. But in the latter case we know further that *sbill* is not an accidental gap like *slib*, but is not a possible word of English because it fails to conform to the permitted phonological patterns of the language. In order to be sure that *slib* is not an English word we happened to be ignorant of, we had to check in the O.E.D.; no such checking was necessary for *sbill* any more than it would be for *ctarinel*. Despite the existence of marginal exceptions to the regular rules, such as *sthenic*, *sphragistics* and *sbirro*, speakers of English seem able to make remarkably consistent judgements about possible and impossible words of English, and a grammar designed to encapsulate all linguistic knowledge must record the principles which underlie such judgements. Hence the lexicon should contain, along with a list of the actual vocabulary a speaker knows, the set of principles which enable him to form new words.

The principles of word-formation govern not only the phonological structure of words, but also their *morphological structure*: that is, the permissible combinations of prefixes, roots and suffixes which go to make up a word. Thus, with a little thought, most speakers of English can see that the words in (10) consist of a single *morpheme* each: contain no prefixes or suffixes which are also used in the construction of other words:

(10) cat, rich, kind, hate, giraffe, platypus, cassowary.

By contrast, they can see that the words in (11) are morphologically complex, in the sense that they contain prefixes or suffixes that may be used in the construction of other words. The component morphemes are here separated by dashes:

(11) cat-s, en-rich, un-kind, kind-ly, giraffe-like, chalk-y,
house-hold, in-suffer-able, retro-rocket, duke-dom-s.

Moreover, they would probably regard the combinations in (12) as yielding possible words of English (even though not listed in the O.E.D.):

(12) non-derive-able, self-flagellate-ing, platypus-dom,
re-cuddle

whereas those in (13) are, like *sbill*, not possible in English at all:

(13) en-rich-en, kind-un, duke-s-dom, hate-y.

Again, the fact that speakers have such knowledge argues that the grammar should state the rules governing permissible combinations of morphemes: for example, that -*dom* is a suffix turning a noun into a noun, that -*ly* is a suffix turning an adjective into an adverb, that -*en* is a suffix turning an adjective into a verb, and so on.[2]

Although much less work has been done in this area than in

2. For some discussion of the distinction between rule-governed word-formation and creative word-coinage, see Chapter 9.

those of phonology and morphology, it might also be possible to argue that there are semantic constraints on word-formation. For example, it is occasionally claimed that there could be no word which designates a scattered object: that though a word like *slib* is phonologically and morphologically possible, it could never be used to designate the object consisting of the front paws and tail of a kitten, or the set of objects which have been in Berkshire for more than ten years. In the absence of more explicit hypotheses about the semantic analysis of words it is hard to test this claim seriously.

So far, we are claiming that the lexicon performs two central tasks: it provides an explicit phonological, morphological, syntactic and semantic analysis of each vocabulary item; and it states the general constraints which the language imposes on the phonological, morphological, syntactic, and perhaps semantic structure of the word. In essence, the former of these tasks amounts to expressing any idiosyncratic properties of particular items, and we end this section with a further illustration of the unpredictable, and hence lexically specified, *syntactic* behaviour of various words; that is, properties which determine their correct incorporation into sentences of the language.

One major syntactic generalization about the structure of English sentences is that the direct object normally follows the verb. We might thus write a general syntactic rule allowing for the combination *verb + direct object* in English sentences. However, if we are to make sure that no ungrammatical sentences result, we will have to mark each actual verb in the lexicon for whether it may or may not take a direct object. Thus, despite their phonological and semantic similarity, the verb *quake* cannot take a direct object, while *shake* may:

(14) a. The children shook in their shoes.
   b. Shake the medicine before swallowing.
(15) a. The children quaked in their shoes.
   b. *Quake the medicine before swallowing.

The distinction between transitive and intransitive verbs is generally marked in standard dictionaries, as it is in the lexicon. However, there are many similar facts which are not so recorded, but which would have to be marked in the lexicon of a fully explicit grammar. For example, some verbs require certain types of adverbial or prepositional phrase: compare (16) and (17):

(16) a. We trudged wearily up the hill.
     b. *We trudged.
(17) a. They often behaved contemptuously towards their neighbours.
     b. *They often behaved towards their neighbours.

Again, certain verbs may be followed by both indirect statements and indirect questions, as in (18), while others, as in (19), allow only the former possibility:

(18) a. I know that you were lonely as a child.
     b. I know why you were lonely as a child.
(19) a. I hope that you have tried to find the answer.
     b. *I hope why you have tried to find the answer.

All these special syntactic facts about individual words would have to be dealt with in the lexicon of a fully explicit grammar, although they are facts which standard dictionaries either ignore or illustrate only tacitly, by use of examples.

So far we have been arguing that the lexicon is the place where special facts about vocabulary items are stored: notably, their particular phonological, syntactic and semantic analyses, and their individual and idiosyncratic possibilities of combining with other words to form sentences. It is perhaps worth mentioning that the relation between the sound, syntax and meaning of a word is largely arbitrary. Apart from a few onomatopoeic words such as *peewee* or *choochoo*, and the possibility of saying words like *squeaky* in a squeaky voice, the association of a particular sequence of sounds with a particular meaning or syntactic category is entirely unpredictable. There is nothing about the sound of the word *flaw* that tells us what it must mean: *flaw* and *floor* have the same pronunciation, but radically different meanings.

Similarly, there is nothing about the meaning of the word *flaw* that uniquely determines its pronunciation: *flaw* and *defect* have the same meaning, but radically different pronunciations. The relation between sound and syntax is no less arbitrary: *floor* may be a noun or a verb, *fly* a noun, verb or adjective, *flat* a noun or an adjective, *flatter* a verb or an adjective, and so on. Finally, the relation between syntax and meaning is also largely arbitrary, though perhaps less so than in the other cases we have considered: words which primarily designate an action are generally verbs, words which designate some object are generally nouns, for example. However, there is nothing about the meaning of *wheat* that tells us that it should be singular while *oats* is plural; nothing about the meaning of *table* that tells us that it should take the feminine article in French whereas *desk* (*pupitre*) takes the masculine article; nothing in the meaning of the adjective *rabbity*, that prevents us from expressing that meaning by a prepositional phrase, *like a rabbit*, or by a participial clause, *resembling a rabbit*, and so on.

By contrast, the grammar proper deals with the phonological, syntactic and semantic properties of the sentence rather than the word. It states the limits within which individual lexical items may pick and choose their possibilities of behaviour; it formulates the rules to which lexical items may occasionally be exceptions, the generalizations which hold 'unless otherwise stated'. If the lexicon is the home of exceptions and idiosyncrasies, the grammar is the home of the significant linguistic generalizations specific to the particular language being described.

To illustrate this distinction, consider the fact already mentioned, that direct objects in English follow the verb. This is a statement correctly recorded in the grammar, since it is a general fact about all lexical items of a particular syntactic type. Contrast this with the information that *quake* is a verb – a special syntactic fact about this particular word; and that it is furthermore a verb that cannot take a direct object – another special syntactic fact. This information is correctly recorded in the lexicon, being unpredictable and idiosyncratic to the particular lexical item *quake*.

In the rest of this chapter we look at the linguistic knowledge used in constructing whole sentences, and not just the individual word of which they are made up. It is at this level that the rule-governed rather than arbitrary nature of linguistic abilities becomes apparent.

Syntax

On the syntactic level, we have already mentioned the fact that verbs in English may be followed by direct objects, prepositional phrases or adverbials. Another obvious type of syntactic knowledge is that which enables one to recognize the subject of a verb. In (20a–e) the noun phrase containing *apples* is in each case the subject of the verb *were*, in spite of the clear differences in syntactic configurations in which they occur:

(20) a. *The apples were* falling heavily on the heads of the passers-by.
   b. There *were apples* in Russell's basket.
   c. *The apples* that Matisse liked to paint *were* Golden Delicious.
   d. *Which apples* did you say the police suspected *were* the ones you stole?
   e. *Those apples*, the witness told the court, the defendant had claimed *were* laced with arsenic before he ever bought them.

There is obviously some general principle which enables speakers to determine which noun-phrase is the subject of a given verb. This is true even when that verb precedes its subject, as in (20b), is widely separated from it as in (20c–e) or when the verb has disappeared completely, as in (21):

(21) The pears were ripe, the apples unripe.

The grammar must somehow replicate this knowledge.

Another domain in which speakers can be made consciously

aware of their syntactic and morphological knowledge relatively easily is that of *agreement*. Two or more items 'agree' if they must both be marked for the same grammatical distinction: singular subject with a singular verb, plural subject with a plural verb, feminine adjective with feminine noun in those languages, such as French, which have grammatical gender; and so on. Examples are familiar to everyone, if only because deviations of the kind seen in the starred sentences below are typical of foreigners' mistakes:

(22) a. Pigs are disgusting.
     b. *Pigs is disgusting.
(23) a. Oats are tasty.
     b. *Oats is tasty.
(24) a. Wheat is tasty.
     b. *Wheat are tasty.
(25) a. These scissors are blunt.
     b. *This scissors is blunt.
(26) a. This week is holy week.
     b. *These week is holy week.
(27) a. More than one of the deputies was seduced.
     b. *More than one of the deputies were seduced.
(28) a. The committee has decided to abolish rape.
     b. The committee have decided to abolish rape.
     c. The committees have decided to abolish rape.
     d. *The committees has decided to abolish rape.
(29) The United States has declared war on Andorra.

In many of these cases neither knowledge of the world (*oats/wheat*) nor logic (*more than one*) will provide an explanation for the agreement found, but the associated intuitions should be clear-cut nonetheless.

Another type of syntactic knowledge enables speakers to tell which of a set of non-adjacent words in a sentence go together, and which do not. For example, the word *all* is often found some distance away from the noun-phrase it semantically modifies.

Thus in (30a–e), the *all* in each case goes with the noun-phrase *the children*:

> (30) a. *All the children* might have been shouting at once.
> b. *The children all* might have been shouting at once.
> c. *The children* might *all* have been shouting at once.
> d. *The children* might have *all* been shouting at once.
> e. *The children* might have been *all* shouting at once.

The grammar must reconstruct the rules which permit this behaviour; and it must formulate them in such a way as to predict also that in (30f) the *all* has moved too far, and can no longer be associated with *the children*:

> (30) f. **The children might have been shouting at once *all*.

Clearly, such knowledge is readily available to each native speaker of English, even though it is not of a type which is ever taught or mentioned in schools; equally clearly, the task of describing this knowledge explicitly is a formidably complicated one, involving the ability to characterize both well-formedness on the syntactic level and identity of meaning on the semantic level.

This last set of examples also shows that in some cases syntactic knowledge may go beyond the confines of a single sentence. Speakers presented with the examples in (30) are able to make judgements not only about the well-formedness of individual sentences but about the relatedness of one sentence to another. The most obvious kinds of related sentence are paraphrases, such as (30a–e), which contain the same words in different orders. By contrast, (31a) and (31b) are neither syntactically nor semantically related: they are not paraphrases, and the two occurrences of *all* are syntactically associated with quite different noun-phrases:

> (31) a. All the girls kissed the boys.
> b. The girls kissed all the boys.

It is also possible for sentences to be syntactically related without being paraphrases. For example, there is a clear sense in which (32) is related to each of the sentences in (33):

(32) The police examined the bullet.
(33) a. The bullet, the police examined.
   b. The bullet is what the police examined.
   c. The bullet was examined by the police.
   d. It was the bullet that the police examined.
   e. The police *did* examine the bullet.
   f. The police did not examine the bullet.
   g. Did the police examine the bullet?
   h. Which bullet did the police examine?

In this range of examples, related pairs consisting of a positive and a negative, or a statement and a question, indicate that the notion of relatedness involved does not amount to identity of meaning. However, each of the sentences in (32)–(33) contains the same words from such major syntactic categories as noun, verb, adjective and adverb, differing only in words such as *not, what, by, did*, etc. If a distinction between these two types of word could be made explicit, it might be possible to construct around it a more exact definition of syntactic, as opposed to semantic, relatedness. In fact, a further caveat needs to be entered here, as some pairs of sentences are felt to be related even though one of them may contain words from major syntactic categories which are absent from the other. For instance:

(34) a. My sister suggested that I marry Esmé, but I didn't want to marry Esmé.
   b. My sister suggested that I marry Esmé, but I didn't want to.

In cases of this kind the requirement that related sentences should contain exactly the same lexical material from major syntactic categories can be relaxed, because the material missing from (34b) is already present elsewhere in the same sentence.

Semantics

On the semantic level, we have already mentioned the speaker's ability to recognize *paraphrase* relations among sentences: that is, cases where two or more sentences, such as those in (30), are identical in meaning. In addition to this, speakers can recognize *ambiguity*, as in (35a), which may be interpreted as either (35b) or (35c):

(35) a. All the guests won't eat the syllabub.
   b. Not all the guests will eat the syllabub.
   c. None of the guests will eat the syllabub.

It is worth stressing at this point that traditional English spelling often obscures the fact that utterances may be ambiguous in the spoken language, even though the written forms of the sentences they correspond to are quite unambiguous. Thus although there is a visible difference between (36) and (37) when written, they would be pronounced in exactly the same way, and only non-linguistic contextual information could tell the hearer which meaning was intended:

(36) We can make your voice great like Rod Stewart's.
(37) We can make your voice grate like Rod Stewart's.

The grammar of English should be able to characterize such examples as ambiguous even if the ambiguity is noticeable only at the phonological level, and even if our background knowledge tells us infallibly that, say, (36) rather than (37) is the only plausible meaning.

Apart from the recognition of paraphrase and ambiguity, a speaker's semantic knowledge extends to the detection of (i) *contradiction* and *anomaly*, properties of sentences which are false in virtue of their meaning, as in (38) and (39):

(38) ?That illiterate can read.
(39) ?The consequence of your argument is purple.

(ii) *tautology* and *analytic truth*, properties of sentences which are true in virtue of their meaning, as in (40) and (41):

(40) That tall man is tall.
(41) All uncles are men.

and (iii) *entailment* relations, as between (42a) and (42b):

(42) a. I learnt to play the triangle.
    b. I learnt to play a musical instrument.

We return to a more detailed discussion of some of these topics in Chapter 7.

Phonology

The correct pronunciation for each word in the language is provided by the lexicon, but there are also phonological properties of units larger than the word which need to be specified by phonological rule. One of these has already been dealt with; namely, the variant pronunciations of *floor*, and other words ending in an *r* in the written language, depending on whether they appear before words beginning with a consonant or vowel. It is clear that the lexicon will have to contain the information about which precise set of lexical items is subject to this variation; however, as the set of contexts in which such items can occur is indefinitely large, the exact realization of this pronunciation in context will have to be specified by rule. The same is true of the difference in stress on words such as *unknown, fourteen*, etc. depending on their position in the sentence, as witness the contrasts in (43) and (44):

(43) a. His whereabouts are unknówn.
    b. Únknown ages will pass before they are discovered.
(44) a. She's nearly fourtéen.
    b. She has fóurteen candles on her cake.

In addition to the stress pattern of individual words in sentences, speakers can also handle possible differences in the overall stress pattern of a whole sentence, where these differences may result either in differences of emphasis, as in (45), or in complete change of meaning, as in (46):

(45) a. My ambition is to *win* a marathon.
    b. My ambition is to win a *marathon*.[3]
(46) a. I *felt* myself again (to see if I had broken anything).
    b. I felt *myself* again (after an illness).

Also within the domain of phonological ability is the speaker's control of *intonational* differences. In 'tone' languages, such as Chinese or the African language Nupe, the different pitch with which a single word is uttered determines its meaning: e.g. Nupe *pá*, on a high pitch (or tone) means 'to paddle a canoe', *pa*, on a mid tone means 'to look after' and *pà*, on a low tone means 'to pound'. In English, fluctuations of pitch are tied to the sentence as a whole rather than to the word, and may serve to distinguish questions from statements, as in (47), where (a) is said on a rising pitch and (b) on a falling pitch:

(47) a. You're happy?

    b. You're happy.

They may also be used to distinguish ironic from neutral utterances, aggrieved from appeasing ones, etc.

We return to a more general discussion of the role of phonology in Chapter 6.

Interactions

So far we have attempted, at least in part, to segregate the different kinds of linguistic knowledge available to speakers of a language. We now want to consider whether any component of this

---

3. We are using an accent ' to mark stress on a particular syllable of a word, and italics to mark the fact that a word as a whole bears heavy stress.

disparate knowledge has priority over any other. Specifically we want to argue that syntax is prior to both semantics and phonology: prior in the sense that there are phonological and semantic processes which depend for their statement on syntactic facts, but no syntactic processes which depend on phonological or semantic facts.[4]

As an example of a phonological rule which needs to refer to syntactic information, consider the phenomenon of 'contraction', the process which provides alternative pronunciations of *is* in (48) and (49):

(48) a. The party is tomorrow.
    b. The party's tomorrow.
(49) a. The party is at midnight tomorrow.
    b. The party's at midnight tomorrow.

Although (50) and (51) look superficially almost identical, leading one to expect contraction to be possible in both, it turns out that contraction may occur in (50), but not in (51):

(50) a. I wonder if the party is tomorrow.
    b. I wonder if the party's tomorrow.
(51) a. I wonder when the party is tomorrow.
    b. *I wonder when the party's tomorrow.

Similar contrasts occur in (52) and (53), (54) and (55):

(52) a. I'll ask whether the party is on Thursday.
    b. I'll ask whether the party's on Thursday.
(53) a. I'll ask where the party is on Thursday.
    b. *I'll ask where the party's on Thursday.

4. Notice that this is not, and could not be, a claim about the order of events that occur in actual speech production or perception. It would clearly be absurd to maintain that speakers had to construct the full syntactic representation of an utterance before deciding what message they wanted to convey. This is yet another reason for maintaining a radical distinction between the rules of a competence grammar and the performance principles used for speech production and perception. While the two types of principle may interact, they are nonetheless distinct.

(54) a. Where do you think the party is happening tonight?
    b. Where do you think the party's happening tonight?
(55) a. Where do you think the party is tonight?
    b. *Where do you think the party's tonight?

Clearly, there is some significant generalization to be made about when contraction can take place and when it can not.

It seems that the correct generalization is not a phonological but a syntactic one. Consider some 'echo' questions related to (50)–(55): that is, questions which request the repetition of a misheard or implausible item. Such questions are formed by placing the *wh*-word (*when* or *where* in these cases) in sentence-internal position rather than at the front of its own clause:

(50) c. You think the party is tomorrow?
(51) c. You think the party is *when* tomorrow?
(52) c. You think the party is on Thursday?
(53) c. You think the party is *where* on Thursday?
(54) c. You think the party is happening *where* tonight?
(55) c. You think the party is *where* tonight?

Here, in contrast with our previous examples, contraction is in all cases possible, as the reader may check for himself.

This behaviour can be explained on the assumption that there are syntactic rules which actually move constituents from one place in a sentence to another. In particular, one might assume that *wh*-words are optionally moved to the front of a clause from sentence-internal position: thus sentences like (50–55c) may be converted into sentences like (50–55a). We can then make the following claim: if a *wh*-word is left in its sentence-internal position, rather than being moved to the front of its clause, contraction applies freely; but if it is moved to the front of its clause from a position *immediately* after *is* (contrast (54) and (55)), then contraction is blocked. The generalization about possibilities of *is*-contraction in English is thus based on syntactic information about whether an item has been moved from a position immediately after *is*: if such movement has taken place, contraction is blocked; if not, then contraction goes through quite freely. This seems to be a clear case where a phonological rule must have access to syntactic information.

We can show that syntactic rules do not normally refer to phonological information by constructing a hypothetical, and perhaps extreme example where they would. Consider the related sentences in (32) and (33) above. It is logically possible, though most linguists would claim that it is linguistically impossible, that the rules creating this relationship would only apply if the subject and direct object nouns of the sentence concerned began with a bilabial consonant (*p*, *b* or *m*). In this case (32) and (33) would indeed be predicted as related, but the examples in (57), which do not contain bilabial consonants, would be predicted as unrelated to (56):

(56) The gendarme studied the weapon.
(57) a. The weapon is what the gendarme studied.
    b. The weapon was studied by the gendarme, etc.

However, we know of no clear cases which would support such a relationship between syntax and phonology: it seems that in general syntactic rules do not need access to phonological information.

Semantic interpretation is clearly dependent on syntactic information. For example, the sentences in (58) all contain the same words, but in different syntactic configurations. These differences in syntactic configuration correlate with differences in meaning:

(58) a. Antigone gave the boy to the slave.
    b. Antigone gave the slave to the boy.
    c. The boy gave Antigone to the slave.
    d. The boy gave the slave to Antigone.
    e. The slave gave Antigone to the boy.
    f. The slave gave the boy to Antigone.

Here the position of a given noun-phrase in the structure will determine whether it is interpreted as the subject, object or indirect object of the verb, with resulting differences in meaning.

However, no syntactic rules seem to be dependent on such semantic properties as tautology, paraphrase, etc. for their operation. To take the case of the movable quantifier *all* illustrated earlier, it is again logically possible, but linguistically impossible, that the quantifier should be separable from its noun-phrase if and only if the sentence involved was tautologous. That is, (59b) would be well-formed, but neither (60b) nor the examples in (30) would be acceptable:

(59) a. All the girls are immature female humans.
    b. The girls are all immature female humans.
(60) a. All the girls are sweet generous brunettes.
    b. The girls are all sweet generous brunettes.

Again, we know of no clear case of such a relationship between syntax and semantics.

The relationships between syntax and phonology on the one hand and syntax and semantics on the other seem to be relatively clear. The relationship between phonology and semantics is not as straightforward. It is obvious that differences of sound correlate with differences of meaning, as witness the kind of examples treated in (45), (46) and (47) above. What is not obvious is whether phonological rules need to refer directly to semantic information or vice versa, or whether all such correlation can be mediated through the syntax. However, there are some examples which seem to indicate that semantic rules need at least to be able to refer to details of stress and intonation. For instance, slight adjustments in stress and intonation on two syntactically identical sentences may induce considerable differences in interpretation: compare (61a) and (61b).

(61) a. The Queen said she was happy to be in Manchester, and then the Duke made a *joke*.
    b. The Queen said she was happy to be in Manchester, and then the *Duke* made a joke.

(61b), unlike (61a), suggests, as one possibility, that saying one is happy to be in Manchester amounts to making a joke. The phonological properties of the sentence are affecting its meaning in some sense independently of the syntactic structure. The reason we are diffident about asserting unambiguously that semantic rules *must* have access to phonological information is simply the difficulty of disproving the reverse possibility: namely that the stress differences in (61) are due to the different meanings.[5]

The arguments given above would suggest setting up a grammar whose components reflect both the major divisions in linguistic knowledge and the 'directionality' among them. The form of such a grammar is sketched in (62):

(62)

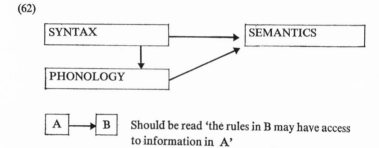

where, furthermore, the lexicon is assumed to be a subpart of the syntax. We shall fill in some of the details of this skeletal structure in the next chapter. In the meantime we want to raise a further problem about the interaction of syntax and semantics.

In previous chapters we have argued for a distinction between linguistic and non-linguistic knowledge. Throughout this chapter, we have been assuming an equally clear demarcation between syntactic and semantic knowledge. We are committed, then, given any sentence that sounds ill-formed, to being able to pinpoint the exact source of its deviance: to say whether it violates syntactic rules, semantic rules, or merely some non-linguistic principles.

Consider, for example, the sentences in (63), all of which are deviant in some way:

5. See Chapter 7 for further discussion of the relationship between phonology and semantics.

(63) a. ?I've just offended a book by Einstein.
 b. ?This pruning-hook argues that Britain should pull out
    of the Common Market.
 c. ?My foot has a headache.
 d. ?The water ran into the basin and bounced.

What these sentences have in common is that they attribute in-compatible properties to objects. Thus, (63a) implies that books are animate objects of a type advanced enough to take offence; (63b) attributes mental qualities to a pruning-hook; (63c) implies that feet are also heads, or that headaches need not be felt in the head; and (63d) implies that water may be solid and resilient. All these implications happen to be false. Sentences like those in (63) are generally claimed to violate *selectional restrictions*: restric-tions designed to prevent the construction of anomalous sen-tences by forbidding certain word-combinations to arise.

If what we have been claiming about the different kinds of linguistic knowledge is correct, we must be able to locate the source of the oddness in (63), and to say whether it should be dealt with in the grammar, and if so by which component, or whether the source of the oddness is non-linguistic. Assuming for the moment that the peculiarity of (63) is linguistic, we are faced with the problem of deciding whether the sentences have violated a syntactic or a semantic restriction. We shall argue for the latter position.

The only reason for thinking that the examples in (63) should be dealt with in the syntactic component is if we can assimilate them to other cases which should clearly be dealt with there. For example, the sentences in (64), which are generally treated as strictly ungrammatical, might also be seen as attributing incom-patible properties to objects:

(64) a. *The children is playing happily on the beach.
 b. *The man are in the next room.

(64a) seems to imply that the children are both singular and plural, and (64b) seems to say something similar of the man.

Surely this is just the same sort of anomaly that we saw in (63), and both types of sentence should be dealt with in the same component of the grammar?

However, there are clear differences in behaviour between strictly ungrammatical sentences, including (64), and the selectional violations in (63). For example, the sentences in (63), when embedded (or inserted) in certain types of clause beginning with *that*, become completely acceptable:

(65) a. It's nonsense to say that you have just offended a book by Einstein.
 b. I dreamed that this pruning-hook was arguing that Britain should pull out of the Common Market.
 c. I almost want to say that my foot has a headache.
 d. I don't believe that the water ran into the basin and bounced.

(65b), although it may be a funny thing to dream, is not a funny thing to say, and we would want the grammar to treat it as perfectly well-formed. If we embed (64), and other strictly ungrammatical sentences, into the same types of *that*-clause, the resulting sentences are still ungrammatical:

(66) a. *It's impossible that the children is playing happily on the beach.
 b. *I dreamed that the man were in the next room.
 c. *I almost want to say that I hope why you have tried to find the answer.
 d. *I don't believe that the children might have been shouting at once all.

In other words, strictly ungrammatical sentences cannot have their grammaticality restored by embedding them into *that*-clauses, whereas selectional violations may be cancelled by judicious embedding. This argues that selectional violations should not be treated as cases of strict ungrammaticality, and should not be dealt with in the syntactic component.

Another reason for coming to the same conclusion is that the sort of information involved in actually stating selectional restrictions seems to be clearly non-syntactic in nature. Syntactic rules generally pick out classes of items by such well-defined properties as being a noun, being a pronoun, being singular or plural, masculine or feminine, definite or indefinite, and so on. The properties one would have to refer to in stating the selectional restrictions needed for (63) are such things as being a foot, being an advanced primate, possessing mental attributes and being a solid and resilient object. Now if such properties are genuinely syntactic, we would expect other syntactic rules, apart from selectional restrictions, to have access to them. We would expect some language to have rules of the following type: 'If the subject of the sentence is a foot, mark the verb with the foot-affix', which is, of course, an exact analogue of the subject-verb agreement rule of English: 'If the subject of the verb is singular, mark the verb with the singular affix; if the subject is plural, mark the verb with a plural affix.' Even though some languages have grammatical classes whose members are defined as long and narrow, or round or red and bovine, no language seems to have such rules as would be required by the examples we have given.

On the other hand, it is obvious that semantic rules must have access to just the properties needed to state selectional restrictions correctly. We have already claimed that the semantic rules must be able to state when a sentence is analytic and when it is contradictory. They must thus be able to mark (67a) and (67b) as analytic, and (67c) and (67d) as contradictory:

(67) a. A headache is a pain in the head.
  b. An object which can bounce is a resilient, solid object.
  c. ?A pruning-hook is a higher primate.
  d. ?One can offend inanimate objects.

If they are able to do this, they must themselves have access to exactly the information needed to state the selectional restrictions for (63). Thus, if selectional restrictions are to be dealt with in the grammar at all, they must be dealt with in the semantic component. The reader may also see why some people argue that selectional restrictions should not be dealt with in the grammar at all: their claim is linked to the wider claim that there is no such thing as analytic truth or analytic falsehood, and that the whole range of knowledge treated under these headings should be excluded from the grammar and treated as non-linguistic, knowledge of the world.

In this chapter, we have tried to illustrate a fair range of linguistic processes which a native speaker of English has at his command. We have argued for a division of the overall grammar into two major parts: the lexicon, which deals with the analysis of the vocabulary of the language, and the grammar proper, which deals with the analysis of the sentence. We have further argued that analyses on both these levels can be separated into three major types: the phonological, the syntactic and the semantic, giving illustrations of phenomena dealt with by each of these components. We have also made a first attempt at showing that of these three components, the syntactic component is logically prior to the other two, which must have access to the output of the syntax. We have as yet said nothing about what the rules of the grammar, or the entries in the lexicon, actually look like, and how we can get them to give explicit descriptions of the various types of knowledge we have surveyed. It is to this task of explicitly formalizing linguistic knowledge that we turn in the next chapter.

4. Formalizing Linguistic Knowledge

In this chapter we outline some of the formal properties of the syntactic component of an explicit grammar. We have argued that this component has two main concerns: it must provide rules which make correct predictions of grammaticality and ungrammaticality over an infinite range of sentences, and, as we saw in the last chapter, it must provide enough syntactic information about each sentence to ensure that the phonological and semantic rules can function correctly. In fact, these goals can be achieved simultaneously.

Constituent Structure

The syntactic rules describe the sentences of a language in terms of syntactic categories such as noun (N), verb (V), adjective (Adj), article (Art) and so on. We assume that each word of English will be assigned to its correct syntactic category in the lexicon; thus, *cat* and *book* are labelled as nouns by being given the syntactic feature [+N], *collect* and *disturb* are labelled as verbs by being given the feature [+V], *purple* and *funny* have the feature [+Adj], *a* and *the* [+Art], and so on.[1] The syntactic rules state which combinations of these categories make up grammatical sentences, and which do not. As an example of such a rule – but a rule which is clearly inadequate – consider the following:

(1) S → N — Adj — Art — V — Adj

1. A syntactic feature is any syntactic property of a lexical item which affects its syntactic or morphological behaviour. Syntactic features are normally represented in square brackets.

This should be read as follows: a sentence (S) may consist of a noun, followed by an adjective, article, verb and adjective, in that order. We can diagram the structure provided by this rule in the form of a *tree*:

(2)

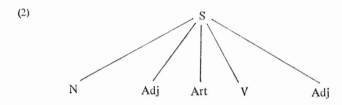

Then, if we insert under each of these category labels a word of the appropriate category from the lexicon, we obtain the following results:

(3) a. *Cat funny a collect purple.
   b. *Book purple the disturb funny.
   c. *Cat purple the collect funny.
   d. *Book funny a disturb purple.

The strings in (3), although they contain genuine English words, have three obvious properties: they are ungrammatical, they are literally meaningless, and they are hard to pronounce with anything approaching normal English stress and intonation contours for sentences. A way of simultaneously accounting for all three properties would be as follows: first, make sure that the grammar of English does not contain rule (1), so that the sentences in (3) will be marked ungrammatical, and second, make sure that the semantic and phonological rules apply only to grammatical sentences. In other words, the syntactic rules will simultaneously specify the grammatical sentences of the language and determine the inputs to the semantic and phonological components.

Now substitute for the inadequate (1) a syntactic rule which *does* produce grammatical sentences:

(4) S → Art — Adj — N — V — Art — Adj — N

(5)

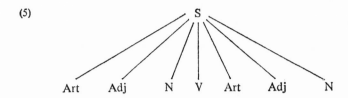

Slotting into this structure words from the appropriate categories, we obtain the following grammatical sentences (with some adjustment for appropriate tense-marking on the verb):

(6) a. The funny book disturbed a purple cat.
   b. The funny cat collected a purple book.
   c. A purple book disturbed the funny cat.
   d. A purple cat collected the funny book.
   e. ?The purple book collected a funny cat.
   f. ?The funny cat disturbed a purple book.[2]

Notice that the sentences in (6), in addition to being syntactically well-formed, are also semantically interpretable, in the sense that we can see what they are claiming, even if some of those claims are necessarily false; they are also pronounceable with the stress and intonation contours of normal English sentences. This further bears out the claim that it is the structures provided by the syntactic rules which are the inputs to the semantic and phonological components.

If we are to take this claim seriously, there is good reason for thinking that (4) is not entirely adequate as a syntactic analysis for the sentences in (6). From the semantic point of view, the two Art–Adj–N sequences mentioned in (4) act as a unit, the first such sequence being the subject of the sentence, and the second the direct object. We might, then, group these items under a new syntactic category of *noun phrase* (NP), to which the semantic

2. Recall our argument in Chapter 3 that sentences like (6e–f) are syntactically well-formed, but semantically deviant, and hence should be produced by the syntactic rules and characterized as anomalous by the semantic component.

rules may refer in determining the subject and direct object of the sentence. We could summarize this information by substituting for (4) the following two syntactic rules:

(7) a. S → NP — V — NP
    b. NP → Art — Adj — N

The resulting trees would look as follows:

(8) a

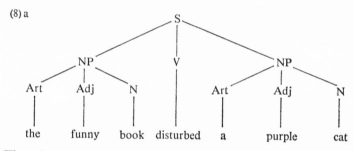

There is an extensive vocabulary for describing trees or parts of trees. A *node* is any point in a tree from which lines emanate; each node is given a *node-label*, such as NP, S or Art in the tree above. Each node *dominates* the element or sequence of elements which occur below it in a tree, and which are linked to it by lines: thus in (8a) the node S dominates the sequence *NP V NP*, and the node V dominates the word *disturbed*. Any element or sequence of elements which is exhaustively dominated by a single node forms a *constituent*: thus in (8a) *the funny book*, which is exhaustively dominated by the NP node, is a constituent of the type NP, but *funny book* is not a constituent, because there is no node which dominates these two words and these two words only. Since they group elements into constituents or phrases, trees such as that in (8a) are called *constituent structure trees* or *phrase structure trees*, and the rules, like (7), which produce them, are *constituent structure rules*, or *phrase structure rules*. Finally, it is perhaps worth mentioning that there is an equivalent representation of (8a), given in the form of the labelled bracketing in (8b), where each pair of labelled brackets corresponds to a node in the phrase-structure tree (8a):

(8) b. $_S[_{NP}[\ _{Art}[\text{the}]_{Adj}[\text{funny}]_N[\text{book}]]_V[\text{disturbed}]_{NP}[_{Art}[\text{a}]$
$_{Adj}[\text{purple}]_N[\text{cat}]]]$

We began with a semantic justification for the constituent NP, arguing that it acted as a semantic unit, and that setting up trees like (8a) would form a basis for explaining this semantic behaviour. However, it is not only for semantic reasons that the elements *Art*, *Adj* and *N* should be grouped together into a single NP constituent. To label a sequence of elements as an NP is to make the explicit prediction that it will bear a syntactic resemblance to any other sequence with the same label. Thus, although our rules do not yet cater for them, and although not all of them contain an article or an adjective, all of the examples in (9) are NPs:

(9) a. you
   b. my girl-friend
   c. all the children
   d. the claim that dinosaurs were endothermic

By giving all these phrases the label NP, we are claiming that they will be able to occur in exactly the same syntactic positions as the NPs, like *the funny book*, which we have already seen. Moreover, in sets of related sentences of the kind illustrated in Chapter 3 (examples (32–33)), the NPs act as syntactic units, in the sense that the elements which constitute them are typically not separated from each other. Thus to (6a) corresponds the set of related sentences in (10):

(6) a. *The funny book* disturbed *a purple cat*.
(10) a. *A purple cat* was disturbed by *the funny book*.
   b. It was *the funny book* that disturbed *a purple cat*.
   c. Did *the funny book* disturb *a purple cat*? etc.

However, in general, (6a) has no related sentences in which the adjective or article is dissociated from the rest of the NP:

(11) a. *It was *purple* that *the funny book* disturbed *a – – cat*.
   b. *A purple* was disturbed by *the funny book cat*.

By setting up such syntactic constituents as NP, and by requiring syntactic rules themselves to refer only to syntactic constituents, we can take account of this typical syntactic behaviour.

The choice of the particular label *NP* rather than, say, *Nominal*, or *Type* 7, is in the first instance merely mnemonic: a *noun* phrase consists of a *noun* and associated material, such as adjectives and articles, relative clauses, etc. However, once the label has been chosen and set up as part of the descriptive machinery of linguistic theory, we are committed to the prediction that comparable categories will recur in the analyses of other languages of the world – in a significant number of cases, all other languages. By 'comparable', we do not mean that it will be possible to give a word by word translation of the sentences in (10) into French or Fante, with each category in English corresponding to exactly the same category in the other language. Rather, it is being claimed that French, Fante, and all languages, will give evidence of the need for a category NP which will consist of a noun and perhaps an article – even though this article may follow the noun as in Swedish, rather than precede it as in English; and that such an NP will occur as the subject and object of sentences, and will undergo comparable syntactic processes. Any descriptive category made available in this way by the theory is termed a *substantive universal*.

The idea that 'universal' means 'occurs in every language' is an oversimplification. A universal is a category necessary for the description of the total set of human languages. Some universals, for instance NP and N, are *strong universals*, which do occur in the grammar of every language. Others, for instance Article, are *weak universals*, which occur in the grammar of some languages, for example English and Swedish, but not in others, for example Russian, where the contrast expressed by our definite and indefinite articles is carried by other devices. It is clear that linguistic theory must provide for a category such as Article in order to account for languages like English. It is equally clear that, until the total inventory of universals is specified, the existence of weak universals may trivialize universal claims, since every apparent counter-example could be accommodated simply by adding a new category to the set of weak universals. One of the main aims of linguistic theory is precisely to limit the membership of the set of universals to a small finite number.[3]

The grouping of words into larger syntactic constituents is necessary for phonological, as well as syntactic and semantic reasons. The NP acts as a phonological unit, so that all the elements of an NP are normally pronounced as a whole, and parenthetical remarks and pauses for breath are typically injected not into the middle of the NP, but only at the beginning or the end:

(12) a. The purple book, Bill said, disturbed the funny cat.

b. The purple book disturbed the funny cat, Bill said.

c. *The, Bill said, purple book disturbed the funny cat.

d. *The purple book disturbed the funny, Bill said, cat.

Again, the claim that the syntactic analysis of a sentence provides information necessary for the semantic and phonological rules is borne out.

Clearly, not all the sentences of English have the structure described in (7). For example, as we saw in Chapter 3, *quake* is an intransitive verb, unable to take a direct object. Inserting it into the structure provided by (7) will always lead to ungrammatical results:

(13) a. *The funny cat quaked the purple book.

b. *The purple cat quaked a funny book.

We can modify (7) to allow for intransitive structures, by using parentheses to indicate that omission of the bracketed constituent is permissible:

(14) a. S → NP − V − (NP)

b. NP → Art − Adj − N

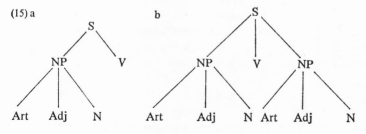

3. For further discussion of this point, see Chapter 12.

Each verb in the lexicon will now have to be marked for which of these structures it can be inserted into. *Shake*, having both transitive and intransitive uses, can be inserted into either of the trees in (15). This is shown in the lexicon by noting not only that *shake* is a verb, [+V], but that it can occur either with or without an NP immediately following it. This is represented by the feature [+ — (NP)] where the position of the underline shows that the verb can be inserted before an (optional) NP. The following sentences will thus be marked grammatical:

(16) a. The purple cat shook.
     b. The purple cat shook the funny book.

A verb like *abandon*, which has only transitive uses, will be marked in the lexicon as *obligatorily* followed by an NP, represented by the feature [+ — NP] indicating that it must be followed by a direct object. A verb like *quake*, which has only intransitive uses, will be marked as unable to occur immediately before an NP, represented by the feature [− — NP], where the minus sign shows that the verb cannot occur before an NP. Similar statements are needed to take account of the other special co-occurrence facts mentioned in Chapter 3: for example, that proper nouns take an article only if they are followed by a modifying clause or phrase, that certain verbs require a prepositional phrase or an adverbial rather than a direct object, and so on. In this way, the phrase-structure rules interact with the lexicon to yield an accurate syntactic analysis of a wide range of English sentences: the phrase-structure rules state which combinations of syntactic categories are permissible, and the lexical entry for a given word will state which of these combinations it actually enters into, and which it does not.

So far, our formal apparatus is still incapable of dealing with anything but single-clause structures in English. Yet clearly, the vast majority of English sentences are much more complex than this. Parallel to the single-clause structures in the (a) sentences below are the multi-clause structures in their (b)-variants:

(17) a. Your argument proves my point.

    b. That the girl is still alive proves that I was right.

(18) a. I know the truth.

    b. I know that he came.

(19) a. That silly claim upset the girl.

    b. That her mother said that she was lying upset the girl.

These examples show that verbs may have as their subjects or objects not just NPs of the type already introduced, but whole clauses, with their own internal subjects and objects. Suppose, then, that we modify the NP rule given in (7) to allow for the re-introduction of an S node:

(20) NP → $\begin{Bmatrix} (\text{Art}) - (\text{Adj}) - \text{N} \\ (\textit{that}) - \text{S} \end{Bmatrix}$

The curly brackets are used to indicate that the NP node may be expanded into either one of the bracketed sequences. That is, an NP may consist of a noun preceded by an article and/or an adjective, *or* it may consist of another sentence optionally preceded by *that*.[4] This immediately provides an analysis for each of the sentences in (17)–(19), as illustrated below in (21):

(21)

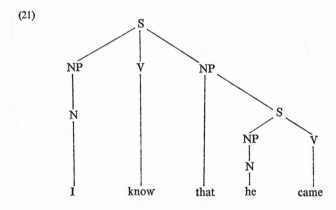

4. Note that we have also modified the first line of the rule to allow for the fact that articles and adjectives are optional rather than obligatory elements of the NP.

This change also accounts for the fact that clauses may act as subjects or objects, since we have already seen that NPs in certain configurations will be so interpreted by the semantic rules. More important, this minor modification in the rules now allows the grammar to produce an infinite range of sentences, simply by reintroducing the S node in one of its expansions of NP, and introducing it again under other NP nodes in a tree. For instance, (22) has the structure (23), where S has been reintroduced twice:

(22) I suspect that the queen thinks beagles are sacred.

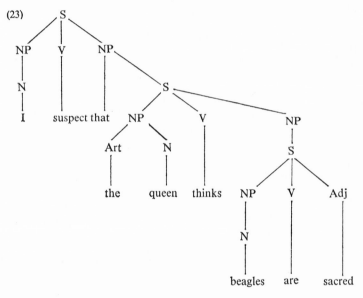

As there is no linguistic limit to the number of times S can be reintroduced in this fashion – cf. (24):

(24) I said that you knew that I thought that you felt that your friends understood that the committee had resolved that the members should be informed that . . . and so on,

it is impossible to construct the 'longest' sentence in English, and hence the number of sentences generated is infinite.

Provided the rules we have illustrated are elaborated to allow for such possibilities as the adjective *sacred* in (22); for prepositional phrases such as *with their friends*, etc., the grammar is capable in principle of providing an explicit syntactic analysis for an infinite set of English sentences, however long and complicated. However, there are still severe limitations in the power of these rules to give a full analysis even of one-clause structures in English. For instance, we have so far failed to take account of the existence of auxiliary verbs. Standard analyses of examples like (25) generally indicate that they contain a main verb (*shake*) and up to three auxiliary verbs (*may, have* and *be*):

(25) a. The tall man shook the bottle.
     b. The tall man may shake the bottle.
     c. The tall man has shaken the bottle.
     d. The tall man was shaking the bottle.
     e. The tall man may have shaken the bottle.
     f. The tall man may be shaking the bottle.
     g. The tall man has been shaking the bottle.
     h. The tall man may have been shaking the bottle.

This raises the question of whether we need a new syntactic category of auxiliary (Aux) in addition to the V category already introduced, and the more general question of how syntactic categories are identified and justified in the first place.

There are some obvious reasons for thinking that we need a separate category of Auxiliary in English. For example, yes-no questions are formed in different ways depending on whether they contain an auxiliary verb or not. Those containing an auxiliary invert it with the subject NP (26–28), while those without an auxiliary (29) insert a 'dummy' *do*, and invert *it* round the subject NP; hence the grammaticality of the (a) sentences below and the ill-formedness of the (b) sentences, where the auxiliaries have been treated as though they were main verbs and vice versa:

(26) a. Have you shaken the bottle?
     b. *Do you have shaken the bottle?

(27) a. May you shake the bottle?

b. *Do you may shake the bottle?

(28) a. Are you shaking the bottle?

b. *Do you be shaking the bottle?

(29) a. Do you shake the bottle?

b. *Shake you the bottle?

(30) a. Did you shake the bottle?

b. *Shook you the bottle?

This seems to indicate that we need a distinction between main verb and auxiliary verb in order to predict the full range of yes-no questions in English.

On the other hand, there are many respects in which main verbs and auxiliaries are alike in their behaviour. For example, the *first* verbal element in a clause changes its form depending on the person and number of its subject NP:

(31) a. He *has* been skiing.

b. They *have* been skiing.

(32) a. He *is* skiing.

b. They *are* skiing.

(33) a. He *skis*.

b. They *ski*.

This is true whether the first such element is an auxiliary verb, as in (31) and (32), or a main verb, as in (33): the agreement rule treats the two identically. Moreover, in certain types of sentence the second of two identical verbal elements may be omitted:

(34) a. One boy ate pastries and the other boy ate fruit.

b. One boy ate pastries and the other boy __ fruit.

(35) a. One boy may eat pastries and the other boy may drink fruit juice.

b. One boy may eat pastries and the other boy __ drink fruit juice.

Again, the rule which governs this omission process seems to treat verbs and auxiliaries alike. Further, in the case of the sentences containing the quantifier *all* that we discussed in Chapter 3, the most obvious generalization is that a quantifier which is separated from its NP may occur immediately to the left of a verb or an auxiliary. Once again, if auxiliaries *are* verbs, as their traditional name 'auxiliary verb' might lead one to expect, then this statement can be correspondingly simplified to allow for the occurrence of the quantifier immediately to the left of a verb. Such evidence suggests that, whatever the superficial differences between them, auxiliaries and verbs should both be treated as belonging to the same syntactic category at some level of analysis. If there is a distinction to be drawn, it is between the *first* verb in a sentence and all the other verbs, rather than between main and auxiliary verbs. Accordingly, we shall treat the auxiliary verbs of English as belonging to the syntactic category V.

The rules in (7) must now be modified to allow for the occurrence of more than one verb per clause. The simplest way of doing this is to introduce a new category of *verb-phrase* (VP), which is parallel to the NP in that it contains a verb and other associated material. This associated material may be a direct object NP, or another VP: the new rules would look as follows:

(36) a. S $\rightarrow$ NP — VP

     b. NP $\rightarrow$ $\left\{ \begin{matrix} (Art) - (Adj) - (N) \\ (that) - S \end{matrix} \right\}$

     c. VP $\rightarrow$ V — $\left\{ \begin{matrix} (NP) \\ (VP) \end{matrix} \right\}$

These rules will generate structures like the following:

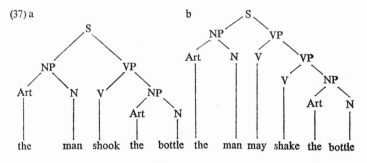

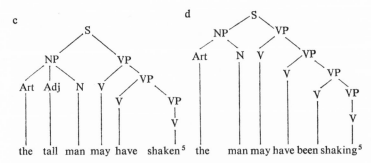

As they stand, the rules in (36) will generate a wide range of ungrammatical sentences, as well as the grammatical ones shown. For example, they will allow for more than one main verb per clause, as in (38a), no main verb at all, as in (38b), and the impermissible sequences of auxiliaries and main verbs in (38c) and (38d):

(38) a. *The man quaked shook the bottle.
    b. *The man may the bottle.
    c. *The man is maying have shaken.
    d. *The man shakes have been mayed.

Some of these structures can be eliminated by the use of the lexical entries for verbs. For example, *shake*, *quake* and other main verbs must always be the last verb in a clause: this condition can be handled by a simple extension of the kind of lexical statement made earlier, that *quake* could optionally be followed by nothing at all except adverbials and prepositional phrases. Thus *shake* and *quake* may be assigned the syntactic feature $[- \_\_ V]$, indicating that they cannot be followed by another verb. On the other hand, auxiliary verbs, which must always be followed by a main verb, and must always be inserted into pre-final position in a clause, may be assigned the feature $[+ \_\_ V]$, showing that they

5. We are assuming that further rules will eventually determine the correct form of the verbs in each structure, so that the past participial form *shaken* occurs after *have*, the infinitive *shake* after *may*, and so on.

must always be followed by another verb. These provisions in the lexicon will rule out (38a), (38b) and (38d).

The problem with (38c) is rather different. Here the main verb has been correctly inserted into final position, and the two auxiliaries into pre-final position, but the two auxiliaries are in the wrong order. English imposes severe constraints on the order of auxiliaries. If there is a modal verb (*can, shall, will, must, may* and their past-tense versions) it must be the first verb in its clause. If there is a perfective *have*, it may be preceded only by a modal, and followed only by a progressive *be* or a main verb. If there is a progressive *be*, it may be preceded only by a modal or *have*, and followed only by a main verb. In other words, the permissible sequences of auxiliaries are the following:

(39) Modal – *have* (perfective) – *be* (progressive)

One straightforward way of guaranteeing that only these sequences are grammatical would be as follows. Allow auxiliaries to be inserted into any pre-final V node, in accordance with the lexical conditions just given. Once they have been inserted into appropriate trees, check their sequence in these trees against the statement in (39). If they are in the order prescribed by (39), treat them as grammatical; if they occur in some other order, mark them as ungrammatical and discard them. (39) is thus being used as a *filter*, applied to the trees produced by the phrase-structure rules and the lexicon, retaining some and discarding others. Such filters seem to be a necessary – though arbitrary – part of the grammar of many languages. Accordingly, something equivalent to (39) might be incorporated into the syntax of English, as a filter which can scan a whole tree produced by the interaction of the syntactic rules and the lexical entries for individual words, and accept it as well-formed or reject it as ungrammatical.

Transformations

With this apparatus, we return to a range of sentences which have already been mentioned a number of times:

(40) a. All the children might have played with their friends.
　　 b. The children all might have played with their friends.
　　 c. The children might all have played with their friends.
　　 d. The children might have all played with their friends.

The rules in (36) can be modified once more, to allow for the optional occurrence of a quantifier *all* (Q) within the NP, and a prepositional phrase (PP) after the verb and its direct object, if any:

(41) a. S → NP — VP

　　 b. NP → $\begin{cases} (Q) - (Art) - (Adj) - N \\ (that) - S \end{cases}$

　　 c. VP → V — $\begin{cases} (NP) - (PP) \\ (VP) \end{cases}$

　　 d. PP → P — NP

(41) now provides a direct analysis for (40a), as in (42):

(42)

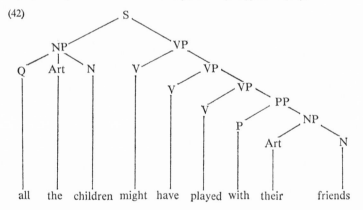

However, by introducing Q only within the NP, we have provided no way of analysing (40b–d). How should these sentences be dealt with?

It seems that no modification of (41) will produce the full range of grammatical sentences without also producing ungrammatical sentences. For example, if we allow for the optional occurrence of a Q before each of the verbs shown in (42), (40b–d) will be correctly produced, but so will the following ungrammatical sentences, each of which contains more than one occurrence of Q:

(43) a. *All the children all might have played with their friends.
b. *The children all might all have played with their friends.
c. *All the children all might all have played with their friends.
d. *All the children all might all have all played with their friends.

But the fact is that though *all* has considerable freedom of occurrence in sentences like (40), it may occur only once for each subject NP that occurs. Phrase-structure rules, such as (41), are incapable of dealing with this type of constraint.

What seems to be needed is a new sort of rule, like a filter in the sense that it can scan a whole tree produced by the phrase-structure rules, but unlike a filter in that, instead of just being able to mark a tree as well-formed or ill-formed, it can actually move items around, into new configurations. The rule needed in this case would be able to detach a Q from within an NP, and move it to the left of any verb in the structure. The tree in (42) would be converted by such a rule to any of the trees in (44)–(46), each corresponding to one of the examples already given:

(44)

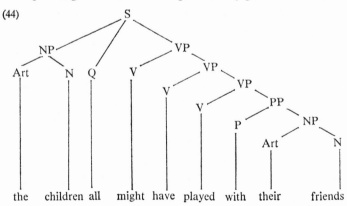

(45)

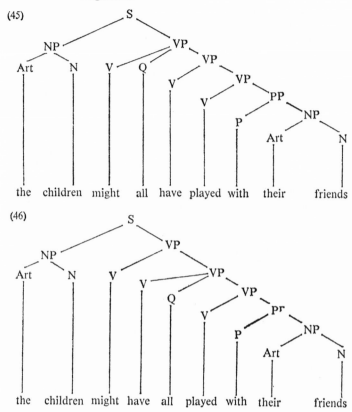

(46)

A rule that can alter trees in this way is a *transformation*. Using a transformation to analyse the sentences in (40) has two obvious advantages over any attempt to analyse them in terms of phrase-structure rules alone. First, it guarantees that if a Q ever occurs in pre-verbal position, as in (40b–d), it will automatically disappear from the subject NP, so that the ungrammatical sentences in (43) will never be produced. Second, it greatly simplifies the task of the semantic rules. The sentences in (40) all mean the same. Suppose that we set up the semantic rules so that they assign a (representation of) meaning to the tree in (42), before the transformation moving the quantifier ever applies. Then the synonymy of

(40a) with (40b–d) will be guaranteed: the operation of the transformation will be irrelevant to the semantic rules; only the structures produced by the phrase-structure rules will be relevant for semantic interpretation.

The formal representation of transformations is fairly straightforward. Each transformational rule describes an input tree, which it converts into an output tree. Thus the transformation of Q-Floating, which we have discussed, will look as follows:

(47) *Q-FLOATING*   *Input tree:* (or: structural description)

$$Q - X - V - X$$

Output tree: (or: structural change)

$$X - Q - V - X$$

The X in these statements is a variable, which can stand for anything at all, or nothing, in a tree. The rule says that any tree which contains a quantifier and a verb, separated by anything at all, may be converted into another tree in which the quantifier immediately precedes the verb, leaving everything else unchanged. The application of this rule to the tree in (42) will automatically produce (44), (45) and (46), depending on which of the Vs in (42) is taken to be the relevant one. In (48) below, each element of the tree in (42) has been associated with some term in the structural description of the transformation given in (47). The output, or structural change, of this transformation will yield the tree in (45): the effect of the transformation is indicated by the dotted line:

(48)

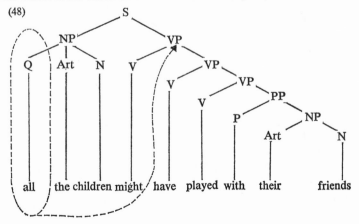

There are different possible analyses of the tree in (42): the reader may check for himself that each one yields a different member of (40a–d) when used as input to the transformation of Q-Floating.

Transformations bring with them such a simplification of both syntactic and semantic rules that they have been very widely used in recent grammars. Just how widely they should be used is a question that is still open, as we shall see in the chapters to come. For the moment, we merely want to illustrate the kind of operations on trees that transformations can be used to perform: they may move items, delete items, or add them to a tree. The transformation in (47) is a *movement* transformation: furthermore, it is one that operates within the bounds of a single clause. Thus, while it is possible to float the quantifier to pre-verbal position in (40), it is not possible to float it across a main verb and into a different clause: thus (49b) is *not* related to (49a), and (50b), despite the existence of (50a), is not even grammatical:

(49) a. All the children said the fireworks might have been stolen.
    b. The children said the fireworks might all have been stolen.
(50) a. All the children regretted that both their parents had been arrested.
    b. *The children regretted that both their parents had all been arrested.

Although Q-Floating is thus restricted to applying within the bounds of a single clause, there are some transformations which can range 'unboundedly' over an indefinitely large number of clauses. Consider an example first used in Chapter 3:

(51) a. The police have examined the bullet.
    b. *Which bullet* have the police examined?

Although the sequence of words in (51b) could be generated by a phrase-structure rule, no such rule could express the fact that the italicized NP *which bullet* is, semantically speaking, the direct object of the verb *examined*. As we have seen, direct objects in

English normally follow the verb. Moreover, the lexical entry for *examine* needs to state not only that it is a verb but that, like *abandon*, it is a transitive verb, which requires a direct object, and should therefore be followed by an NP, as it is in (51a). These points can be dealt with simultaneously and simply on the assumption that *which bullet* starts out from direct object position immediately to the right of *examined*, as in the echo question (52):

(52) The police have examined *which* bullet?

and is moved to the front of the sentence by a transformation of *Wh*-Movement. This rule would convert the tree in (53a) to that in (53b):

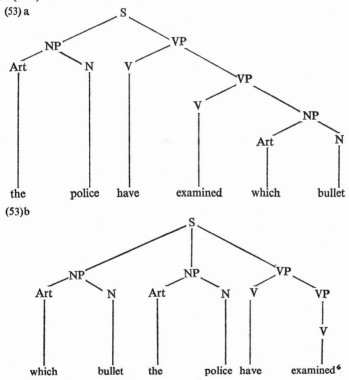

6. A further rule inverting *the police* and *have* is independently needed to account for the word-order of (51b).

This particular case involves only a single clause, but crucially, there is no limit to the complexity of material across which such a questioned constituent can be moved. This is shown by the pair of sentences in (54), where the NP *which offence* has been taken from its original position after *overlook* and moved across four other NPs:

(54) a. The plaintiff suggested the police had advised the criminal to bribe the judge to overlook *which offence*?
   b. Which offence did the plaintiff suggest the police had advised the criminal to bribe the judge to overlook?

Similar unbounded rules are used in the formation of relative clauses, as in (55), and topicalized sentences, as in (56):

(55) a. She was supposed to get her brother to find someone to give a cake to *the boy*.
   b. The boy she was supposed to get her brother to find someone to give a cake to had vanished.
(56) a. I will on no account ever allow you to bring caterpillars to the service.
   b. Caterpillars I will on no account ever allow you to bring to the service.

Apart from being able to move constituents around, transformations can also *delete* items. A typical example of the effects of such deletion was seen in examples (34) and (35) above repeated here for convenience:

(57) a. One boy ate pastries and the other boy ate fruit.
   b. One boy ate pastries and the other boy __ fruit.
(58) a. One boy may eat pastries and the other boy may drink fruit juice.
   b. One boy may eat pastries and the other boy __ drink fruit juice.

The simplest analysis of such sentences would involve generating only the (a) sentences by phrase-structure rules, but setting up a transformation which would optionally delete the second of the two identical verbs, yielding the related (b) sentences. Such an analysis would make the explicit claim that these sentence pairs were syntactically related. It would also support the general claim that all clauses contain a verb at some level of syntactic analysis. Moreover, the verb which is eventually deleted makes an obvious contribution to the semantic analysis of (57b) and (58b): (57b), for example, must be interpreted as meaning the same as (57a): it cannot be interpreted as meaning that one boy ate pastries and the other boy picked fruit. This would follow naturally from the assumption that (57a–b) and (58a–b), being syntactically related, share their semantic analyses, and are thus predicted as synonymous.

Finally, transformations may *add* syntactic features to a tree. The agreement rules found in many languages provide evidence for this. For example, in English the subject and verb of a sentence must agree in number: a singular subject goes with a singular verb, and a plural subject with a plural verb. Assuming that noun-phrases can be either singular or plural – can contain the syntactic feature [+singular] or [−singular] – this relationship could be handled in the following way. A transformation could be set up to copy the feature [+singular] or [−singular] from the subject NP onto the verb, guaranteeing the correct agreement. The form of the verb would in all cases be determined by the form of the subject. Other agreement rules in other languages could be handled in similar ways.

In this chapter, we have outlined a transformational grammar of the following form. It contains three components: syntactic, semantic and phonological; the semantic and phonological components have access to the output of the syntactic component, but not vice versa. The syntactic component itself falls into two major sub-parts. There are *phrase-structure* rules like those in (41), which state what basic combinations of syntactic categories are permissible within the sentence, using labels like S, NP, V, Art, Adj, PP and so on. Into the trees thus created, words from the appropriate categories may be inserted from the *lexicon*. At this stage, certain *filters* may be applied to weed out ungrammatical combinations, as in the case of auxiliary verbs already discussed. The resulting trees are the *deep structures* of English. The other major type of syntactic rule is the *transformation*, which converts trees produced by the phrase-structure rules into other trees. All transformations are *structure-dependent*: that is, they operate not simply on arbitrary strings of words, but on strings analysed into syntactic categories and constituents which determine the applicability of transformations. Transformations perform three basic types of operation. In the case of Q-Floating, the relevant operation was one of moving a Q from within a subject NP to immediately before a verb, leaving the rest of the tree unchanged. As we have seen, transformations may also delete, and occasionally insert material into a tree. The tree which results from the application of a transformation is a *derived structure* and the tree resulting from the application of all transformations is the *surface structure*. Strictly speaking, then, the syntactic component produces two outputs for each sentence: a deep structure, and a surface structure.

The question then arises: which of these two outputs is the one relevant to the semantic and phonological components? In the case of the phonological component, the answer is clear: only the surface structure is relevant. This is because the phonological component must assign different pronunciations, stress and intonation contours to each of a range of sentences which may share their deep structure. Thus the examples in (40), which share a deep structure, are phonologically distinct from each other. It is only at the level of surface structure that their differences will become apparent – differences in word-order and constituent structure in this case. Hence it must be the syntactic surface structure which is available to the phonological rules.

In the case of the semantic component, the answer is not so clear cut. In the classical version of transformational grammar set out in Chomsky's *Aspects of the Theory of Syntax* (1965), it was claimed that only syntactic deep structure was relevant to the semantic interpretation of sentences. We reiterated that claim when dealing with the examples in (40), arguing that it would be

simpler for semantic interpretation to take place before the transformation of Q-Floating performed its operations, separating the
quantifier from the NP which it is semantically associated with.
However, we have also argued, in Chapter 3, that the semantic
rules must have access to the phonological structure of a sentence – in particular to its stress pattern. Since stress patterns are
not normally available at the level of deep structure, this seems to
indicate that a semantic component which has access only to deep
structure will not be entirely adequate. Ignoring for the moment
the relationship between semantics and phonology, the form of
grammar presented in this chapter might be summed up in the
following diagram:

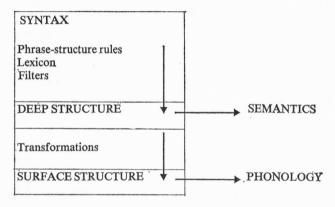

The phonological, syntactic and semantic components could then
be seen as specifying, for each sentence, a means of relating sound
to meaning and meaning to sound, via the levels of deep and surface structure.

For many reasons, it seems that this extremely elegant conception of the form of a transformational grammar cannot be correct. The problems centre on the nature of deep structure and its
role in syntax and semantics. In the next chapter we look at these
problems in more detail, and sketch out some alternative conceptions of grammar.

5. For and Against Deep Structure

In the last chapter, we suggested that the syntactic component has two outputs: a deep structure produced by inserting words from the lexicon into trees created by the phrase-structure rules, and a surface structure produced by applying transformations to the deep structure trees, adding, deleting or moving material around. In this chapter, we want to look more closely at the arguments for a syntactic level of deep structure, and its relation to surface structure and to semantics. We first illustrate some of the classical arguments used to motivate this level of syntactic analysis, and then discuss some of the objections and modifications that have been formulated in recent years.

Arguments for Deep Structure

There are two main types of justification for the level of deep structure: first, that having such a level simplifies the statement of semantic rules, and second, that having such a level simplifies the statement of syntactic rules. In other words, having a level of deep structure makes it easier to formulate significant linguistic generalizations on both the syntactic and semantic levels. We have already given one example of this with respect to the rule of Q-Floating, which brings with it a wide range of correct predictions about both the syntactic and semantic properties of sentences containing *all*.

To take the semantic arguments first. A fairly basic assumption about the semantic component is that in order to work properly it must be able to recognize the subject and object of each verb in a sentence. Hence a first step towards the semantic interpretation of (1) and (2) would be the discovery that the subject and object roles are reversed between them:

(1) The diver fascinated the dolphins.

(2) The dolphins fascinated the diver.

It is also obvious that the notion of subject and object relevant for semantics is not that of surface structure subject, but rather that of underlying or logical subject. In (1) and (2) the surface subjects and logical subjects coincide; however in (3a) and (3b), where the italicized surface subjects differ, the logical subject is felt to be the same:

(3) a. *Where the robbers have their hideout* is still unclear.

b. *It* is still unclear where the robbers have their hideout.

Similarly, the surface subjects differ in (4a) and (4b), but the logical subjects do not:

(4) a. *He* was eaten by an antelope.

b. *An antelope* ate him.

The notion of logical subject corresponds to some traditional definitions of the subject: doer of the action, experiencer of the state, etc. One task of the grammar, then, and a task relevant for semantic interpretation, is to determine logical subjects and objects for each verb in a sentence.

Another assumption made in classical Chomskyan grammar is that it is not necessary or desirable to label the logical subject and object as such at any point in the syntactic analysis of a sentence. So the grammar would never provide trees like the following for (1):

(5)

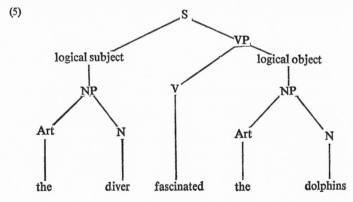

It would provide the same tree, but without the subject and object labels. The claim underlying this assumption is that there is never any syntactic rule which applies only to logical subjects or objects and not to other NPs: for example, to logical subjects and objects and not to surface subjects and objects. *Logical subject* and *logical object* are not categories to which the syntax ever needs to refer.

If these two assumptions are correct, then one of two further claims must also be correct. Either logical subjects and objects can be determined directly by inspection of surface structures, or there is another level of representation at which logical subjects and objects can be directly determined. To show that the second of these claims – which would motivate a level of deep structure – is plausible, we must discredit the first claim: the claim that logical subjects and objects can be determined by examination of surface structures with no subject and object labels.

We can at least show that it would be a rather complicated job to find logical subjects and objects direct from surface structure, without subject and object labels. For example, in the following sentences, the italicized NPs all bear the logical subject relation to the verb *leave*:

(6) a. *The man* left last night.
   b. *Which man* did John say left last night?
   c. The woman left yesterday and *the man* today.
   d. *The man* who I thought left last night was your uncle.
   e. *The man* wanted to try to leave last night.
   f. *The man* was thought by many to have been supposed to leave last night.
   g. Leaving, *the man* tripped over the doorstep.

It seems that in surface structure there is no easy rule which will determine the logical subject for a given verb. In some cases the verb precedes its subject, and in others it follows. In some cases the verb is next to its subject, and in other cases it is far away from it. In some cases the verb is in a different clause from its subject, and in others in the same clause. Moreover, the relation of logical subject to verb is not the same for all surface configurations and all verbs. Thus, *the man* is the logical subject of *leave* in (7a), but not in (7b), although the surface trees for both sentences are the same:

(7) a. The man is anxious to leave.
   b. The man is difficult to leave.

In (8a), which is ambiguous, there is one interpretation on which *the man* is the logical subject of *leave*, as in (8b), and one on which it is the logical object, as in (8c):

(8) a. The man was good to leave.
   b. It was good of the man to leave.
   c. It was good to leave the man.

Notice too that it is frequently not purely semantic considerations which determine what is the logical subject of a verb. Thus, the only way to make sense of (9) is to assume that *the man* is the logical subject of *leave*; but the syntax of the sentence does not permit this interpretation:

(9) ?The departure lounge was said to have left the man.

Hence, although we are assuming that there is no need for a label 'logical subject', i.e. no syntactic rule which would apply to all and only the italicized NPs in (6), and although the relation of logical subject to verb cannot easily be defined over surface structure trees, it seems that the determination of subject-verb relations is largely a syntactic matter.

Chomsky's elegant resolution of this problem was to posit a level of syntactic deep structure at which subject-verb relations could be very simply defined, and then to provide syntactic rules which would transform these deep structures into the actually occurring surface strings. The logical subject of a verb would be defined as the NP immediately preceding it in deep structure; the logical direct object would be the NP immediately following it. Between deep and surface structures, syntactic rules could delete NPs or verbs, could move NPs over verbs, as in passive sentences, or move them to the front of whole clauses, as in relative clauses and questions, and hence account for the widely differing configurations of surface structure. This simultaneously makes sense of the judgement that logical subjects and objects are syntactically determined, and the seemingly conflicting judgement that no syntactic rule ever refers to a node labelled 'logical subject' or 'logical object'.

To take just one example of how judgements about logical subjects and logical objects suggest deep structures of a particular form, consider (10), and its standard deep structure (11):

(10) The party was hard for Bill to leave.

(11)

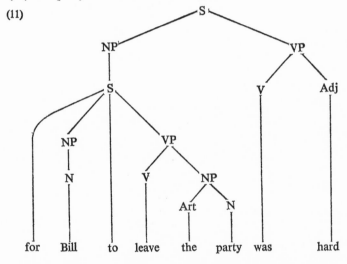

Contrary to what the surface structure suggests, the logical subject of *was hard* in (10) is not *the party*, but the whole clause *for Bill to leave the party*. This fact is represented in deep structure by making the whole clause the subject of the VP *was hard*. In the subject subordinate clause itself, *Bill* is made the subject of *leave*, showing that it is Bill who does the leaving; and again contrary to what the surface structure suggests, *the party* is made the direct object of *leave*, showing that it is the party that gets left. The transformation needed to convert this tree into the surface structure in (10) is called Tough-movement (because it applies only in sentences containing one of a small class of adjectives including *tough, hard, difficult, easy*). It removes the NP *the party* from its subordinate clause position to become the surface subject of the VP *was hard*, shifting the remainder of the subordinate clause to the end of the sentence. The resulting surface structure would look as follows:

(12)

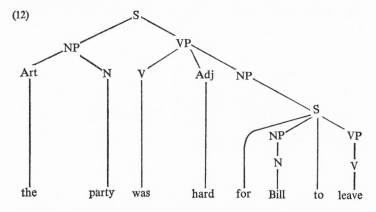

The strategy for writing deep structures based on this line of argument is to find the logical subject and object of each verb in a sentence, and to provide a deep structure in which the logical subject appears immediately before its verb, and the logical object immediately after it. One would then set up syntactic rules to transform this deep structure into the actually occurring surface string, and semantic rules which would make use of the deep structure information about subjects and objects in providing a semantic representation for the sentence. Notice that this commits us to finding identical deep structures for any range of sentences all of which contain the same words and express the same subject-verb-object relations. Thus the deep structure for (10) will also be the deep structure for the synonymous (13) and (14):

(13) For Bill to leave the party was hard.

(14) It was hard for Bill to leave the party.

The surface structure for (13) is essentially the same as its deep structure, while (14) motivates a rule of Extraposition, which moves a subject clause to the end of the sentence, replacing it with the dummy subject *it*. By allowing the semantic rules access only to deep structures, one would thus automatically simplify their task: since (10), (13) and (14) are indistinguishable from each other at the level of deep structure, they would necessarily be predicted as synonymous.

Having seen how the postulation of a level of deep structure can greatly simplify the task of the semantic component, we now look at some evidence that it can also greatly simplify the task of the syntactic component, making it possible to state generalizations that would not be statable at the level of surface structure alone. In general, arguments of this type reinforce the conclusions reached via arguments of the first type. Consider the behaviour of *there* in sentences such as (15):

(15) a. There is an elephant in the garden.

b. There appeared a mistake in our final draft.

It is clear that this word is distinct from the *there* in (16):

(16) He sat down *there*.

in that it behaves like an NP rather than an adverb. For instance, like other NPs, it inverts with the first verb of a sentence to form yes/no questions:

(17) a. The elephant was in the garden.

b. Was the elephant in the garden?

(18) a. There was an elephant in the garden.

b. Was there an elephant in the garden?

Like subject pronoun NPs, it is repeated at the end of 'tag-questions' like (19):

(19) a. *The elephant* was in the garden, wasn't *it*?
  b. There was an elephant in the garden, wasn't there?

Thus it seems that *there* should be labelled in the lexicon both as a pronoun and as an NP.

However, *there* also shows marked divergencies from the behaviour of other pronominal NPs such as *it*, *he*, etc. For example, it cannot appear in anything but subject position in a sentence:

(20) a. I like him.   *I like there.
  b. I gave her a book.   *I gave there a book.
  c. I left with it.   *I left with there.

Moreover, it can appear only as the subject of the verb *be*, or one of a small number of other verbs such as *appear* and *arise*:

(21) a. *There crawled a baby upstairs.
  b. *There trumpeted three elephants in the cage.

Furthermore, the NP which is in fact the logical subject of a sentence which contains *there* – the NP that appears immediately after *be* – should normally be indefinite:

(22) a. There may be a flaw (*the flaw) in this argument.
  b. There appeared a mistake (*the mistake) in the final draft.

It seems, then, that the entry for *there* in the lexicon, if it is to take account of all these restrictions on the appearance of *there* in sentences, would have to be very complex indeed.

Rather than trying to build all these restrictions into the lexicon, it might be simpler to account for the behaviour of *there* by means of a transformation. This transformation would optionally insert *there* into a tree which already has precisely the relevant properties, namely an indefinite subject and the verb *be*, *appear*, *arise*, etc. That is, it would convert a tree of the form (23a) into one of the form (23b):

(23) a

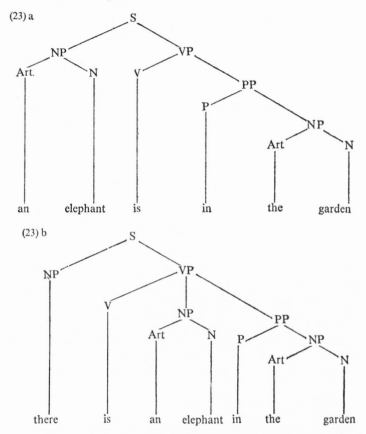

(23) b

All of the grammatical sentences mentioned above would be generated by means of this transformation, and none of the ungrammatical ones. On the assumption that all occurrences of *there* in surface structure result from this transformation, the divergencies between the behaviour of *there* and other pronominal NPs would have a straightforward explanation.

In fact, there is further syntactic and semantic support for this analysis, from sentences involving verbs like *seem, happen* and *appear*. For any sentence of the form (24) there is a corresponding sentence of the form (25):

(24) It seems that the heron eats frogs.

(25) The heron seems to eat frogs.

Any anomaly in a sentence of the first type is matched by an exactly comparable anomaly in a sentence of the second type, as in (26):

(26) a. ?It seems that this triangle has eloped.

   b. ?This triangle seems to have eloped.

Furthermore, there are no grammatical sentences of the type shown in (27), where *seem* and *eat* have distinct surface subjects:

(27) a. *They seem that the heron eats frogs.

   b. *The heron seems that the stork eats frogs.

In other words, there is a dependency between the subject of *seem* and the subject of the verb which immediately follows it in surface structure. If the subject of *seem* is *it*, then the following verb may have a surface subject, as in (24). If the subject of *seem* is a non-pronominal NP like *the heron*, then the following verb must have no subject at all, as in (25). In no case may both *seem* and its following verb have full NP subjects, as in (27).

All these facts could be explained on the assumption that there is a transformation which relates sentences like (24) to sentences like (25). Specifically, it would convert the deep structure in (28a), which underlies both (24) and (25), to the tree in (28b), which is the surface structure of (25):

(28)a

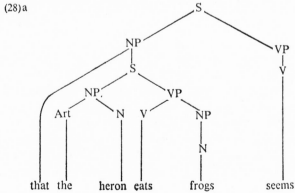

(28) b

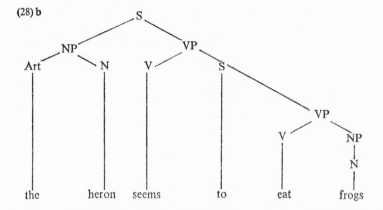

This new transformation, Raising, takes the logical subject of a subordinate clause and makes it the subject of a verb like *seem* in the next clause up, shifting the remainder of the subordinate clause to the end of the sentence. It thus does for logical subjects of subordinate clauses what Tough-movement did for logical objects.

Such a rule would provide an explanation for the superficially puzzling distribution of data in (29):

(29) a. The otter seemed to swim effortlessly through the water.
     b. The otter seemed to be swimming effortlessly through the water.
     c. There seemed to be an otter swimming effortlessly through the water.
     d. *There seemed to be the otter swimming effortlessly through the water.
     e. *There seemed to swim an otter effortlessly through the water.

That is, *there* may occur as the subject of *seem* only if the verb immediately after *seem* is *be* (*appear*, *arise*, etc.), and only if the logical subject of this following verb is indefinite. Given a grammar which contains both There-insertion and Raising, and given that There-insertion applies before Raising does, the distribution of data in (29) will be automatically predicted. For example, (29c) will be derived in two stages from the underlying structure in (30):

(30)

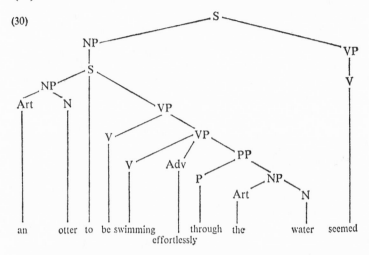

First, There-insertion will apply to the subordinate clause, inserting *there* as the subject of the verb *be*; second, Raising will remove this new subject and make it the subject of *seem*, as in (29c). (29d) and (29e) will not be derived, because of the constraints on the application of There-insertion that we have already seen.

Thus, a grammar incorporating a level of deep structure and these two transformations makes it possible to give a simple treatment of a rather complex set of facts. Accounting for the ungrammatical sentences in (21), (22) and (27) in a grammar with no level of syntax deeper than surface structure would be quite difficult; this is mainly because of the possibility of embedding a number of verbs from the *seem* class under one another, so that the *there* may be indefinitely far removed in surface structure from the *be + indefinite phrase* that must ultimately justify its existence. Thus (31) is grammatical , but (32) is not:

(31) There often seem to happen to turn out to *be difficulties* with such analyses.

(32) *There often seem to happen to turn out to eat snails in France.

Any difficulty which arises in stating the behaviour of *there* using a level of surface structure alone tends to make grammars with a level of deep structure look more attractive.

A similar type of argument for deep structure, this time not depending on the notions of logical subject and object, is the following. Sentences of type (33)–(37) are all grammatical:

(33) A friend of Bill's came in.
(34) Some friends of Bill's came in.
(35) Those friends of Bill's came in.
(36) All those friends of Bill's came in.
(37) Several fat friends of Bill's came in.

Although (38) is also grammatical, sentences of type (39)–(42) are not:

(38) The friend of Bill's that you wanted me to meet came in.
(39) *The friend of Bill's came in.
(40) *All the friends of Bill's came in.
(41) *Some of the friends of Bill's came in.
(42) *The fat friends of Bill's came in.

Parallel to (39)–(42), and with the same meaning, are the following grammatical sentences:

(43) Bill's friend came in.
(44) All Bill's friends came in.
(45) Some of Bill's friends came in.
(46) Bill's fat friends came in.

To take account of (33)–(46) in a grammar without deep structure, one would have to set up rules generating (33)–(38), further rules vetoing the parallel structures (39)–(42), and still further rules permitting (43)–(46). This treatment, while fairly complicated, would still miss the fact that (43)–(46) are both syntactically and semantically related to the ungrammatical (39)–(42). If one instead set up rules generating both (33)–(38) and (39)–(42) as deep structures, and a further rule converting the ungrammatical (39)–(42) into (43)–(46), there would be a number of immediate linguistic advantages. First, as in most other sentences in English, *the* could be treated as forming a class with *a, several, some, this, that,* etc., entering into the same structures and performing the same types of semantic function: its exceptional surface behaviour would not be accounted for by a special syntactic rule. Second, there would be a considerable simplification of the syntactic rules in the grammar. Third, the ungrammaticality of (39)–(42) would be explicitly related to the grammaticality of (43)–(46), since the one set of sentences would be derived from the other. Fourth, the grammar would now express the fact that the meaning of (43)–(46) is exactly the meaning that would have been predicted for (39)–(42) if these sentences had been grammatical. Thus the deep structure treatment of this type of phenomenon seems to have clear advantages over the surface structure treatment.

The strategy for constructing deep structures based on this line of argument would be as follows. Find a range of sentences which are all grammatical except for a small, ungrammatical subclass. Find a further range of sentences which 'fill the gap' in the paradigm – in other words, which are grammatical and mean the same as the ungrammatical subclass. Set up deep structure rules which directly generate the whole paradigm, ungrammatical sentences included; then set up a syntactic rule or rules converting the ungrammatical subclass into the related grammatical sentences. A classic example of this type of gap-in-paradigm argument has been used to justify the syntactic rule of reflexive:

Paradigm	you washed		
		me	*myself
		*you	yourself
		him	*himself
		her	*herself
		it	*itself
		them	*themselves

Procedure   a) Well-formed deep structure: NP V NP.

b) Syntactic rule: if the two NPs are identical,[1] convert the second into the related reflexive pronoun.

Generalizations a) The syntactic rule relates the grammatical paradigm containing one ungrammatical member to the ungrammatical paradigm containing one grammatical member, predicting both paradigms correctly.

b) It explains why *I washed myself* means what *I washed me* would mean if it were grammatical.

c) It captures the generalization that reflexive pronouns in English only occur if they have an identical antecedent NP.

On the basis of these two types of argument – subject-object arguments and economy and generality of syntactic rules – a large number of compelling generalizations have been achieved, both about the grammar of English and other languages, and about syntactic organization in general. However, within the same broad framework first elaborated by Chomsky, there are at least two possible approaches to syntactic and semantic generalization which make no appeal to a level of deep structure as Chomsky defined it. We now turn to a discussion of these alternative approaches.

Arguments against Deep Structure

Since 1965, when Chomsky published *Aspects of the Theory of Syntax*, many linguists have come to the conclusion that classical

1. In fact identity might appear to be too strong a condition. *I* is not identical to *me*. However, at the stage when reflexivization occurs there is no distinction between I/me, she/her and so on. That is, the lexicon needs to contain only *one* of each of these pairs, and the other can be predicted by rule.

deep structure cannot exist. *Generative semanticists* have argued that there is no clear-cut distinction between syntactic and semantic rules, and hence that the level of syntactic deep structure defined as the input to both cannot be defended. Their solution is to set up syntactic-semantic rules which take semantic representations as their input and yield surface structures as their output, with no intervening level of deep structure. *Interpretive semanticists* have successively abandoned the defining assumptions which underlay the level of deep structure, transferring more and more of the work of the syntactic rules into the semantic component, so that 'deep structure' has gradually moved nearer and nearer to the surface syntax of the sentence. We thus need to look at two types of argument against classical deep structure: the first designed to show that it is not deep enough, and the second designed to show that it is too deep.

(a) *Deep structure is not deep enough.* In general, this type of argument against deep structure takes the classical arguments *for* deep structure, and carries them a stage further. Hence, if one believes the original arguments for deep structure, one is eventually forced, by arguments of the same type, to conclude that deep structures are deeper than was first thought.

One of the defining features of deep structure in Chomsky's (1965) model was that deep structures contained actual words inserted from the lexicon, and that once a word had been inserted into a tree, it could not subsequently be turned into another word, although it could undergo certain morphological changes which could, for example, realize it as a participle or gerund rather than in finite form.[2] No deep structure containing the verb *give* could be transformed into a surface structure containing the verb *receive*, for example. Yet there seems to be a semantic argument that *give* and *receive* **should** be explicitly related.

Consider the relationship between active and passive in (47) and (48):

2. It was also possible for elements such as *by* and *to* to be inserted by transformation. Crucially, however, no nouns, verbs, adjectives or adverbs could be changed or inserted by transformation.

(47) John gave a book to Bill.
(48) Bill was given a book by John.

(47) and (48) are synonymous, in the sense that they express the same subject-verb-object relationships: in both sentences John is the giver, and Bill the receiver. These facts would be correctly predicted by giving (47) and (48) the same deep structure, and formulating a rule of Passive which optionally converts this into the surface structure in (48). But now consider the relationships between the following sentence pairs:

(49) John gave a book to Bill.
(50) Bill received a book from John.
(51) I consider your suggestion insulting.
(52) Your suggestion strikes me as insulting.
(53) Maria sold Harry an icebox.
(54) Harry bought an icebox from Maria.

Each of these pairs may also be regarded as synonymous: (49) and (50), for example, both express the fact that John is the giver and Bill the receiver of a book. Surely, then, these pairs too should be given common deep structures, and related by transformations to their different surface structures, as active and passive forms of the same underlying meaning? If the argument for giving a common deep structure to (47) and (48) is a good one, it should also apply to (49) and (50), and the other sentence pairs.

However, because of the way deep structure was defined, only (47) and (48) can be given a common deep structure, because only they contain the same words. The remaining sentence pairs cannot be handled in this way, since they contain different words. The claim made by the generative semanticists is that this definition of deep structure forces us to miss the obvious relationships between (49)–(54). They conclude that deep structures must be abstract enough to permit us to derive *all* active-passive pairs from a common source, even if this means dropping the claim that deep structures actually contain words instead of, say, a representation of the meanings of words.

Once it is admitted that sentences containing different words may share the same deep structure, the way is open for wholesale adoption of much deeper deep structures than the classical model ever permitted. For example, if one thinks about sentence (55):

(55) John killed Bill.

one sees that although *Bill* is the logical object of *kill*, at a deeper level it is also the logical subject of an unexpressed verb *die*. So an underlying structure for (55) which a generative semanticist might defend is (56):

(56) John caused Bill to die.

Here logical subjects and objects are explicitly represented, as required by classical deep structure, but some semantic analysis of the verb *kill* has also been performed – a type of analysis which is not permitted at the level of classical deep structure. It can be seen quite clearly that in this case the dispute about the deepness of deep structure could be resolved by deciding whether such semantic analysis of verbs is required in the grammar of English. If it turned out that it was not only not required, but not possible, the generative semantic position would collapse into the classical 1965 position. In other words, if *kill* does not in fact mean *cause to die*, then we will be left with a standard deep structure for *John killed Bill*. If such semantic analysis *is* required, then the debate about deep structure remains open.

Another assumption implicit in the classical arguments for deep structure is that to every sentence with two or more distinct meanings correspond two or more distinct deep structures. For example, the standard analysis of the ambiguous (8a) above – *The man was good to leave* – yielded a different deep structure for each possible interpretation of that sentence. To take another example, consider (57):

(57) My friendly neighbour will talk to anyone.

This has two distinct interpretations, corresponding to (58) and (59):

(58) My neighbour, who is friendly, will talk to anyone.
(59) My neighbour who is friendly (as opposed to the ones who are hostile) will talk to anyone.

According to the 1965 model, the fact that (57) has two distinct interpretations must lead us to assign it two distinct deep structures. In this case the standard solution has been to represent (59) as having an underlying relative clause structure, while (58) is represented as a conjunction, having the same underlying structure as (60):

(60) My neighbour is friendly and my neighbour will talk to anyone.

Given this assumption that an ambiguous surface structure requires two different deep structures, we are immediately committed to finding two deep structures for such sentences as (61) and (62):

(61) Everyone in the room loves some pop-star.
(62) John wants to fly an aeroplane over the North Pole.

(61) has two possible interpretations: one on which there is some particular pop-star whom everyone in the room loves, and one on which everyone in the room loves a pop-star, but the pop-star differs in each case. (62) also has two possible interpretations, one on which there is a particular aeroplane which John wants to fly over the North Pole, and no other will satisfy him, and one on which he wants to fly an aeroplane over the North Pole, but any old aeroplane will do. If these two different interpretations do reflect differences in meaning, then we need two different deep structures to capture this fact. But classical deep structure analysis will only provide one deep structure for each of these sentences. They have the same subject-verb-object relations on both interpretations, and both interpretations seem to be syntactically identical. To provide different underlying structures, we must go deeper than classical deep structure, and provide some such paraphrases as (63)–(66):

(63) There is some pop-star whom everyone in the room loves.
(64) Everyone in the room loves some pop-star or other.
(65) There is an aeroplane which John wants to fly over the North Pole.
(66) John wants to fly some aeroplane or other over the North Pole.

Again, the conclusion must be that deep structures are much deeper than was believed at the time of the 1965 model, and that linguistic theory must be modified accordingly.

(b) *Deep structure is too deep.* In general, this type of argument takes the motivations for classical deep structure, and tries to show that they were not strong enough to warrant the conclusions that were drawn from them, and hence that deep structures should be seen as lying much nearer the surface than was thought in 1965. Chomsky's own recent writings have tended to favour this conclusion. One such argument might run as follows.

Because of arguments to do with underlying logical subjects and objects, backed up by considerations of economy, the 1965 model assigned the same deep structure to the active and passive sentences (67) and (68):

(67) John abandoned all hope.
(68) All hope was abandoned by John.

A Passive transformation was then introduced, which would derive (68) from the structure underlying (67), and any passive sentence from its related active version. As was pointed out in section (a), the same type of arguments could, if sound, lead us to derive (70) from (69), (72) from (71), and (74) from (73):

(69) John caused Bill to die.
(70) John killed Bill.
(71) Mary caused the door to open.
(72) Mary opened the door.
(73) It is probable that Manchuria will annex Wales.
(74) Manchuria will probably annex Wales.

However, instead of drawing the conclusion from these facts that deep structure should be much deeper than was classically supposed, it is possible to draw the different conclusion that the original arguments for deep structure were not good enough, and that the generalizations that were captured by positing a level of deep structure could be captured without reference to any such level. Classical deep structure forbids us to posit a transformational relationship between the pairs in (69)–(74). Yet there is clearly some relationship between these pairs, which we would want the grammar to state. In the 1965 model, these relationships would be stated, not at the level of deep structure, but in the lexicon, where any idiosyncratic fact about any lexical item would be listed. Thus, for intransitive verbs like *open*, it would be mentioned in the lexicon that there was a transitive counterpart, having the meaning 'to make open', which was generally morphologically related. Similarly, for adjectives such as *probable* which can occur with a sentential complement, as in (73), it could be stated that there was a related adverb which could occur in that sentence which acted as a complement to the *adjective*, and had the same meaning, as in (74). The reason for handling these relationships in the lexicon rather than by a syntactic transformation rule was, first, that classical deep structure did not permit a transformational handling of such cases, and second and more important, that not every verb or adjective enters into such relationships: it has to be stated for each verb whether or not it has a transitive causative form. Thus *open* does, cf. (71)–(72), but *creak* does not, cf. (75)–(76):

(75) Mary caused the door to creak.
(76) *Mary creaked the door.

Likewise, it has to be stated for each adjective whether or not it has a related adverb: beside (73), (74) we have:

(77) It is impossible that Manchuria will annex Wales.
(78) *Manchuria will impossibly annex Wales.

The reason for *not* handling passives, for example, in the same lexical fashion was first, that classical deep structure permitted a transformational treatment in this case, and second, that almost every transitive verb *does* have a related passive.

However, against this second point, it should be noticed that there are certain verbs which enter into structures of the type NP V NP, but which do *not* have related passives. (79)–(84) are examples:

(79) That book cost a lot of money.
(80) *A lot of money was cost by that book.
(81) John resembles your mother.
(82) *Your mother is resembled by John.
(83) Mary became President.
(84) *President was become by Mary.

It would be perfectly straightforward to account for these facts, as well as for the regular passive versions of active sentences, by simply stating in the lexical entry for each passive-forming verb that if a structure of the form (85)

(85) $NP_1 - V - NP_2$

is well-formed, so is the corresponding sentence (86)

(86) $NP_2 - is - V\text{-ed by } NP_1$

and where there is no passive form of a verb, such a statement will simply be omitted.

If it is objected that such a treatment misses the obvious generalization that transitive verbs typically passivize, this fact can be easily incorporated into the grammar by stating once for all in the lexicon that *any* verb which can occur in a structure of the form (85) will also be able to occur in a structure of the form (86), unless it is explicitly marked as being unable to. This would have the effect of leaving the general case, e.g. *open*, unmarked, and only the exceptions, such as *cost*, marked in the lexicon. Such statements are known, rather misleadingly, as *redundancy* rules, because they enable one to avoid the repetition in each lexical

entry of redundant, or predictable, information. Such a statement of lexical relationships would capture essentially the same
set of facts as the deep structure treatment, but without any mention of a level of deep structure itself. Hence deep structure can be
abandoned, not because it is not deep enough to handle all the
facts, but because it is deeper than is necessary.

We have looked at one way of arguing against deep structure,
by allowing some of its role in grammar to be taken over by the
lexicon. Another way of reaching the same conclusions would be
to show that many of the functions performed by classical deep
structure – a syntactic construct – were in fact not syntactic at all,
and would be better handled by the semantic component. In both
types of argument the resulting output of the grammar is the
same – the same generalizations are captured, and the same
sentences are generated – but the mechanics by which the results
are achieved differ. Earlier in this chapter it was mentioned that
sentences such as (87) would on the 1965 model be transfor-
mationally derived from sentences with underlying structures like
those of (88):

(87) John washed himself.
(88) John washed John.

Hence there would be a transformational rule of Reflexive, which
would turn the second of two identical NPs, by a syntactic operation, into its related reflexive. An alternative way of handling the
same set of facts would be to generate both (87) and (88) by
means of phrase-structure rules, and to set up a semantic rule
which would tell us that (87) meant something like (88). This
would involve seeing the relationship between (87) and (88) as
semantic rather than syntactic, and dispensing with the claim that
(87) had the same deep structure as (88). A reason for moving
towards this last position is provided by the repeated failure of
the combined efforts of linguists to formulate a syntactic rule of
Reflexive which would in fact handle all known cases of grammatical sentences containing reflexive pronouns. Hence the move
away from deep structure was not arbitrary, but resulted from the

failure of the model in which classical deep structure was incorporated to handle all of the facts which it was designed to handle.

On the basis of the sort of arguments presented here, most linguists since 1965 have abandoned classical deep structure, adopting instead either grammars in which underlying structures are much deeper and closer to semantic representations than was envisaged in *Aspects*, or else grammars in which underlying structures are much shallower and closer to surface structure than was previously envisaged, and with much richer lexical and semantic components than in earlier years. In many ways, although these two types of model which have grown out of *Aspects* look superficially very different, and their supporters have engaged in fairly acrimonious debate, their resulting outputs are very similar, and anything that one type of model can handle the other type can handle too.

It would be a mistake to think that the current state of controversy within generative grammar means that the work of the last twenty years is being abandoned wholesale. The classical model of transformational grammar (and its various extensions) uncovered a great wealth of facts and relationships, and for the first time provided an explicit overall theory within which such facts received not only a description but a partial explanation. The specific analyses involving Tough-movement, Raising, There-insertion, etc., which we have used here to illustrate the reasons for setting up a level of deep structure, will certainly be superseded. But whatever takes their place will have to account for this well-defined set of problems in terms either of a more satisfactory syntactic theory, or of a better-developed semantics, or both. The contribution of deep structure has been two-fold: on the one hand it has forced us to ask questions about grammars and grammar that we could not previously frame; on the other hand, it has given us a theoretical tool by reference to which we can make generalizations not merely about sets of sentences in individual languages, but about types of rule across languages. We have so far restricted ourselves to English, but we turn to a wider field in

Chapter 9, and we return to the difference between description and explanation in the last two chapters of the book. In the meantime, we continue our survey of the form and organization of grammars.

6. Phonetics and Phonology

So far, we have said very little about the sound system of language, apart from claiming that the pronunciation of each word must be represented in the lexicon, and that the pronunciation of whole sentences must be dealt with by phonological rules which take syntactic surface structures as input. In this chapter, we look more closely at what the phonological component of a grammar should actually look like.

A theory of phonology has two main tasks: first to provide a means of representing the pronunciation both of lexical entries and of whole sentences; second, to state how surface syntactic structures which contain lexical items are related to their *phonetic representations*, or pronunciations, and to describe the form and function of the phonological rules which relate them.

In demanding that the grammar give a phonetic representation to each sentence of a language, we immediately come up against the problem of deciding precisely what such phonetic representations should describe. Not only do no two people sound exactly the same, as witness our ability to identify large numbers of our friends and acquaintances merely on hearing them utter a brief greeting such as 'hello' on the telephone, but also no two utterances of 'hello' by the same speaker are physically identical on separate occasions. The differences may be extremely small: the *h* may be pronounced on one occasion a few milliseconds longer than on another, for instance, but the problem of principle remains. The solution, both in traditional and generative grammar, is in the first instance to include in a phonetic representation all and only those features of pronunciation which can serve to distinguish one word or sentence of the language from another. For example, consider the pronunciation of (1):

(1) There's no floor in that building.

It makes no difference to one's understanding whether the underlined *r* is pronounced with the roll characteristic of Scots, with the '*er*' like sound of most Southern British speakers, or the uvular rasp of the Northumberland burr. What does matter is that some form of *r* be there to distinguish (1) from (2):

(2) There's no flaw in that building.

where no *r* is pronounced.[1] The differences among the various possible pronunciations of *r* are *phonetic* differences; the difference between the presence and absence of *r* is a *phonological* difference, because it serves to distinguish two different sentences. To make the same point with different speech-sounds, consider the contrasts among the items: *sat*, *pat* and *bat*. The fact that these three words are different lexical items, with different syntactic and semantic properties, but are felt to be phonologically identical except for their initial element, indicates that these initial elements are distinctive: that is, using *p* rather than *b*, for instance, gives rise to a different word, or possible word, of English. In this case, the phonetic difference of *voice* – whether a sound is pronounced with concomitant vibration of the vocal cords, as in *b*, or without such vibration, as in *p*[2] – is also *phonologically* (or *phonemically*) relevant; and *p* and *b* are said to be *phonemes* of English. Phonemes are traditionally put between slashes, so the phonemic representation of *pat* is /pat/.

1. For dialects where *r* is pronounced in both (1) and (2) the point we are making can be established equally easily by reference to slight differences in the pronunciation of any other speech-sound: e.g. each of the variant pronunciations of *hello* mentioned earlier, as opposed to the pronunciation of *help*.

2. In fact the most important characteristic of 'voicing' is *voice onset time*: i.e. the exact point when the vocal cords start vibrating, rather than the simple presence or absence of voice.

If we take three words such as *pat*, *spat* and *tap*, there are still audible phonetic differences in the pronunciation of the /p/ in each of them, but this time the difference is not capable of distinguishing between different words, and is not something we need to learn separately for each lexical item; as we need to learn separately that *bat*, *bin* and *bray* begin with a /b/, while *pat*, *pin* and *pray* begin with /p/. Rather it is a predictable fact about English words that /p/ is *aspirated* (pronounced with a puff of air following the opening of the lips) when initial in the word as in *pat*, but unaspirated after /s/ as in *spat*; and when final, as in *tap*, the lips don't even need to open at all. Sounds which differ in this predictable way are called *allophones* of the phoneme under discussion, and are standardly put between square brackets. Thus the aspirated allophone of /p/ that occurs in initial position is written [pʰ], the unaspirated allophone of /p/ that occurs after /s/ is written [p], and the allophone which sometimes occurs in word-final position with the lips kept shut is represented as [p˃]. In final position the phoneme /p/ may be pronounced either as [p˃] or as [p], that is, with the lips opening but without aspiration. When either of two such sounds may occur non-distinctively in the same place, they are said to be in *free variation*. Where there exists only one possible pronunciation for a phoneme in each of two or more different positions, as with [pʰ] initially and [p] after /s/, the sounds, or allophones, are said to be in *complementary distribution*. The English word *pap* has the phonemic representation /pap/ but possible phonetic representations: [pʰap˃] or pʰap]. A phonetic representation gives more detail than a phonemic representation and usually includes differences that the non-phonetician finds hard to hear. The reason for this is simply that whereas substituting one phoneme for another gives rise to a different word, e.g. *bat* instead of *pat*, substituting one allophone for another merely gives rise to a funny pronunciation of the same word – for instance, [pat] instead of [pʰat] for *pat*. We are sensitive to such substitutions inasmuch as they are characteristic of some dialect speakers' and foreigners' pronunciation of English; but we are sensitive to them unconsciously, whereas our awareness of phonemic differences such as the contrast between /p/ and /b/ is normally completely conscious and instant.

From this it is clear that not all languages have the same phonemic system. What is phonemically distinctive in one language may be a predictable allophonic variant in another language, and vice versa. For instance, in English the phonetic contrast between [p] and [b] is phonemically distinctive; in the Athapaskan languages of North America the two sounds occur in free variation, with the result that an alternative name for the group is the Athabaskan languages; in Dyirbal, and many other Australian languages, they are allophones of one phoneme, [p] occurring finally and [b] everywhere else. Conversely, although English has *phonetic* contrasts between aspirated and unaspirated consonants, [pʰ] and [p] in *pin* and *spin* respectively, and between voiced and voiceless consonants, [b] and [p] in *bin* and *spin*, there are only two *phonemic* possibilities: /p/ and /b/. In Hindi and many other Indian languages, however, there is a four-way phonemic contrast among /p/, /pʰ/, /b/ and /bʰ/.

It follows from the foregoing discussion that the inventory of symbols which phonological theory has to provide must be rich enough to represent all the phonemic contrasts possible in every language of the world, and also capable of refining these representations sufficiently to distinguish the phonetic differences between, for instance, the English *pat* and the French *patte*, 'paw'. Both of these, within their respective systems, would be represented as /pat/, but the English /p/ is aspirated, the French unaspirated; the English /t/ is alveolar (articulated with the tip of the tongue against the ridge behind the top teeth), the French dental (articulated with the tip of the tongue against the top teeth); and the vowel is clearly different in the two languages: front in English, further back in French. Thus although the phonemic representation of the two words looks the same, the phonetic representations would be very different: English [pʰæt], French [pat]. The question we raised earlier about what to include in a phonetic representation has a dual answer: it must take account of all the phonological contrasts in the language and ultimately – even though very little progress has been made in this direction – it must be able to state the limits within which speakers can differ from each other in their pronunciation, both of different languages and of the same language.

Distinctive Features

We turn now to look at the form of phonetic and phonological representations, and the alphabet used in constructing them. Consider first the representation of words in the lexicon. One might contemplate representing them using the ordinary alphabet of English, or more realistically a phonemic alphabet based on it, but in which all and only those sounds capable of distinguishing one word from another are represented. In such a system, words of English would be represented as follows:

(3) *pin* – /pin/
   thin – /θin/
   thing – /θiŋ/
   box – /bɔks/
   dread – /dred/

This is roughly the system adopted by good traditional dictionaries.

The defect of such a system is that it is unable to show that certain speech sounds are more or less closely related to others. It is intuitively clear that some sounds share certain characteristics with others. For instance, /p/, /b/, and /m/ are all bilabial, involving closure of the lips, while /t/, /d/ and /n/ are not; however, these latter three are similar in that they are all pronounced with the tip of the tongue touching the alveolar ridge (behind the teeth). Further, /m/ and /n/ are nasal, pronounced with air passing through the nose rather than the mouth, /f/, /s/ and /θ/ (*th* as in *thin*) are voiceless, whereas /v/, /z/ and /ð/ (*th* as in *this*) are voiced. In other words, a sound such as /m/ is related to other sounds on the basis of certain properties: it is nasal like /n/, it is bilabial like /p/ and /b/, and it is voiced like /b, d, n, v, z, ð/, etc. Each of these properties, whose presence or absence can be used to distinguish between phonemes, and hence between lexical items – e.g. *pan, ban, man, Dan, than* – may be used to define a *distinctive feature.* Any speech-sound is then definable as consisting of a specified set of distinctive features, normally represented as a *matrix* with each relevant feature marked with the positive value +, or the negative value −. Thus /p/ is represented as in (4) (features and bundles of features are usually enclosed in square brackets):

(4)   p

$$
\begin{bmatrix}
+ \text{ consonantal} \\
- \text{ coronal} \\
+ \text{ anterior} \\
- \text{ voiced} \\
- \text{ nasal} \\
- \text{ strident} \\
- \text{ continuant}
\end{bmatrix}
$$

This matrix then shows how the first phoneme of *pin*, etc. is represented in the lexicon, and /i/ and /n/ have comparable specifications.

The definition of distinctive features is given in articulatory terms, with acoustic and auditory correlates where there is sufficient evidence available to provide these. Thus [voiced] sounds are those produced with vibration of the vocal cords (but cf. fn. 2 on page 126 above); [strident] sounds are those produced with greater acoustic noise than the non-strident equivalents. The informal designation 'bilabial' used earlier is replaced in (4) by the two features [coronal] and [anterior]. [Coronal] consonants are those pronounced with the front of the tongue as the active articulator: /t, d, s/ and /tʃ/ (*ch* as in *church*); [anterior] consonants are those pronounced further forward in the mouth than /tʃ/, and so on. Some of these features, such as [voiced], and [coronal], are exploited systematically to provide a large number of distinctive consonant pairs in nearly all languages; others, such

as [lateral], are used minimally – in English only /l/ is given a +
specification for this feature; and some features, such as that used
for describing the clicks of certain South African languages such
as Xhosa, do not occur in the description of English at all.

Each phoneme must differ from all others by reference to at
least one distinctive feature: e.g. /p/ differs from /b/ by reference
to the feature [voiced], from /t/ by reference to the feature
[coronal], from /k/ by reference to the feature [anterior], from /m/
by reference to both [nasal] and [voiced], from /s/ by reference to
[coronal], [strident] and [continuant] and so on. The more features two phonemes have in common the greater their phonetic
similarity. Thus /p/ is closer to /b/ than either of them is to /s/.

All features are standardly held to be *binary*; that is, there are
only two possible choices for any phoneme with respect to a
particular feature: + or −. Thus /b/ is [+ voiced], /p/ is [−
voiced] and there is no third possibility. The number of distinctive features needed for the description of all the distinctive speech
sounds in the phonological systems of the world's languages is in
the region of thirty, although any one language uses only about
half this number. The features used for describing vowels are
partly disjoint from those for describing consonants, and we delay
discussion of them until Chapter 10.

So far, we have dealt only with phonological *contrasts* and have
neglected the specification of fine points of phonetic detail. For
instance, in neither French nor English is there a phonological
contrast between dental and alveolar plosives, although there is
such a contrast in many Indian languages. However, as we
pointed out earlier, the pronunciation of /t/ in French and English differs consistently, the former being dental, and the latter
alveolar. Each language has only one voiceless coronal stop, /t/,
and so the same distinctive features can be used to characterize
it in each. This equation of the two *t*'s is not arbitrary, as they are
articulatorily close and native speakers of the two languages
identify them as equivalent. To represent the phonetic difference
between them, the previously binary features are broken down
into multivalued (*n-ary*) features. In the present case the feature

[coronal] is graded into an arbitrarily fine numerical scale stretching from interdental to dental to alveolar to post-alveolar to retroflex. As yet no generally accepted values for such gradations have emerged: a plausible first approximation might make the dental French [t̪] [2 coronal] and the alveolar English [t] [3 coronal]. Similar specifications will be made for all features other than those such as [consonantal] which by definition allow of no gradation. Although the transition from binary to n-ary feature specifications appears to coincide with the contrast we have drawn between distinctive and non-distinctive sounds, it has sometimes been suggested that distinctive features should have n-ary specifications at the phonological as well as the phonetic level. We leave the question open here, but we shall present some evidence in favour of such a view in our discussion of language change in Chapter 10.

In addition to their function of delimiting the set of possible phonemes and phonemic systems, distinctive features are also involved in the statement of phonological rules. It is to these rules that we now turn.

Phonological Rules and Underlying Forms

The main task of the phonological rules is to provide a phonetic representation for each word on the basis of its phonological representation in the lexicon and the syntactic configuration in which it occurs at surface structure. We need to justify any divergence between the phonological (lexical) representation of items and the phonetic form they finally adopt. Giving this kind of justification will also help to illustrate the sorts of process that phonological rules must be capable of carrying out.

The simplest example of the need to allow for divergence between lexical (or phonological) and phonetic representation is provided by *assimilation*: that is, when one phoneme takes on features of a preceding or following phoneme. For instance, the word *ten* differs in the pronunciation of its final, nasal, phoneme in that this adopts the same point of articulation as the initial consonant of the next word:

(5) *ten tops*   is pronounced   [ten tɔps]
    ten men   is pronounced   [tem men]
    ten kings   is pronounced   [teŋ kiŋz]

Given that precisely the same assimilation takes place with all words ending in /n/ and is not restricted to the items illustrated, and given further that the pronunciation of *ten* in isolation (its 'citation form') is always [ten] and never [tem] or [teŋ], there is no point in putting the predictable information about the different forms of the word in the lexicon. Rather the lexical entry can correspond to the citation form and the other variants can be predicted by a phonological rule changing the features specifying the point of articulation of the phoneme concerned.

A second example of different realizations at the phonetic level is given by the varying pronunciation of words ending in clusters of consonants. Thus *soft* is usually pronounced [sɔft] in isolation and before words beginning with a vowel, but as [sɔf] before words beginning with a consonant and before the suffix *-en*:

(6) *soft eiderdown* → [sɔft aidədaun]
    soft toys   → [sɔf tɔiz]
    soft feathers → [sɔf feðəz]
    soft-en   → [sɔfən]

In this case the most economical solution is again to enter in the lexicon the citation form of the word and delete the final consonant by a general rule in specified environments. As before, the process is not restricted either to *soft* or to the range of words illustrated above:

(7) *waste of time*   → [weist əv taim]
    waste paper   → [weis peipə]
    lost opportunity → [lɔst ɔpətjuːnitiː]
    lost children   → [lɔs tʃildrən]
    moist-en   → [mɔisən]

A third example of the role of phonological rules is stress assignment. Traditionally, stress in English was treated as distinctive: i.e. as essentially unpredictable, because of the variation in the placement of stress in such items as:

(8) *macaróon, devélop, aspáragus, pénitently*

where stress occurs on the last, penultimate, antepenultimate and preantepenultimate syllables respectively; or the contrast in stress between compounds such as:

(9) *yéllow-hammer, blué-stocking, chéap-jack*

and phrases containing apparently the same words:

(10) *yéllow hámmer, blúe stócking, chéap jáck*

However, in a theory where phonological rules have access to syntactic and morphological information as well as purely phonological data – i.e. where phonology is interpretive – the position of stress becomes very largely predictable. Thus the differences among *devélop, aspáragus* and *pénitently* are a function of the differences between verb, noun and adverb (compare *astónish, América, calámitously*), the final stress in *macaróon* is attributable to the long vowel in that syllable (compare *Japanése*), and the difference between *blúe-stocking* and *blúe stócking* is due to their difference in syntactic structure: while both consist of an adjective followed by a noun, in the former these unite to form a *compound noun*, in the latter an NP, categories independently needed in the syntax. This last example is more significant than simple examples of word stress, as the latter, being finite, could be handled entirely within the lexicon. The configurational differences between *blúe-stocking/blúe stócking* or *George has pláns to leave/George has plans to léave*, however, can only be the result of phonological rules which have access to syntactic information; the set of possible forms to which such rules can apply is infinite, and therefore in principle not treatable by lexical listing.

A final example of divergence between lexical and phonetic representation is given by the relation between certain forms in adult and child speech. Presented with words such as *wasp, desk, ask* and so on, children often metathesize the final two consonants to produce [wɔps], [deks] and [aːks]. Given that this is a regular process and not merely the reflection of a mishearing on the part of the child, it must be accounted for by rule. The implication is that we need phonological rules that can change the position of phonemes.

In these four examples we have seen that the rules of the phonological component can add features (e.g. of stress, cf. the third example), can delete features, indeed whole phonemes (cf. the second example), change the value of individual features (e.g. in assimilation, cf. the first example) and change the position of whole phonemes (cf. the last example). Indeed there seems to be no conceivable operation they could not carry out, and to the extent that this great versatility predicts the existence of phonological rules which are apparently not needed for any language, the theory is defective, as it is failing to delimit narrowly enough the notion 'possible human language'. Let us look at an example of a phonological rule which is less plausibly motivated than the four cases just given, and see what general principle or principles could distinguish it from the preceding ones.

Certain words in English are exceptions to the stress rules. Extending the analysis of stress illustrated briefly above, we can say that in nouns stress falls on the final syllable if it contains a long vowel, e.g. *boutíque, redóubt*, and on the penultimate syllable if the vowel in the final syllable is short, e.g. *cábbage, tórrent, rábbit*. In words of more than two syllables, cf. *aspáragus, América* above, the stress may be further to the left if all vowels are short: note, for instance, the couplet *ábdomen/abdómen* where stress shifts according to the length of the vowel. Words like *cemént, burlésque, ellípse* are predicted by this statement to be stressed on the first (i.e. penultimate) syllable, which is wrong. One solution that has been proposed is simply to add an extra syllable, in the form of an abstract element represented by /e/ to the lexical representation of these words so that they are trisyllabic not disyllabic. The stress rule then applies to stress the penultimate syllable and a later rule deletes the final /e/. Thus the derivation of *cement* would be:

(11) Lexical representation – cemente
Stress assignment   – ceménte
Deletion of /e/   – cemént

which is close to the correct phonetic form.

The trouble with this analysis is that the device of adding an /e/ is arbitrary. The same effect could have been obtained by any number of equivalent stratagems: e.g. adding a nasal vowel at the end; making the second vowel of *cement* long and then shortening it by a late rule; adding a feature, say [+ unusual] to the specification of the second vowel and making the stress rule apply to any [+ unusual] vowel, etc. As the postulated /e/ never appears in the phonetic representation there is no means of testing the validity of the claim implicit in its appearance. Whereas all the distinctive features have some definable articulatory or acoustic correlate; and phonemes, as bundles of these features, do likewise, the /e/ has no such correlate beyond the difference in stress it was invented to account for, and *in principle* never could have such a correlate. Such examples of 'absolute neutralization', i.e. where a contrast in lexical representation is *always* wiped out by the time we get to the phonetic representation, are felt to be theoretically objectionable by many phonologists and are accordingly disallowed by the theory. Banning absolute neutralization, like various other constraints which have been suggested, has as its ultimate motivation a desire to maximize the *naturalness* of the phonology.

Naturalness in Phonology

What is needed is a phonological theory which not only provides a reasoned link between syntax and sound, but does so in terms which are externally validated. In principle the categories and processes made available by the theory should be explicable by reference to physical or psychological facts: specifically the theory should not only exclude 'impossible' analyses of the sort we have just looked at, but should also provide an explanation in functional, or auditory, acoustic and articulatory terms for those phenomena which do occur. This implies that some phenomena are predictable, or more to be expected than others.

The nature of this predictability ranges from total to statistical. Total predictability would be given by a universal statement about what features can combine to constitute a phoneme; statistical predictability would be given by a statement of the *usual*, but not invariable, value for particular features either in isolation or in defined contexts. An example of the universal kind is the requirement that:

(12) Vowels are non-strident.

or

(13) Bilabial consonants are not trilled.

An example of the statistical kind is:

(14) Vowels are voiced.

The first of these, (12), is a matter of definition, and reflects properties of the human vocal tract. (13) appears to be a brute fact about phonological and not even phonetic representations. Voiced and voiceless bilabial trills do occur, either as non-linguistic reactions to cold, or as the realization in children's language of the clusters /br/ and /pr/. That they never appear distinct from such clusters is probably accidental. (14) is overwhelmingly true, except that in whisper everything is voiceless including what are still recognizable as vowels; and in a few languages voiced and voiceless vowels are reported to be contrastive.

Perhaps the most important concept in generative phonology, the phonology used in generative grammar, is that of *natural class*. A natural class is a set of phonemes which can be specified more economically (in terms of fewer distinctive features) than any subset of that class. For example, English has three nasal phonemes /m/, /n/ and /ŋ/. The class consisting of precisely these three phonemes and only these can be referred to as [+nasal]: i.e. the set of elements sharing the property [nasal]. To refer to /m/ alone we need to specify not only [+nasal] but also [−coronal] to distinguish it from /n/ and [+anterior] to distinguish it from /ŋ/. The major claim of distinctive feature theory is that the usual case in phonology is for processes to range over natural classes of phonemes rather than subsets of those classes. A typical example is provided by the phonetic rule which nasalizes vowels before the nasal consonants /m, n, ŋ/: e.g. the *a* in *ram, ran* and *rang* is somewhat nasalized, whereas the *a* in *rap, rat* and *rack* is not. This process can be stated with maximal simplicity and naturalness as occurring before the class of consonants marked [+nasal]. If the rule applied only before /m/ or /n/ and not before /ŋ/, its statement would be more complex, even though describing the process by reference to a list of phonemes would make it appear simpler in such a case.

It follows from this that a natural rule is one, like vowel nasalization, which is stated over natural classes. A second example is provided by the different forms of the plural affix in English, /-iz, -s, -z/, seen in *horses*, *cats*, and *dogs*, which occur after strident, voiceless and voiced consonants respectively. That is, the form /-iz/ occurs in all and only those cases where a strident consonant /z/ or /s/ would otherwise be immediately adjacent to another strident consonant /s, z, ʃ, ʒ, tʃ, dʒ/ – i.e. in the environment 'after any phoneme marked [+strident]'. The form /s/ occurs after all other voiceless phonemes /p, t, k, f, θ/ – i.e. in the environment 'after a phoneme marked [−voiced]'; and /z/ occurs everywhere else. Each of these statements is simpler as it stands than it would be if the conditioning environments consisted of any other sets of consonants: e.g. if /-iz/ occurred after /p, b, f, v, m/, and so on. Moreover, the rule is natural in the further and more important sense that the sequences resulting from the operation of the rule are themselves to be expected. That is, in *cats* [kats], the final consonant cluster [ts] is voiceless throughout, and in *dogs* [dɔgz] it is voiced throughout [gz], so that the articulation of these sequences is simpler in terms both of the number of commands from the brain necessary to bring about changes in the vocal cord vibration, and in the muscular execution of that vibration. In the case of *horses*, where the plural marker has an [i] intervening between /s/ and /z/, the explanation is auditory rather than articulatory. A sequence of [ss] or [zz], and to a lesser extent of [tʃs, dʒz] etc. in final position would be extremely hard to hear: the presence of the vowel eliminates that difficulty.

To characterize the natural domain of phonological rules we need to consider the phonological *units* used in the grammar.

Phonological Units

Within generative phonology it is generally assumed that the only unit of description is the distinctive feature, and that the traditional phoneme, as described at the beginning of this chapter, is either superfluous or undesirable, as reliance on it leads to a loss of generalization. Accordingly, with the exception of the categorial information represented by labelled bracketing inherited from the syntax, all phonological rules are stated exclusively in terms of distinctive features. We want to argue that the phoneme is a useful unit in addition to the distinctive feature, and that both these and perhaps further units are necessary for a satisfactory description of phonology.

The standard argument against the phoneme is that its use prevents the statement of linguistic generalizations. For instance, consider again the example of nasal assimilation given in (5) above. In these examples, a phonological rule converts one phoneme into another: the /n/ of *ten* is converted into or replaced by an /m/ in *ten men* and by an /ŋ/ in *ten kings*. Accordingly this rule is classed as 'morphophonemic' – one dealing with changes of phoneme. However, if we look at a wider range of examples, the issue is not so clear-cut. Thus, if we put *ten* before *things* or *facts* we still have nasal assimilation to the point of articulation of the following consonant: [ten θiŋz], [tem̩ fæks] (where [n̩] represents a dental nasal, and [m̩] a labio-dental nasal). However [n̩] and [m̩] are not independent phonemes of English (no two words can differ simply because of a contrast between [n̩] and [n] or [m̩] and [m] in the way that *ram*, *ran* and *rang* are distinct), they are rather allophonic variants of the phonemes /n/ or /m/. But this means that a theory which sets up the phoneme as a crucial level of representation, with one class of processes taking place *before* the level of the phoneme is reached, and another class taking place *after* the level of the phoneme is reached, must split up nasal assimilation into two processes, whereas it is patently a single unified process that should be stated in a unitary way. A treatment using a single rule, formulated in terms of distinctive features, and relating the level of lexical representation directly to the level of phonetic representation, does precisely what is wanted without making any mention of the phoneme.

This is a very strong argument in favour of the use of distinctive features for the statement of nasal assimilation. It is not necessarily a good argument against the use of phonemes or some equivalent segments in other circumstances. Consider another of the examples of rules given above: namely, metathesis, which relates the forms /desk/ and [deks]. In terms of distinctive features this involves a permutation of two matrices, that for /s/ – [+consonantal, +coronal, +anterior, −voiced, +continuant, +strident] and that for /k/ – [+consonantal, −coronal, −anterior, −voiced, −continuant, −strident]. Such a permutation clearly allows us to describe the switch of segments, but it seems intuitively odd that we should have to specify all those features. Worse, it makes the explicit prediction that metathesis could equally well range over not just whole segments but individual features within a phoneme, in the same way that individual features are affected in assimilation rules. In the present case we should predict not only that /desk/ could become [deks], but that [desk] could also become [detx] for instance, where only the value for [continuant] has switched. It could even be claimed that such a change is simpler, as one would need to specify only a single distinctive feature from each phoneme. Except in the speech of aphasics, however, we do not find instances of metathesis involving only a subset of the distinctive features of a segment; rather it is virtually always the *whole* phoneme which is involved. The implication is that some phonological processes, e.g. metathesis, have as their natural domain units the size of phonemes, not units the size of distinctive features. Given that phonemes are viewed as bundles of distinctive features it is clearly always *possible* to use the latter instead, but it is not always insightful.

Further, if we look at a special kind of metathesis, the phenomenon of spoonerisms, we can also find evidence that rules which range over larger units (phonemes) must precede those ranging over smaller units (distinctive features). Take for instance the following slip of the tongue where 'it's gone bad' was pronounced 'it's bon gad'. 'Gone bad' is pronounced [gɔm bæd] with assimilation of /n/ to [m] before the /b/; the metathesized variant is pronounced as [bɔŋ gæd] with assimilation not to the displaced /b/ but to the /g/ which has replaced it. Therefore the metathesis must take place before the assimilation. This is not a case of an ordering that must be specified in the grammar of English. The ordering here is the result of a general convention on rule application stated once for all languages. That is, the claim is that application of a metathesis rule will always take precedence over application of an assimilation rule, in all languages.

Various suggestions have been made for incorporating units larger than the distinctive feature and the phoneme into phonological theory: the syllable, the foot, the phonological phrase, etc. The status of these is even less clear-cut than that of the phoneme, so we shall ignore them for present purposes and continue this section with a brief discussion of some tonal and intonational phenomena which, while clearly phonological, are more closely related to the rest of the grammar and are equally clearly not best described in terms of phonemes and distinctive features, but seem to require a specification of phonological properties partially independent of the sequence of phonemes represented in distinctive feature matrices. That is, whereas words or morphemes consist of (sequences of) distinctive features, we now need a unit which is not arranged hierarchically with respect to the other units, but is parallel to it and is mapped onto it separately by a set of special conventions.

Phonology and Syntax

All languages use variations in pitch to signal some aspect of the message. If the domain of this pitch variation is the sentence, as in English, then the language is said to be intonational, and we have contrasts such that:

(15) John married an Amazon.

can, by changing the intonation, be pronounced either as a simple statement, or as a question, or as an outraged exclamation, and so on. Even if the sentence in question consists of only one word, e.g. 'yes', the range of possible intonation patterns remains substantially the same as for a sentence containing a large number of words such as (15). If the domain of pitch variation is essentially the word or lexical item, then the language is said to be tonal, and we have contrasts such as the following from Nupe:

(16) bá (said on a high pitch) means 'to be sour'
ba (said on a mid pitch) means 'to be against'
bà (said on a low pitch) means 'to pray'

The number of tonal contrasts varies from language to language: some, such as Ewe, have just two; others, such as Miao, have eight or nine. We shall have no more to say about the many interesting problems raised by tone languages, but we want to spend a little more time on the interaction of the phonological processes of stress and intonation with syntactic processes, since this has implications for the structure of the grammar as a whole.

Whichever of the possible intonational patterns for (15) one uses, the neutral stress pattern is that in which the major stress falls on *Ámazon*. That is, unless one is using stress contrastively to oppose *John* or *married* to *Bill* or *loved*, the stress rules of English must be so formulated that they assign primary stress to the rightmost constituent in a sentence. The rule which does this is normally referred to as the Nuclear Stress Rule. Consider now, however, the sentences in (17) and (18):

(17) a. George has *pláns* to leave.
 b. Margaret left *diréctions* for George to follow.
(18) a. George has plans to *léave*.
 b. Margaret left directions for George to *fóllow*.

where, assuming non-contrastive stress still, (17a) means that George has documents to deposit, whereas (18a) means that he intends to leave; (17b) means that George is to follow an explicit set of directions, whereas (18b) means simply that he is to follow. Clearly the stress rule we have just assumed, namely one that assigns stress to the rightmost lexical item in the sentence, cannot be correct for (17), and no single rule couched in as simplistic a way as this one could ever cater for both (17) and (18).

Joan Bresnan has suggested an elegant solution to the problem presented by such sentences, but one which entails that the simple structure of the grammar assumed heretofore, one where all syntactic rules precede all phonological rules, is wrong. Her suggestion depends crucially on allowing the rules of stress assignment to refer to information that is no longer available by the time surface structure is reached. In the case of (17) and (18) above, this information correlates with the fact that the two verbs *follow* and *leave* are being used alternately transitively and intransitively: a fact which is reflected directly at deep structure, but not at surface structure, by the transitive verbs having their object (*plans/directions*) overtly present. The syntactic underlying structure for (17b) would be as in (19):

(19) ₛ[Margaret left ₙₚ[directions ₛ[for George to follow directions]]]

where there are two occurrences of *directions*, of which the second is deleted by a syntactic transformation. The structure underlying (18b) on the other hand would be as in (20):

(20) $_S$[Margaret left $_{NP}$[directions $_S$[for George to follow]]]

with *no* second occurrence of *directions*. The structural difference between the sentences is clear, and Bresnan suggested that the stress difference between them could be explained by making the rules assigning stress be interspersed among the syntactic rules. That is, in (19), primary stress is applied to the second occurrence of *directions*, the rightmost element of the most deeply embedded constituent in underlying structure, but this item is then deleted by a syntactic transformation. The stress rule subsequently reapplies to the next biggest constituent to assign stress correctly to the remaining instance of *directions*.[3] In the case of (20) stress is assigned to *follow* in the usual way and because no syntactic rule subsequently affects *follow* in any relevant way, it keeps its primary stress. Such an analysis is not without its problems, but it does offer a convincing account of otherwise recalcitrant data.

The wider implication of allowing some phonological rules to precede some syntactic rules is, as indicated above, that the simple compartmentalized view of the structure of a grammar is no longer tenable. It is *not* the case, however, that all constraints on organization are abolished. The only kinds of phonological rule which can precede any syntactic rule are those dealing with pitch and stress. It may even be the case that *all* such rules have to be intercalated among the syntactic rules: if so, we in fact have just as strong a constraint on the structure of our grammar as before.

Earlier in the discussion we deliberately excluded contrastive stress from the analysis of examples like (17) and (18). If we allow

3. Technically the assignment of primary stress to a word entails the simultaneous reduction of stress in all other words within the domain of the rule. Thus in (19) each of *Géorge, fóllow* and *diréctions* has primary stess as indicated. The Nuclear Stress Rule then restresses *diréctions* and reduces the stress on *George* and *follow* to secondary. When the NSR reapplies to the larger constituent [directions [for George to follow]] primary stress is assigned to the rightmost word which still has primary stress, i.e. *diréctions* not *follow*.

contrastive stress to play a role, the apparent regular relation between form and meaning disappears. That is, the preferred interpretation of the (a) and (b) examples is as indicated; but with contrastive stress on any item, either interpretation becomes possible for any of the sentences. Now, the cause of contrastive stress in a sentence such as (21):

(21) *Helen* left directions for George to follow, not Mary.

is usually not linguistic, but pragmatic: for instance, as a mark of denial; and this raises the question whether the phonological rules are sensitive not only to syntactic but also to pragmatic information. The answer is clearly no. The rules of the phonology, wherever they are situated in the grammar, must allow for the contrastive stressing of any item, and it is then up to a theory of performance to ascribe a relevant interpretation to a string containing such an item. We return to a discussion of contrastive stress in Chapter 8.

The Innate Basis of Phonology

We end this chapter with a brief discussion of how much specific phonological knowledge the child brings to bear on the task of learning his language. We suggested in Chapters 1 and 2 that human beings were innately predisposed to learn language, and it is in the realm of phonetics and phonology that some of the clearest evidence for this claim appears.

To a large extent children seem to be genetically programmed to respond to precisely the correct range of auditory stimuli: they possess innate *templates* for certain speech sounds. Experiments with infants between the ages of one and four months suggest that they perceive in terms of the same phonological categories necessary for the description of adult language, and not simply in terms of arbitrary distinctions along a physical continuum. For instance, if they are presented with two phonemically distinct stimuli, e.g. [p] and [b] in a speech context, infants of this age can readily tell them apart. If, however, they are presented with two stimuli, e.g. two occurrences of [b] with different voice onset times, which are categorially identical but acoustically as far apart as the earlier pair, they are *unable* to tell them apart. The physical differences between the pairs of sounds are kept constant, and since the child seems to perceive at least some speech events in the same categorial manner, and since at one month he has had minimal exposure to language, it is assumed that the mechanisms by which he perceives speech are innate. Further, these mechanisms seem to be particular to *speech* in that when pairs of sounds embodying the same categorial and non-categorial contrasts are presented in isolation, instead of in a speech context, the child's discrimination is the same for all contrasts whether within a single category or across phoneme boundaries. Research in this area is still in its early stages, but there is a good chance that the set of distinctive features necessary for the description of the world's languages may be innate.

There have also been speculations to the effect that we are not only equipped to perceive in terms of a specific number of discrete categories, but we are innately predisposed by the shape of our vocal tract and the nature of our mental endowment to apply certain phonological *processes* such as assimilation. Learning to speak one's first language would then consist largely in learning how to inhibit general processes in favour of language specific deviation from universal regularity. Thus we saw above that consonant clusters in English as manifest in *cats* and *dogs* are characterized by identity of voicing: either all voiced or all voiceless. Such combinations are predicted as easy to learn for the child (or not really in need of learning at all) by contrast with other combinations such as *spend* vs. *spent* where, in the latter case, there is a switch of voicing half-way through the cluster, so that sequences involving *nt* would appear later in language acquisition, be more liable to simplification in rapid speech and more likely to change in the history of the language. The idea that phonetic processes are identical in language acquisition, in fast speech, and in language change, is extremely appealing, but a major problem for any linguistic theory is that the best theoretical machinery for treating one aspect of language is not always optimal in the description of other aspects. For instance it is not always the case that processes typical of language acquisition are equally typical of historical change. To take but one example: whereas assimilation occurs in all aspects of language, the process of *dissimilation* – where one of two similar sounds changes to be *unlike* the other – occurs in fast speech and historical change but *not* in language acquisition. The implications of such heterogeneity for the whole of phonological theory are dismaying, and tend to belie the frequent claim that we understand more about phonology than other areas of language.

We shall return to the subject of innateness in our treatment of language acquisition in Chapter 10.

7. Semantics and Meaning

The competence-performance distinction, introduced in Chapter 2, implies as a special case a distinction between the meaning of a sentence and the interpretation of an utterance. Sentence-meaning, dealt with by the semantic component of a competence grammar, is only one among many factors involved in the interpretation of utterances in context. Others include the beliefs of speaker and hearer, the nature of the occasion, and the principles which underlie conversational exchanges themselves. In this chapter and the next, we examine some of the factors, both linguistic and nonlinguistic, which affect the interpretation of utterances.

The central problem for both semantics and pragmatics is to explain how a sequence of sounds can be used to convey a message; more particularly, how a comparatively short sequence of sounds can convey a rather substantial message. The information conveyed by (1), for example, is only partially expressed in (2a–j):

(1) My son threw a brick at the window.
(2) a. Someone threw a brick at the window.
    b. My son threw something at the window.
    c. I have a son.
    d. I have a child.
    e. My child threw a brick.
    f. My son did something.
    g. My child threw a brick at something.
    h. Someone threw a brick at something.
    i. Someone's son threw a brick at the window.
    j. Something happened.

On particular occasions of utterance, (1) will convey considerably more than this, often including information which is semantically unrelated to (1) itself. For example, appropriately stressed, it might be used by a respectable middle-aged parent to deny an accusation that he himself had been throwing bricks; or that his son had been throwing bricks at passers-by; or that a hand-grenade had been used. We want to argue that the literal meaning of (1) can be distinguished from the information (1) may, on certain occasions, be used to convey; that literal meaning falls within the scope of a grammar while other aspects of utterance interpretation do not.

We may regard the meaning of a sentence as a set of *propositions*. Propositions are abstract objects designed to represent semantic structure while ignoring syntactic and phonological form. Hence two synonymous sentences of English may be said to express the same propositions, regardless of their syntactic or phonological differences; and two synonymous sentences, one from English and one from French, may also be said to express the same propositions. We shall use underlined English sentences to represent propositions; thus part of the meaning of (1) is expressed by the propositions represented in (2a–j), and part of the meaning of (3) and (4) is represented in (5):

(3) The football game is over.
(4) The football game has finished.
(5) The football game has ended.

We may also regard the interpretation of an utterance as a set of propositions. As we have seen, some of these propositions will be supplied by semantic rules, as the interpretation of an utterance of (1) will contain (2a–j). However, there may – and in general will – be certain further propositions in the interpretation of an utterance, which are *not* supplied by semantic rules alone. For example, suppose you and I both know that the Nobel Prize committee is going to choose between Barbara Cartland and Patrick White for the Literature Prize, and we are discussing the likely outcome:

(6) *Me*: I wonder who they'll give the Prize to.
 You: Well, it won't be Patrick White.

Among other things, your utterance will convey to me that you think Barbara Cartland is going to get the Literature Prize. But clearly, though your utterance conveys this message on this occasion, we would not want to set up rules of grammar which relate sentence (7) to the proposition expressed by (8):

(7) Well, it won't be Patrick White.
(8) Barbara Cartland will win the Literature Prize.

(8) is here a clear example of a proposition that forms part of the interpretation of (7) on one possible occasion of utterance, but does not form part of the literal meaning of (7). In other words, the interpretation of an utterance is not always fully determined by the rules of a competence grammar alone. One of the central problems for the theory of communication in general is to build a coherent picture of the clearly heterogeneous processes by which utterances are interpreted. We shall have more to say about the non-linguistic aspects of interpretation in the next chapter; for the remainder of this chapter we shall be concerned with semantics proper.

Entailments and Meaning

Returning to the domain of purely linguistic meaning, how is it that an utterance of (1) can convey the information in (2)? Or, to ask the question in slightly more revealing terms, how is it that the speaker of (1) commits himself to the truth of (2a–j)? The notion of *entailment*, definable in logic, seems to provide a basis for answering a number of questions both about speaker-commitment and about sentence meaning.

The entailments of a declarative sentence are those propositions that can be inferred from it in isolation from any context: that must be true whenever the sentence itself expresses a true claim. So for example (9) entails (10):

(9) We've just bought a dog.
(10) <u>We've just bought something.</u>

There are no circumstances in which (9) could be true and (10) false: thus by definition (9) entails (10) (and (10) is an entailment of (9)). Not only is (10) an entailment of (9), it also seems intuitively correct to say that (10) expresses part of the meaning of (9). The claim that the entailments of a sentence form part of its semantic analysis seems, in this case at least, to be justified. By contrast, consider the relation between (11) and (12), which we have already argued is not to be dealt with in the grammar:

(11) It won't be Patrick White.
(12) <u>Barbara Cartland will win the Literature Prize.</u>

Clearly, (11) does not entail (12). There are many circumstances in which (11) would be true but (12) false; thus, by definition, (12) is not an entailment of (11). Moreover, as we have already argued, (12) is not part of the literal meaning of (11). Thus the claim that *only* the entailments of a sentence form part of its semantic analysis seems, in this case at least, to be justified.

If the meaning of a sentence simply turned out to be the set of propositions it entailed, there would be a number of advantages for linguistic theory. First, we could explain why, by uttering a sentence, a speaker tacitly commits himself to the truth of a large number of propositions. If the meaning of a sentence is just its set of entailments, then a speaker could not consistently assert the sentence and deny one of its entailments; when he utters the sentences, he automatically commits himself to the truth of everything it entails. Second, the study of entailments, and of the concept of entailment itself, is already well advanced within philosophy and logic. If linguists could take over this well-established theory, a large amount of their work in semantics would have been done for them, and all that would remain would be actually to write the rules that relate the sentences of natural language to their semantic sets of entailments.

The third advantage of a semantic theory based on entailments is that it seems able to provide definitions of some of the fundamental semantic terms and relations which a grammar should be able to reconstruct. For example, we argued in Chapter 3 that the semantic component of a grammar should be able to state which sentences of the language were synonymous, which were contradictory or anomalous, which were tautological or analytic, which were ambiguous, and which entered into entailment relations. We have already defined a notion of entailment: it turns out that using this basic definition we can go on to define many of the other fundamental semantic terms.

Two sentences may be said to be *synonymous* if and only if they have exactly the same set of entailments; or, which comes to the same thing, if and only if they entail each other, so that whenever one is true the other must also be true. By this definition, (13) and (14), which entail each other, will be correctly predicted as synonymous:

(13) John and Mary are twins.
(14) Mary and John are twins.

There are no circumstances in which (13) could be true and (14) false, or in which (14) could be true and (13) false. By the definition of entailment, then, (13) and (14) entail each other; by the definition of synonymy, they will be synonymous.

Two sentences may be said to be *contradictories* if each entails the negation of the other. Thus (15) and (16) are contradictories:

(15) No one has led a perfect life.
(16) Someone has led a perfect life.

Whenever (15) is true, (16) must be false, and whenever (16) is true, (15) must be false. They are thus, by our definition, contradictories. Similarly, a single sentence may be said to be a *contradiction* if it has contradictory entailments. Thus (17) is a contradiction, because it entails both (18a) and (18b):

(17) ?I have no brothers, but my elder brother is tall.
(18) a. I have no brothers.
     b. I have a brother.

(18a) and (18b) are themselves contradictories; by our definition (17), which entails them, is a contradiction. *Anomaly* is merely a special case of contradiction, and we shall not attempt to define it more narrowly here.

A sentence may be said to be *analytic*, or *analytically true*, if its denial is a contradiction. Thus (19) is analytically true, because its denial is the contradictory (20):

(19) A spinster is a woman.
(20) ?A spinster is not a woman.

(20) is, of course, intuitively a contradiction. To see that it is also a contradiction by our definition, we need to look a little more closely at the notion of entailment. By our definition, if (20) is a contradiction, it must carry contradictory entailments. The entailments we have in mind are (21a) and (21b):

(21) a. An unmarried woman is not a woman.
b. An unmarried woman is a woman.

It is fairly easy to see that (20) entails (21a): that whenever (20) is true (21a) must also be true. However, it is less easy to see that (20) entails (21b). The fact is that (21b), being a logical truth, will be true in all conceivable circumstances; in particular it will be true whenever (20) is true, or indeed when (17), (18) or (19) is true. By the definition of entailment, then, it follows that (20) entails (21b) as well as (21a), and hence, by the definition of analyticity, that (19) is analytic. This fact about entailment – that a logical truth is entailed by any sentence at all – helps with the characterization of analyticity, as we have just seen; however, it causes serious problems for a semantic theory based on the notion of entailment, as we shall shortly demonstrate.

Finally, a sentence may be said to be *ambiguous* if it may be conjoined to its own denial without the result being necessarily a contradiction. Thus, for example, (22a) is ambiguous, as is borne out by (22b):

(22) a. I felt myself.
(b) I felt myself, but I didn't feel myself.

(22b) is not a contradiction if the first clause is interpreted as entailing (23a) while the second is interpreted as entailing (23b):

(23) a. I felt the way I normally do.
     b. I didn't run my hands over myself.

Thus, by our definition, (22a) is ambiguous.

In spite of its advantages, there are a number of serious problems with this approach to meaning. However, it seems that they are not insoluble problems: in fact their solutions provide valuable insights into the form of semantic descriptions and the nature of semantic knowledge. Because of this, we shall spend some time discussing them, and outlining some recent proposals about how to solve them.

As we have shown, the theory of meaning as entailments makes the prediction that all sentences which entail exactly the same set of propositions must be synonymous. As we have also seen, there are many cases like (13) and (14) where these predictions are correct. However, there also seem to be a number of types of case where two sentences do share their entailments, but are nonetheless not obviously synonymous. This raises two separate questions: first, how do we decide whether two sentences which share their entailments are in fact synonymous; second, if synonymy cannot be fully defined in terms of shared entailments, how *is* it to be defined?

As an example of two sentences which share their entailments but are not necessarily synonymous, consider (24) and (25):

(24) *Jane* spoke to Alex.
(25) Jane spoke to *Alex*.

(24) and (25) share exactly the same set of entailments; in particular, both entail (26a) and (26b):

(26) a. Someone spoke to Alex.
     b. Jane spoke to someone.

However, these entailments play different pragmatic roles when (24) and (25) are uttered in context. For example, someone uttering or interpreting (24) will generally take (26a) for granted, while someone uttering or interpreting (25) will generally take (26b) for granted. For this reason the two sentences, although true in exactly the same set of contexts, will be appropriate to rather different contexts. This does not, of course, prove that (24) and (25) are semantically distinct, but it does leave us with the onus of explaining how two sentences which share their entailments can behave so differently when uttered in context. If it could be shown that (26a) and (26b) play different *semantic* roles in the analysis of (24) and (25), the further pragmatic differences between these sentences would receive a natural explanation.

As a slightly different case of sentences which share their entailments, consider the following pair:

(27) I met your sister last week, and she is very intelligent.
(28) Your sister, who I met last week, is very intelligent.

Since (27) and (28) share exactly the same set of entailments, they will be predicted as synonymous on the theory we have outlined. However, there are clear differences in their pragmatic interpretations. For example, both sentences entail (29) and (30):

(29) I met your sister last week.
(30) Your sister is very intelligent.

However, someone who utters (27) will generally indicate that he regards (29) and (30) as equally important or relevant, whereas someone who utters (28) will generally indicate that he considers (29) to be less important or relevant than (30). These differences in turn affect the interpretation of denials or questionings of (27) and (28). Someone who denies or questions (27) may equally well be seen as rejecting either or both of (29) and (30); however, someone who denies or questions (28) will normally be taken as denying or questioning (30) rather than (29). That these differences between (27) and (28) are not just pragmatic differences is shown by embedding them into (31) and (32):

(31) John knows that I met your sister last week, and that she is very intelligent.

(32) John knows that your sister, who I met last week, is very intelligent.

It is perfectly possible to imagine circumstances in which (32) would be true and (31) false: for example, if John does not know that I met your sister last week. In other words, (31) and (32) actually differ in their entailments, and cannot, therefore, be synonymous. Since the only difference between these two sentences is that one contains (27) where the other contains (28), it seems that the difference in meaning between (31) and (32) must be attributable to some difference in meaning between (27) and (28) themselves. It must be concluded that, in spite of the predictions of the entailment theory, (27) and (28) cannot be treated as synonymous.

In the two cases just considered, the meaning differences involved have been slight. There are further cases where the semantic differences between two sentences are much more noticeable, but where the entailment theory will mark them as either synonymous or partially synonymous. The problem raised by these cases is that, on the entailment theory of meaning, *every* entailment of a sentence must be considered part of its meaning. Yet there are many propositions which are logically deducible from a sentence which are intuitively felt *not* to be part of its meaning. This seems to indicate that the definition of meaning in terms of entailment cannot be quite right.

For example, consider the relations between (33) and (34):

(33) Shelley was a poet.
(34) Either Shelley was a poet or Ibsen was a clown.

In fact (33) entails (34): whenever (33) is true (34) must also be true. According to the entailment theory, then, the meaning of (34) will be seen as included in the meaning of (33): each entailment of a sentence is seen as part of its semantic analysis. Intuitively, this is quite wrong: if anything, the meaning of (33) is included in the meaning of (34), rather than the reverse. Moreover, one would not want to produce a *grammar* which included the meaning of (34) in its semantic description of (33), any more than one would want a grammar to relate (7) above to the meaning of (8). If these intuitive distinctions are correct, it seems that there must be a difference between rules of logical entailment in general – which relate (33) to (34) – and rules of semantic entailment in particular – which do not; and the entailment theory of meaning is unable to express this difference.

As a final case where the entailment theory of meaning leads to unpalatable results, consider the following pair:

(35) All parents are parents.
(36) If John and Bill are here, then John is here.

Clearly, (35) and (36) differ in meaning. Unfortunately, however, they entail each other, and thus, on the entailment theory, will be predicted as synonymous. Since (35) is a logical truth, as we have already seen, it will be true in all possible circumstances, and in particular, it will be true whenever (36) is true; hence (35) entails (36). Similarly, (36) is a logical truth, and will be true in all possible circumstances; in particular, it will be true whenever (35) is true; hence (36) entails (35). These two sentences – and in fact all necessary (or logical) truths – will thus be predicted as synonymous. That they are not synonymous should be obvious, but it can be demonstrated by embedding them into (37) and (38):

(37) Joe regrets that all parents are parents.
(38) Joe regrets that if John and Bill are here, then John is here.

(37) and (38) are not synonymous: it is perfectly possible for one to be true while the other is false. Since the only difference between (37) and (38) is that one contains (35) where the other contains (36), it follows that (35) and (36) must themselves differ in meaning, in order to account for the differences in meaning between (37) and (38). Again, the only conclusion to be drawn from these examples is that the meaning of a sentence cannot be adequately captured merely by specifying its set of entailments.

The problems with the entailment theory of meaning might be summarized as follows. First, this theory takes no account of the fact that certain of the entailments of a sentence seem to be pragmatically more important than others, so that two sentences which share their entailments may nonetheless differ in the pragmatic order of importance they assign to these entailments, and hence be appropriate to different contexts. Second, it is forced to treat any proposition which is logically deducible from a sentence as part of its meaning, allowing no place for a distinction between rules of logical inference and rules of semantics proper. Third, it falsely predicts all necessary truths (and by the same token all necessary falsehoods) as synonymous, being unable to distinguish between two sentences which are true (or false) in all possible circumstances. Various solutions to these problems have been attempted in the philosophical and linguistic literature. In the next section, we shall outline the one that seems to us most adequate.

Ordered Entailments

If the basic insights of the entailment theory of meaning are to be preserved, what is clearly needed is some method of distinguishing between two sentences which share their entailments, but are nonetheless not synonymous. What we are going to argue is that the semantic rules of the grammar impose an internal structure on the entailments of a sentence, and that two sentences which share their entailments, but structure them differently, should no longer be regarded as synonymous.[1] We shall also make use of the idea that the structure of entailments affects pragmatic interpretation processes, so that two sentences which share their entailments but structure them differently will be appropriate to different contexts, and will receive different pragmatic interpretations. If something like this approach is correct, we need to provide answers to two questions: first, what type of structure is involved in the semantic analysis of a sentence, and second, what mechanisms are used for imposing this structure? We shall argue that the structure involved is essentially a logical one, and that the

1. In this section we are summarizing forthcoming work by Wilson and Sperber.

mechanisms used for deriving it involve the lexical, syntactic and phonological form of the sentence under analysis.

Turning first to the mechanisms by which entailments may be derived, notice that a small subset of the entailments of a sentence may be obtained by performing a simple operation on its surface syntactic structure. Consider (39), with the surface structure given in (40):

(39) John stole three horses.

(40)

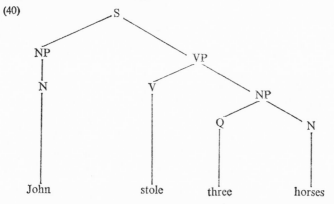

By substituting an appropriate indefinite phrase, such as *someone, something, do something*, for each surface structure constituent in (40), we obtain the following series of entailments:

(41) a. Someone stole three horses.
  b. John did something to three horses.
  c. John stole some number of horses.
  d. John stole three things.
  e. John stole something.
  f. John did something.
  g. Something happened.

(41a) is obtained by substituting the indefinite phrase *someone* for the NP *John* in (40); (41b) substitutes the indefinite phrase *do something to* for the verb *stole*; (41c) substitutes the indefinite phrase *some number of* for the quantifier *three*; (41f) substitutes the indefinite phrase *do something* for the VP *stole three horses*; and (41g) substitutes the indefinite phrase *something happened* for the sentence *John stole three horses* as a whole. Each of the entailments in (41), then, is the result of a substitution operation on the surface syntactic structure of (39), and all such possible substitutions are listed in (41). We shall call the set of entailments obtained from surface structure in this way the *grammatically specified entailments* of a sentence, and claim that they play a particularly important role in the semantic analysis and pragmatic interpretation of the sentence.

How are we to decide which is the appropriate indefinite phrase to substitute for a given surface constituent? How, for example, did we decide that *someone* was the appropriate indefinite phrase to substitute for the NP *John*? This is not a trivial question, and we shall do no more than indicate a rough answer here. Notice that (39), with stress on *John*, would be an acceptable answer to the question in (42):

(42) Who stole three horses?

(42) itself bears a semantic relationship to (43):

(43) Someone stole three horses.

(43) in some sense specifies the range of acceptable answers to (42), in that any acceptable answer to (42) must itself entail (43). Thus (39), which entails (43), is an acceptable answer, while (44), which does not, is not:

(44) ?The earth is flat.

This suggests that a good way of determining the appropriate range of indefinite phrases to associate with a given sentence, such as (39), would be to consider the range of questions to which it would be an acceptable answer. These questions would in turn bear a semantic relationship to sentences containing the appropriate indefinite phrase for substitution, as (42) does to (43). Thus (39), with stress on *three*, would also be a possible answer to (45a), which in turn bears the relevant semantic relationship to (45b):

(45) a. How many horses did John steal?
     b. John stole some number of horses.

Hence *some number of*, in (45b), is an appropriate indefinite phrase to substitute for the quantifier *three* in (39). Along these lines, we think an adequate account of the substitution mechanism could be found.

The grammatically specified entailments of a sentence have an internal logical structure: certain of these entailments entail, or are entailed by, others. The internal logical structure of the grammatically specified entailments of (39) is shown in the following diagram, where downward arrows link entailing propositions with the propositions they entail:

(46)

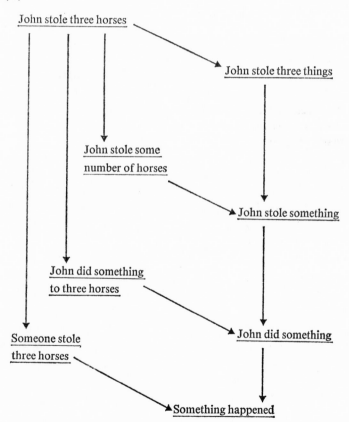

John stole three horses

John stole three things

John stole some
number of horses

John stole something

John did something
to three horses

Someone stole
three horses

John did something

Something happened

Each downward path through (46) picks out a series of propositions in which each member entails its successor and is entailed by its predecessor. Thus the type of structure imposed on the entailments of (39) by the surface substitution mechanism is a partial logical ordering, in which higher-ordered entailments themselves entail lower-ordered ones.

What (46) provides is a sort of semantic skeleton onto which the remaining entailments of (39), derived by lexical and other semantic rules, may be grafted into positions determined by their logical relations to the propositions already present in the structure. Before turning to these further aspects of semantic analysis, however, we might look at the effect of phonological information on the semantic structure itself. It seems that phonological information does not so much contribute new entailments to the semantic structure of a sentence, as effect a re-ordering of the grammatically specified entailments, promoting some to positions of special prominence, and demoting others to more minor roles. The main phonological factor involved is that of stress: the more ways there are of stressing a sentence, the more varied its possible interpretations will be.

We noted in Chapter 6 that English allows its speakers great freedom in where they put the heaviest stress in a given sentence. Thus all of (47a–d) are possible pronunciations of (39) (with heavy stress represented by italics):

(47) a. *John* stole three horses.
    b. John *stole* three horses.
    c. John stole *three* horses.
    d. John stole three *horses*.

Clearly, although (47a–d) share all their entailments, they will be appropriate to rather different contexts, and will be interpreted as suggesting rather different things. For this reason, we might want to assign them different semantic structures: the question is how stress patterns may affect the basic semantic structure of a sentence and provide for its different possible interpretations.

The answer seems to be that different stress-assignments will pick out different members of the set of grammatically specified entailments, and promote them to higher positions in the semantic ordering. Take (47a), for example. By substituting the indefinite phrase *someone* for its most heavily stressed constituent, entailment (48) is obtained:

(48) Someone stole three horses.

This entailment lies on a unique downward path through (46), and is a member of the following logically ordered series:

(49) a. John stole three horses.
     b. Someone stole three horses.
     c. Something happened.

We shall call (48) the *background* entailment of (47a), and the series (49a–c) the *focal scale* for (47a). We want to make the following claim: entailments on the focal scale are promoted to higher positions in the semantic ordering than all other entailments of a sentence, and are in fact the only entailments which are invariably involved in the pragmatic interpretation of that sentence in context. The precise role of the background and focal scale in pragmatic interpretation will be considered in Chapter 8.

(47c) selects a different background and a different focal scale. Its background, obtained by substituting the indefinite phrase *some number of* for the heavily stressed quantifier *three*, will be (50):

(50) John stole some number of horses.

Its focal scale, the only downward path on (46) which includes (50), will be (51a–e):

(51) a. John stole three horses.
     b. John stole some number of horses.
     c. John stole something.
     d. John did something.
     e. Something happened.

The semantic structure of (47c) will thus differ from that of (47a), since its highest ordered entailments will be those in (51) rather than those in (49). This difference between the two semantic structures will make it possible to predict differences in the pragmatic interpretations of (47a) and (47c) in context. This in turn will solve one of the problems we saw in the entailment theory of meaning: that two sentences which shared their entailments might nonetheless be appropriate to different contexts.

There are certain cases where the stress pattern of a sentence does not determine a unique interpretation. (47d) is an example:

(47) d. John stole three *horses*.

By substituting an indefinite phrase *things* for the noun *horses*, the following entailment is obtained:

(52) John stole three things.

This in turn determines the following focal scale for (47d):

(53) a. John stole three horses.
   b. John stole three things.
   c. John stole something.
   d. John did something.
   e. Something happened.

Accordingly, the entailments in (53) will be promoted to highest position in the ordering, allowing for differences in the interpretations of (47a), (47c) and (47d). The reason why (47d) does not itself have a unique interpretation is that it is not entirely clear from the stress pattern exactly what syntactic constituent is being selected for special emphasis. So far, we have assumed that the constituent being emphasized was always the smallest possible constituent bearing the heavily stressed item. However, in the case of (47d) it is clear that the emphasized constituent could have been the noun *horses*, or the NP *three horses*, or the VP *stole three horses*, or the sentence as a whole. The selection of the background, if it is to play a genuine role in the interpretation of utterances, must be determined, not by the *smallest* constituent bearing heaviest stress, but by the constituent actually selected for special emphasis by this stress-assignment. This specially emphasized constituent is normally referred to as the *focus* of a sentence, and (47d) has more than one possible focus. Accordingly, (47d) has more than one possible background, obtained by substitution of an indefinite phrase for each possible focus. Thus (53b), (53c), (53d) and (53e) would all be possible backgrounds for (47d). Since, as will be seen in the next chapter, the background plays a crucial role in the interpretation of utterances, even the fact that it selects a unique focal scale, as (47d) does, will not reduce the possible interpretations of an utterance in context to a single one.

The role of stress, then, affects the semantic structure of a sentence in the following way. It picks out a small number of syntactic constituents as possible focuses of the sentence; it simultaneously picks out a small subset of entailments – the focal scale – and promotes them to highest position in the ordering, thus assigning them a crucial role in the pragmatic interpretation of the sentence. Actual choice of a focus, which may be determined by partly non-linguistic factors, will simultaneously select a background entailment which will also determine certain crucial aspects of the pragmatic interpretation of the sentence. Sentences which differ in their stress patterns will thus receive different semantic analyses, enabling them to play different pragmatic roles, and be appropriate to different pragmatic contexts.

What we have been calling the background entailment of a sentence with a given stress pattern is often referred to as its *presupposition*. Presuppositions are logically distinct from entailments: a presupposition is generally defined as a proposition which must be true if the sentence which presupposes it is to be either true *or* false. So, for example, on the assumption that (54) is a presupposition of (55) and that (55) is false, (54) must necessarily be true:

(54) <u>Someone stole three horses.</u>

(55) *John* stole three horses.

Now while it is clear that (55) entails (54) – that (54) must be true whenever (55) is true – it does not seem at all clear that (54) must be true whenever (55) is false. For example, it seems perfectly consistent to deny both (54) and (55), as in (56):

(56) *John* didn't steal three horses; *no one* stole three horses.

The possibility of such denials is ruled out on the assumption that (55) presupposes (54). Since we find (56) fully acceptable and grammatical, we shall deny that (55) presupposes (54), and continue to maintain that there is an entailment relation between the two. Hence our choice of the term *background entailment* rather than the term *presupposition*.

We now turn to the third major factor in semantic analysis: the *grammatically unspecified* entailments derived by lexical and other semantic rules, and their positions in the overall semantic structure of a sentence. In Chapter 3 we suggested that word-meaning would be handled by giving each word a semantic entry in the lexicon: this entry would contain all the information necessary for its semantic interpretation. We can now give slightly more substance to that account. If meaning is to be described in terms of entailments, then the semantic entry for a word must state what contribution it may or must make to the entailments of sentences in which it occurs. Two words will be synonyms if they make exactly the same contribution to the entailments of sentences in which they occur; they will be partial synonyms if every contribution made by one is also made by the other; and so on.

How is the semantic analysis of a word actually arrived at? Essentially, by examining the entailments of sentences which contain it. Suppose that we want to analyse the word *horse*. It is immediately obvious that the first member of each of the following pairs entails the second:

(57) a. That is a horse.
   b. <u>That is an animal.</u>
(58) a. <u>I bought a horse.</u>
   b. <u>I bought an animal.</u>

(59) a. A horse bit him.
   b. <u>An animal bit him.</u>

We could record this entailment relationship simply by stating in the semantic entry for *horse* that a horse is an animal, and allowing the semantic rules which derive the entailments of a sentence, whenever they derive an entailment of the (a) form above, to derive an extra entailment of the corresponding (b) form. Many words will, of course, have more than one such entry. It is unclear at the moment just how many entries a word like *horse* should have, or even whether it should have more than the one just given. This is one of the places where there is a genuine problem about whether and where the line between linguistic and non-linguistic knowledge can be drawn. We have no contribution to make to this issue; we are inclined to be conservative about it, and to attribute as little as possible to the side of linguistic knowledge: we will therefore assume that the semantic relation between *horse* and *animal* is the only one available in the lexical entry for *horse*.

With this one semantic entry for *horse* we can derive a considerable number of further entailments from the sentence we have been analysing (repeated here for convenience):

(39) John stole three horses.

The following entailments will be among them:

(60) a. <u>John stole three animals.</u>
   b. <u>John stole some number of animals.</u>
   c. <u>John did something to three animals.</u>
   d. <u>Someone stole three animals.</u>

(60a–d) are not grammatically specified entailments of (39), but each of them is entailed by one grammatically specified entailment in the diagram (46), and entails another. Each thus fits naturally into a particular position in the overall semantic structure. We might represent the results as follows:

(61)

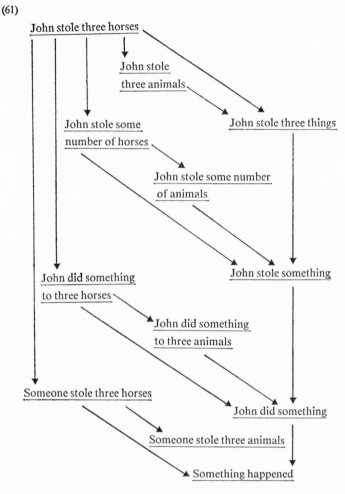

When stress assignment picks out a particular focal scale and promotes it to the highest position in the semantic ordering, the entailments which bear some logical relationship to the focal scale will be promoted at the same time, allowing for still further differences in the semantic structures of sentences with the same entailments but different stress patterns. Thus with the stress pattern in (47a), (62a) and (62b) may play a part in pragmatic interpretation:

(47) a. *John* stole three horses.
(62) a. John stole three animals.
    b. Someone stole three animals.

With (47c), it will be (63a) and (63b) which are promoted; and so on:

(47) c. John stole *three* horses.
(63) a. John stole three animals.
    b. John stole some number of animals.

The richer the semantic entry for a particular word, the more entailments it will contribute to the overall semantic structure, and the richer that semantic structure will be in consequence.

There are still other entailments, from other sources, to be fitted into the structure. For example, (39) entails (64a–c):

(39) John stole three horses.
(64) a. John stole.
    b. John existed at the time referred to by (39).
    c. There were horses at the time referred to by (39).

(64a) can be fully integrated into the structure, since it is entailed by *John stole something*, and in turn entails *John did something*. (64b) and (64c) must be less fully integrated, in the sense that they are entailed by other entailments of (39), but themselves entail no others. The existence of such entailments implies that the semantic structure of (39) will be a partial ordering rather than a full ordering, with certain arrows pointing out of the diagram altogether. The existence of such entailments also implies that in addition to the lexical entries for words and the various ordering mechanisms we have discussed, there must be additional semantic rules which read off certain entailments like those in (64a–c) from a mixture of syntactic and lexical cues.

Within the framework we have just outlined, we can solve some of the problems for the entailment theory of meaning outlined earlier in this chapter. For example, the entailment theory predicted falsely that all necessarily true sentences were synonymous. If we now modify the definition of synonymy so that only sentences which share their grammatically specified entailments are synonymous, this difficulty is overcome. For example, although the necessarily true (35) and (36) entail each other, they do not share their grammatically specified entailments:

(35) All parents are parents.
(36) If John and Bill are here, then John is here.

Among others, (35) has the grammatically specified entailment (65), which (36) lacks:

(65) <u>Some proportion of parents are parents.</u>

Similarly, (36) has the grammatically specified entailment (66), which (35) lacks:

(66) <u>If John and Bill are here, then someone is here.</u>

For this reason, according to the new definition of synonymy, (35) and (36) will not count as synonymous, even though they entail each other.

We have also made a distinction between semantic and logical rules, so that there may be logical entailments which are not obtained through the application of any semantic rule. It is by logical rather than semantic rule that (34) is obtained from (33):

(33) Shelley was a poet.
(34) <u>Either Shelley was a poet or Ibsen was a clown.</u>

This means that, according to the arguments of this section, (34) will not form part of the semantic analysis of (33), even though one may be obtained from the other by logical rule.

Finally, we have shown how a single syntactic structure, alternatively stressed, will receive alternative semantic analyses, and have argued that in terms of these alternative semantic analyses we can explain differences in their pragmatic functions: this matter will be taken up in the next chapter.

In this chapter, we have tried to survey some of the factors involved in the semantic interpretation of a sentence. In doing this, we have taken a stand on the issue of how semantic rules relate to the other components of a grammar. In particular, we have argued that semantic rules must have access both to surface syntactic structure and to stress contours. We have not taken a stand on whether certain semantic rules must also have access to deep structures; we have left this matter entirely open. Our positive claims have been the following: the basis for semantic description is the notion of entailment; however, the meaning of a sentence cannot be regarded as merely an unstructured set of entailments. Many problems of semantics can be solved by assuming that the meaning of a sentence is a structured, partially ordered set of entailments, with the structure being determined by a combination of syntactic, lexical, phonological and logical considerations. Within this framework, it is possible to distinguish between sentences which share their entailments but nonetheless exhibit different semantic and pragmatic potentialities. It is to these pragmatic potentialities, and the factors involved in the interpretation of utterances in context, that we turn in the next chapter.

8. Pragmatics and Communication

With the last chapter, we completed our survey of the types of linguistic knowledge embodied in a grammar, and of the role of grammar itself in verbal communication. The object of a grammar is to pair sound sequences with meanings, which we are now construing as structured sets of propositions. We have emphasized two aspects of sentence meaning: it is context-independent, and it deals with the range of propositions which a speaker who asserts a sentence cannot consistently deny. It is clear, however, that a theory of verbal communication which dealt with only these aspects of meaning would be sadly lacking. It would have nothing to say about those propositions which are conveyed by an utterance in one context, but not in another; nor about those propositions which are suggested, though not actually entailed, by the utterance of a particular sentence in context, nor about the dimension of appropriateness, relevance and informativeness which we have rigorously excluded from grammar. All of these aspects of communication involve non-linguistic knowledge and non-grammatical principles: in this chapter, we allow such factors a small amount of the consideration we have been denying them.

Pragmatic Implications

In the last chapter we saw a case where part of the message conveyed by an utterance was context-dependent, and hence ignored by the grammar. It was a case where the utterance of (1), in suitable circumstances, would convey (2):

(1) It won't be Patrick White.
(2) <u>Barbara Cartland will win the Nobel Prize for Literature.</u>

The semantic component as we are conceiving it could not, in principle, deal with such a message, because (1) does not entail (2). Nor would we want the grammar to represent (2) as part of the meaning of the *sentence* (1), because of the vast majority of occasions where speakers would utter (1) without any intention of conveying (2). However, virtually every utterance does convey a message which is not dealt with by the grammar, as (1) conveys (2) in the circumstances we have described. What factors are involved in this type of communication, and how do speakers exploit them?

In the case of (1) and (2), the factors involved are rather obvious. First, speaker and hearer must know or believe that either Barbara Cartland or Patrick White will get the Nobel Prize for Literature; second, they must know or believe that (1) excludes the possibility of Patrick White getting it; and third, they must know that given two alternatives and the assumption that one is false, it follows that the other is true. If this background of shared knowledge and belief is allowed to play a role in inference, (2) is easily deducible from (1), and would thus be part of what the speaker of (1) committed himself to by uttering it. We shall call (2) a *pragmatic implication* of (1) in the context described, meaning by this that it does not follow from (1) alone, but it does follow from (1) together with a suitable body of background knowledge or beliefs.

From this example, it appears that a basic model of verbal communication must involve the following factors, which speakers and hearers would share:

(a) A body of linguistic knowledge (a grammar).
(b) A body of non-linguistic knowledge and beliefs (an encyclopedia).
(c) a set of inference rules (a logic).

Given these, an utterance would be analysed as conveying two different types of information:

(a) A set of propositions deducible from the sentence uttered by purely linguistic (semantic) rules.

(b) A further set of propositions deducible from the sentence uttered, together with some item(s) of non-linguistic knowledge shared by speaker and hearer, and a set of shared inference rules.

The full message conveyed by an utterance in context would thus consist of its set of semantic entailments together with its set of pragmatic implications. While there is nothing particularly wrong with this as the basis for a theory of communication – indeed some model of knowledge and inference could act as a basis for most theories of human mental activity – it does not nearly begin to account for the variety and complexity of actual conversational exchanges, and the subtlety of the principles underlying them.

Consider the following exchange:

(3) A: Where's my box of chocolates?
   B: Where are the snows of yesteryear?

B's reply is not a direct response to A's question. Under the right circumstances, however, it would convey an indirect response: it would convey that his question was unanswerable, or less directly still, that his box of chocolates was gone. Yet how could this message be logically deducible from any item of background knowledge, together with B's reply? Intuitively, it is clear what is going on. B responds to A's question with another. The answer to this second question is somehow construed as giving an answer to the first; thus depending on the answer to B's question, an answer to A's will follow. More or less direct responses to the same question are conveyed in (4)–(7):

(4) A: Where's my box of chocolates?
   B: I was feeling hungry.
(5) A: Where's my box of chocolates?
   B: I've got a train to catch.
(6) A: Where's my box of chocolates?
   B: Where's your diet sheet?

(7) A: Where's my box of chocolates?
    B: The children were in your room this morning.

All of (3)–(7) are perfectly reasonable conversational exchanges; most of them would convey some sort of a reply to A's question, given the right circumstances, but the reply will sometimes be indirect, and it is unclear what role shared knowledge and inference are playing in the move from overt reply to tacit message. What is clear, however, is that something more than mere systems of knowledge and inference must be involved.

Ten years ago, in a series of influential lectures that have only recently been published, Paul Grice drew attention to the crucial role played by judgements of relevance in the interpretation of utterances. Consider (3), for example. We said that B's question might well suggest that A's chocolates had been eaten. However, it will not convey this suggestion unless it is construed as a relevant response to A. If it is construed as irrelevant – for example as the start of a poetry reading, a genuine inquiry in its own right, or a rhetorical response to a quite different question – then no such suggestion will arise. Similarly, if B's remark in (7) is construed as a relevant answer to A's question, it will suggest that the children may have eaten his chocolates, or may know where they are. If it is construed as an attempt to change the subject or to dismiss A's question for some other reason, no such suggestion will arise. In other words, the interpretation of an utterance will depend on the hearer's judgement about how relevant it was intended to be. If he decides that it was intended as relevant, he will go to considerable lengths to interpret it as such, even if this means reading into it a certain amount of information which it does not overtly convey. (3), (4) and (7) may be seen as examples of this indirect conveying of information. If the hearer decides that the utterance was *intended* as irrelevant, he may still be able to gather some relevant information from it. For example, in (5) B's remark that he has got a train to catch may be taken as implying that he has more important things to do than answer A's question; or that he has guilty knowledge about the chocolates and is refusing to answer the question for that reason. In either case, his answer gives an indirect response to A's question, in the form of a refusal to answer it. Examples (6) and (7) could also be taken in this way. The point here is that even an overtly irrelevant remark may be interpreted as conveying some relevant information, as long as it is seen as directed at the previous remark. The third possibility of construal is, of course, that the remark in question was indeed irrelevant, but accidentally so: for example, because the previous remark was misheard, or itself irrelevant or unworthy of consideration, or for some other reason. Examples (3), (5) and (7) could be taken in this way. In short, a hearer will attempt to get out of a remark just what he believes the speaker put into it, and his judgement about its intended relevance will crucially affect the amount of work he is prepared to do to get a message out of it.

The notion of relevance, then, will play a central part in any theory of pragmatic interpretation. An informal definition of relevance might run as follows.[1] The participants in a conversation have a stock of shared knowledge, assumptions and beliefs. Remarks which add new information to the stock of shared knowledge will be informative; those which add no new information will be uninformative. Relevance seems to involve a special type of informativeness. Intuitively speaking, one remark is relevant to another if the two combine to yield new information which was not derivable from either in isolation. For example, (8b) is relevant to (8a):

(8) a. If John is prepared to pay £10, Bill will tell him the answer.
    b. John is prepared to pay £10.

Together, (8a) and (8b) entail (9), which does not follow from either in isolation:

(9) Bill will tell John the answer.

1. This definition, together with much else in this chapter, is taken from forthcoming work by Sperber and Wilson.

In the vast majority of cases, of course, the stock of shared knowledge will have to be called on in deriving the new information required. For example, by our definition (10b) may or may not be relevant to (10a):

(10) a. <u>Whenever Susie sees a cat, she screams.</u>
　　 b. There's a cat coming round the corner.

For (10b) to be relevant – to combine with (10a) to yield new information – there will have to be additional assumptions: that Susie is present, that she is in a position to see the cat, and so on. If these assumptions are made, then (11) will follow from (10a) and (10b):

(11) <u>Susie</u> $\left\{\dfrac{\text{may be}}{\text{is}}\right\}$ <u>going to scream.</u>

Without something like these assumptions, although (10b) may be informative, it will not be relevant to (10a), because nothing will follow from (10a) and (10b) together that does not follow from each in isolation. We might thus give an informal definition of relevance as follows:

> A remark P is relevant to another remark Q if P and Q, together with background knowledge, yield new information not derivable from either P or Q, together with background knowledge, alone.

This definition excludes a number of cases of relevance which we would obviously like to include: relevance to an occasion or context, relevance to a general purpose, relevance to a topic, and so on. However, it gives the notion enough content for our present purposes.

　　The assumption that a remark was intended as relevant will dramatically reduce its possibilities of interpretation in context. Essentially, its only relevant pragmatic implications will be those that follow from it in conjunction with the immediately preceding remark, together with any items of shared knowledge needed as extra premises in the deduction. The task of the hearer is, quite simply, to find the relevant pragmatic implications. In the case of (1)–(7), (8) and (10), this task is fairly easily accomplished, the result being the pragmatic implications we have mentioned, which will supplement the semantic interpretation provided by the grammar, to yield a fuller interpretation of the utterance in context. In certain other cases, however, the task will be more complex. Consider (12), for example:

(12) A: Your son's really taken to Annette.
B: He used to like playing with snails when he was a child.

On the assumption that B's remark was intended as relevant, the hearer must set about finding its relevant pragmatic implications. Now nothing directly follows from A and B together that does not follow from either in isolation; moreover, on fairly normal assumptions about background knowledge, there will be no item of shared knowledge which could be used as an additional premise establishing a connection between A and B. What is to be done? A hearer who persists in regarding B as relevant might reason as follows. B's remark was intended as relevant. Therefore there must be some additional premise I could use to derive relevant information from A and B together. Since I know of none, I'll have to construct one. He might construct one as follows. B's remark suggests that his son has strange tastes. If liking Annette was also a strange taste, then B's remark would carry a further implication: a normal person would not like Annette. Therefore there must be something wrong with Annette. The final result of this reasoning is a pragmatic implication derived from A and B together, and thus establishing the relevance of B's remark. Of course, this is not the only possible interpretation, but most are along similar lines: for example B's remark might be taken as implying that Annette is like a snail. What is important is that the hearer has to supply additional premises of his own, premises which he does not necessarily believe, yielding pragmatic implications which he also need not necessarily believe. Nor could the speaker be accused of *saying* something nasty about Annette, although he has certainly conveyed his dislike. These extremely indirect implications, which constitute the real point of remarks like (12B), Grice calls *conversational implicatures*: pragmatic implications which follow from a remark only on the assumption that it was intended as relevant, together with additional premises which do not form part of shared knowledge, but which the speaker expects the hearer to construct for himself. And of course these additional premises themselves will form part of the pragmatic implications of a remark.

It can thus be seen that beyond its literal semantic interpretation, provided by the grammar, an utterance has three main types of pragmatic implications. First, those that follow from the utterance itself together with a preceding remark and any item of shared knowledge needed to establish a connection between the two; second, those additional premises, not already part of shared knowledge, needed to establish this connection; third, those that follow from these additional premises, together with the utterance itself, the preceding remark and any necessary item of background knowledge. All of these may contribute to establishing the relevance of the utterance as intended by the speaker; none will follow unless the utterance is treated by the hearer as relevant.

As we have seen, any utterance carries an enormous number of entailments and implications. If utterances are interpreted along the lines just suggested, a vital stage in the interpretation process will involve identifying the particular entailments on which the relevance of the utterance depends: the particular entailments which will combine with items of shared knowledge to yield the new information which the speaker intended to convey. We have also seen how the assumption that the utterance *is* relevant will narrow down the search for the relevant entailments to some extent, since they must in some way connect up with the interpretation of the preceding remark to yield some relevant item of new information. However, this still leaves hearers a considerable degree of latitude in interpretation. It seems that there are a number of overt linguistic cues which speakers may use to guide the hearer towards the intended interpretation. These cues form an interesting subject of study in their own right; with their aid, it is perhaps less surprising that speakers and hearers manage to communicate unspoken messages so successfully.

Consider the following exchange:

(13) A: I really disliked that man you introduced me to.
     B: He's your new boss.

There are a number of ways B's remark could be taken, even with the proviso that it was intended as relevant, and that it must thus combine with A to yield new information. It could be construed as a warning, an exhortation, a suggestion or a diagnosis. There are in fact a number of overt indicators which B could use to bring out his intentions more clearly: for example (14)–(18) each suggests a slightly different interpretation:

(14) A: I really disliked that man you introduced me to.
     B: Actually, he's your new boss.
(15) A: I really disliked that man you introduced me to.
     B: Anyway, he's your new boss.
(16) A: I really disliked that man you introduced me to.
     B: After all, he's your new boss.
(17) A: I really disliked that man you introduced me to.
     B: Still, he's your new boss.
(18) A: I really disliked that man you introduced me to.
     B: Well, he's your new boss.

(14B) suggests that A should reconsider his statement, (15B) suggests that his dislike is irrelevant, (16B) suggests that he dislikes the man *because* he's the new boss, (17B) suggests that he should make the best of things, and (18B) suggests that he's got problems. It seems that any language will contain a similar range of words used to indicate how a given remark relates to preceding remarks: whether confirming them, modifying them, contrasting with them, contradicting them or even substituting for them entirely. Such words fit naturally into the framework for pragmatic interpretation that we have been outlining. Another overt indicator, this time phonological, would be the intonation pattern chosen; again, this has an obvious pragmatic function.

Pragmatic Effects of Semantic Ordering

In the last chapter we suggested a further way in which the linguistic form of an utterance might be geared to its pragmatic function. We argued that the semantic interpretation of an utterance should consist, not of an unordered set of entailments, but of an ordered set, with the semantic ordering reflecting aspects of syntactic, lexical and phonological form. If such a semantic ordering does exist, we can now begin to see why. As we have seen, any sentence carries a very large number of entailments. Not all of these will be equally relevant for pragmatic interpretation: some will already form part of shared knowledge, and will thus contribute no new information, while others will vary in the amount of new information they bring. It seems natural that a speaker should have some means of indicating which of the entailments carried by his utterance are the most relevant, and hence the most worthy of his hearer's attention. One way of looking at the semantic ordering of entailments is as a device for indicating the degrees of relevance of these various entailments, with the highest ordered entailments being the most relevant. This would in turn explain, in the light of our remarks on relevance, why sentences which shared their entailments but ordered them differently could nonetheless be interpreted in radically different ways. We now turn to a more detailed investigation of the effects of semantic ordering on the pragmatic interpretation process.

It will be recalled that the semantic component of a grammar divides the entailments of a sentence into two classes: the grammatically specified ones, produced by substitution rules applied to surface syntactic constituents, and the grammatically unspecified ones. Among the grammatically specified entailments will be a series of focal scales, each associated with a particular heavily stressed item in surface structure. Any syntactic constituent containing the heavily stressed item may be chosen as the focus of the sentence. Choice of a focus will in turn select a background entailment, obtained by substitution of an indefinite phrase for the focus of the sentence; it will also promote the focal scale which contains the background entailment, to the highest position in the semantic ordering. The grammatically unspecified entailments of the sentence will themselves fall into three classes, depending on their logical relations to the background entailment: whether they entail it, are entailed by it, or neither. We now want to show that all these semantic distinctions have a role to play in pragmatic interpretation.

In terms of the semantic ordering, the highest ordered entailments of an utterance will be those above the background in its focal scale. If the ordering is in turn interpreted as imposing degrees of relevance on the entailments of an utterance, it will follow that the entailments above the background should be the most relevant. These entailments are the ones which should combine with the preceding remark to yield the further information which constitutes the main point of the remark. We can in fact make a stronger claim: *only* these entailments have to be relevant: the background entailment, and all entailments below it in the ordering, must be irrelevant – must *not* be used to establish the main point of the remark.

Consider (19), for example, with background (20):

(19) *Jem* stole your book.
(20) <u>Someone stole your book.</u>

Someone who utters (19) generally takes (20) for granted. His main point would be not that *someone* stole your book, but rather that that someone is Jem. The natural context for uttering (19) would be where speaker and hearer both know that the book has been stolen, but only the speaker knows who the thief is. If we assume that the background entailment may *not* contribute to the point of an utterance – may not count as one of its relevant entailments – we can explain this appropriateness to context very naturally. As we have seen, a relevant entailment must be an informative one. If (20) is uninformative, then, it can never be relevant; moreover, if it already formed part of the shared knowledge of speaker and hearer, it would automatically be uninformative. Thus the fact that (19) is often treated as presupposing, rather than asserting (20), receives a natural explanation if we *require* the background of an utterance to be uninformative. By the same token, we can explain why it would be inappropriate to utter (19) in a context where the hearer was not already aware that his book had been stolen. In those circumstances, (20) would be extremely relevant: probably more relevant than any of the other entailments of (19). It would therefore be most inappropriate to choose the form of utterance in (19), which as we have seen requires the *ir*relevance of (20).

If what we have said about the irrelevance of the background entailment is true, it follows that the relevant entailments of the utterance must lie above the background in the semantic ordering, and that the main point of the utterance must lie in the information which has to be added to the background to obtain the entailments of the utterance as a whole. Thus the point of (19), with background (20), will be to identify the person who stole the book as Jem. It follows, too, that a necessary condition for correctly interpreting an utterance, and grasping its point, is the identification of its background. Since alternations in stress and syntactic form will in turn alter the background, the speaker has considerable freedom, by manipulating the form of his utterance, to indicate to hearers exactly how he wishes it to be taken.

It should follow, of course, that misidentification of the intended background should lead to misinterpretation of the intended point, and there do seem to be cases where this is true. For example, consider the following question, said with normal sentence stress on the last word, to a doctor who has just suggested that his patient go on a diet:

(21) Could I not eat *breakfast*?

As we have seen, there are a number of different possible focuses for (21), depending on which syntactic constituent is construed as the domain of the heaviest stress. In particular, with normal sentence stress, its focus could be the NP *breakfast* or either of the

VPs *eat breakfast* and *not eat breakfast*. The interpretations which result will be, respectively, as follows:

(22) There's something I'd like to eat – breakfast. Could I eat it?

(23) There's something I'd like to do – eat breakfast. Could I do it?

(24) There's something I'd prefer not to do – eat breakfast. Could I skip it?

There is a fairly radical difference between the first two interpretations and the last – a difference which may have significant consequences if the doctor gives a fairly neutral reply, such as *I don't see why not*, so that any misinterpretation which has arisen is not detected. Clearly, on most occasions either intonation or background knowledge will play a part in determining which interpretation is most appropriate. Equally clearly, in the absence of such special factors, even the full resources of semantic ordering are not enough to guarantee perfect communication.

Another point at which the semantic ordering of entailments may help with pragmatic interpretation is in the case of denials. Consider, for example, an utterance of (25a), with background (25b):

(25) a. *Arsenal* will beat Everton.
    b. Someone will beat Everton.

Now imagine that a hearer responds to (25a) by saying *That's not true*. The natural interpretation of this denial would be as in (26):

(26) Someone will beat Everton, and it won't be Arsenal.

In other words, a natural denial of (25a) would preserve the assumption that (25b) was true. What we have said about the pragmatic role of background entailments will provide automatically for this interpretation. Someone who denies (25a) will naturally be taken as denying its *relevant* entailments. Thus, under normal conditions, a denial of (25a) would be interpreted as conveying (26). On the other hand, someone who is prepared to dispute the truth of (25b) will have to deny not only the truth of (25a), but also its relevance. Thus (27) is not only a denial of (25a), but questions the speaker's right to have said it at all:

(27) No one will win the Cup.

The role played by background propositions in pragmatic interpretation is thus a crucial one, and the distinction between background entailments and those above them in the focal scale seems to be empirically justified.

The grammatically unspecified entailments of an utterance also seem to play different roles in pragmatic interpretation, depending on which of the following categories they fall into:

(a) Grammatically unspecified entailments which themselves entail the background.

(b) Grammatically unspecified entailments which are themselves entailed by the background.

(c) Grammatically unspecified entailments which neither entail, nor are entailed by, the background. Consider (28), for example:

(28) A: Marcus is allergic to fish.
     B: He's just eaten *a plate of háddock*.

The most relevant entailment in (28B) is clearly (29):

(29) <u>Marcus has just eaten a plate of fish.</u>

This entailment will combine with (28A) to yield the new information that Marcus is likely to suffer an allergic reaction. (29) is not a grammatically specified entailment of (28B): it is a grammatically unspecified entailment which falls into category (a) above, since it entails the background of (28B):

(30) <u>He's just eaten something.</u>

It seems, then, that entailments falling into this category *may* contribute to the main point of the utterance. That they do not *have* to is shown by the exchange in (31), where entailment (29) would play no part at all in establishing the relevance of (31B):

(31) A: What sort of fish does Marcus eat?
   B: He's just eaten *a plate of háddock*.

Clearly, the information in (29) would not be relevant to the interpretation of (31B), which is intended to identify the type of fish that Marcus eats, rather than merely conveying that he eats fish. Thus, unlike the grammatically specified entailments above the background on the focal scale, which *must* contribute to the point of an utterance, grammatically unspecified entailments belonging to category (a) may, but do not have to, contribute to that point.

Grammatically unspecified entailments belonging to category (b) play a complementary role to those in category (a): they may, but do not have to, contribute to the background of an utterance. Consider (32), for example:

(32) Harry bought Bill's *car*.

As we have seen, there is more than one possible focus-background pair for (32), as illustrated in (33)–(36):

(33) a. Harry bought Bill's *car*.
   b. Harry bought something of Bill's.
(34) a. Harry bought *Bill's car*.
   b. Harry bought something.
(35) a. Harry *bought Bill's car*.
   b. Harry did something.
(36) a. *Harry bought Bill's car*.
   b. Something happened.

There are contexts in which one of the grammatically unspecified entailments of (32) will contribute to determining which focus-background pair should be used in its interpretation. Suppose that speaker and hearer both know that Harry is a friend of Bill's, and that Bill has been selling his property off cheaply to his friends. In that case, (37) might well form part of the shared knowledge of speaker and hearer:

(37) Bill sold Harry something.

(37) is a grammatically unspecified entailment of (32), contributed by the semantic relationship between *buy* and *sell*. Because it already forms part of shared knowledge, some interpretation of (32) must be found which does not imply that (37) is relevant. The only such interpretation is (33), on which (37) is entailed by the background (33b), and must thus, like the background itself, be irrelevant. On all alternative interpretations, (37) will be above the background in the ordering, and will have to be treated as a potentially relevant entailment of (32). Thus the hearer is guided towards the correct interpretation of (32) by his pragmatic knowledge of its grammatically unspecified entailments falling into category (b) above.

Another way in which such entailments play a different pragmatic role from those in category (a) is in the interpretation of denials. We have seen that denial of an entailment in category (a) may amount to denial of the truth of the entailing utterance, but not its relevance. Denial of an entailment in category (b), by contrast, will involve a rejection of the background of the utterance, and will thus amount to denial of the relevance of the utterance itself. Consider the following exchange:

(38) A: Your little boy's *really grówn*.
　　 B: He's not my little boy.

A might be naturally interpreted as an intended compliment to B; but it will only succeed as such if B really is the mother of the little boy. (38B) denies this. It thus denies a grammatically unspecified entailment of (38A), and one which is entailed by the background (39):

(39) Your little boy's done something.

(38B) thus denies not just the truth of (38A), but also its relevance. It thus amounts to a much stronger rejection of (38A) than (40), which does not deny the background entailment of (38A):

(40) He hasn't grown much.

The third category of grammatically unspecified entailments –

those that neither entail nor are entailed by the background – play a different pragmatic role again. It seems that such entailments should normally play no part in the interpretation of the utterance. If pragmatic considerations force the hearer to call on them in his interpretation, he will regard the utterance as infelicitous or inappropriate in some degree; denial of an entailment in this category would also amount to a very strong rejection of the entailing utterance. Consider (41), for example:

(41) A: *My ex-húsband*'s waiting outside.
     B: I didn't know you were divorced.

(41B) may be a mild rebuke. Because of its form, (41A) presents the grammatically unspecified entailment (42) as irrelevant, part of shared knowledge:

(42) <u>The speaker of (41A) is divorced.</u>

(41B) indicates that it was *not* part of shared knowledge, and *was* considered by the hearer to be relevant. Entailments such as (42) fall into category (c) above: it thus seems that their truth should play no role in the normal interpretation of utterances, and if they do turn out to be relevant, their entailing utterance will be perceived as infelicitous. Denying an entailment of this category will amount to a very strong rejection of the entailing utterance, as in (43):

(43) A: I saw a *ghost* last night.
     B: No one's ever seen a ghost.

Notice, though, that (43B) may leave the background of (43A) intact:

(44) <u>I saw something last night.</u>

It would thus not amount to a denial of the *relevance* of (43A), but it would deny both its truth and its appropriateness.

What we have tried to do in this chapter is outline some of the main linguistic and non-linguistic factors which interact to provide a full interpretation of a given utterance in context. The main linguistic factor involved is the semantic ordering of entailments, itself determined by the syntactic, lexical and phonological form of the utterance. The main non-linguistic factors are the body of knowledge shared by speaker and hearer, and judgements of relevance. Judgements of relevance are in turn affected by the semantic ordering of entailments, and by the body of shared knowledge. All these factors interact in ways we have tried to illustrate, so that the actual message conveyed by an utterance in context goes well beyond its purely linguistic meaning.

It is often claimed, by both linguists and others, that there can be no strict separation between linguistic and non-linguistic knowledge: that any attempt to draw a dividing line between them must inevitably falsify the rich and subtle process of communication. On the contrary, we have tried to show that only on the assumption that there *is* such a dividing line can the variety and subtlety of the communication process be done full justice. For example, the semantic ordering of entailments can be justified on purely linguistic grounds: it is needed to distinguish sentences which share their entailments but do not share their meaning. Once this ordering is established, we can go on to investigate its pragmatic function, its effect on judgements of relevance, and thus its role in pragmatic interpretation. The fact that it has a purely linguistic justification means that it must fall on the linguistic side of the dividing line between linguistic and non-linguistic knowledge; the fact that it also plays a role in pragmatic interpretation gives us a valuable insight into the interpretation process itself, and into the interaction between linguistic and non-linguistic knowledge. Thus everything we have said in this chapter supports the claim we have been making throughout the book: that grammars are self-contained systems which can be studied in their own right, and that an investigation of their properties may shed real light on the organization of human knowledge and the use to which it is put.

9. Language Variation

In Chapter 1, we argued that it is highly likely that no two speakers of a language possess identical grammars, and that furthermore the grammar of an individual might vary through time. However, we also argued that there are limits on the ways in which grammars can differ from each other, and that these limits are in many cases innately determined. In this chapter we look more closely at language variation, considering three main aspects: variation in the individual, in the community, and across languages.

Variation in the Individual

Often, a speaker who wants to convey a given meaning can choose among a number of different ways of doing so. Often, too, there is no way of predicting which alternative he will choose: either is equally well-formed. So, for example, the same situation may be described equally well by (1a) or (1b), and there is no linguistic reason for preferring one form to the other:

(1) a. The juror wrote down the details in his pocketbook.
   b. The juror wrote the details down in his pocketbook.

(1a) and (1b) demonstrate the existence of *free variation* in language, where free variants are generally defined as expressions which are semantically and stylistically equivalent but syntactically, lexically or phonologically distinct.

As a further example of syntactic free variation, compare (2a) and (2b):

(2) a. Your son seems happy at school.
   b. Your son seems to be happy at school.

The inclusion or omission of the words *to be* seem to make no difference to the meanings of (2a) and (2b), which appear to be synonymous and freely intersubstitutable. As an example of free variation on the phonological level, consider the alternative ways of stressing *princess* in (3a) and (3b):

(3) a. A príncess is a pearl.
   b. A princéss is a pearl.

In (3a) heavy stress falls on the first syllable of *princess*; in (3b) it falls on the second. It would be quite hard to predict which stress pattern would be chosen by a given speaker on any given occasion: moreover, the choice actually made would have no effect on the meaning of (3). A similar alternation is possible for many speakers in the pronunciation of the adjective *fifteenth*: compare (4a) and (4b):

(4) a. The fifteénth attempt was successful.
   b. The fífteenth attempt was successful.

As an example of lexical free variation, one might take any case of synonymy. For instance, *old man's beard* and *traveller's joy* are alternative ways of referring to the wild clematis, and many speakers have both expressions in their vocabulary. Moreover, although surprisingly few words are full synonyms, there are many sentences where substitution of one word for another will have no effect on meaning. Thus, although *begin* and *start* are not exact synonyms, either could be selected without change of meaning in (5):

(5) a. Daylight saving time starts at midnight tonight.
   b. Daylight saving time begins at midnight tonight.

The examples of free variation in (1)–(5) merely show that the grammar of a given individual may provide more than one phonological realization of a given meaning: in other words, they merely provide further evidence for the existence of synonymy and paraphrase relations in natural language. Slightly more interesting examples, from our point of view, are cases of *stylistic variation*. We might define stylistic variants as expressions which share all their entailments but differ in acceptability or appropriateness to context. We have already seen a number of such cases: for example, (6a) will generally be preferred to (6b), not because of any difference in grammaticality or meaning between the two, but because of a stylistic principle ultimately based on performance strategies:

(6) a. The juror wrote down in his notebook the details of this tedious case of blasphemy, which heartily bored him, and which had already gone on for several weeks.
   b. The juror wrote the details of this tedious case of blasphemy, which heartily bored him, and which had already gone on for several weeks, down in his notebook.

The stylistic principle concerned rejects utterances in which a verb (e.g. *wrote*) is too widely separated from its associated particle or prepositional phrase (e.g. *down, in his notebook*). This stylistic principle itself might arise out of a desire to make sentence-comprehension easier for the hearer; we have already argued that such principles should be accounted for on the level of performance, rather than competence.

As a slightly different case of stylistic variation, it might be claimed that in certain contexts (7a) would be more appropriate than (7b), while in other contexts the reverse would be true:

(7) a. The children came into the room.
   b. Into the room came the children.

As a response to the fairly prosaic questions *Who came into the room?* or *What happened next?*, (7a) would appear to be rather more appropriate. (7b) would normally be preferred to (7a) only when the speaker wants to elicit some dramatic reaction from the hearer to the news that the children came into the room. Again, this difference in appropriateness to context does not have to be treated in the grammar: few people would seriously claim that there were contexts in which one member of the pair would actually be ungrammatical while the other would not. However, there is a general point which might be worth making on the contrast between (7a) and (7b).

The structure of (7b), with a prepositional phrase in sentence-initial position and the subject coming after the verb, is a mildly unusual one for English. In many cases, it is unusual structures, like that of (7b), which are used for dramatic or figurative effect. On the assumption that (7b) is derived from (7a) by an optional transformation, we could go on to make the following claim: one of the reasons for having optional transformations in the grammar may precisely be to provide syntactic structures which can be used to dramatic effect in communication. If this is true, it demonstrates once again the close interaction between linguistic and non-linguistic principles. The notion of 'dramatic news' is clearly not a linguistic one: it involves the notion of relevance, as well as the non-linguistic knowledge and beliefs of speaker and hearer. The notion of 'optional transformation' clearly is a linguistic one. What we are suggesting is that one of the reasons for having optional transformations in the grammar may be a non-linguistic one, based on the use to which they may be put in the process of communication. This should in no way blur the distinction between linguistic and non-linguistic knowledge, which we have maintained throughout this book; nor does it in any way diminish the possibility of studying the relationship between the two.

In certain cases, the choice between stylistic variants may be determined by the degree of formality of the occasion, the age, social status or occupation of speaker and hearer, or other aspects of the context. Such variation is *conditioned* rather than free, and is often given the special name of *register variation*. We have already argued that an utterance which violates contextually imposed, performance requirements should be classed as unacceptable rather than ungrammatical. We would place utterances which violate constraints on register variation in this class. For example, the fact that in one religious context it is appropriate to refer to the *Pentateuch* and in another to the *Torah*, that on one occasion one refers to the *Carmelite Fathers* and on another to the *White Friars*, that *old man's beard* is more likely to be heard on informal occasions and *clematis vitalba* on formal ones, is of no import as far as the set of sentences containing these nouns is concerned. All the grammar has to do is provide lexical entries for each of these terms, stating their syntactic, semantic and phonological properties. It is a matter of encyclopedic, non-linguistic information to record which of them is appropriate to which occasion – just as it is a matter of encyclopedic, non-linguistic information to record which forms of behaviour are appropriate to which occasion. Knowing the conditions under which it would be appropriate to greet the Prime Minister with *Wotcher mate* seems to us no more a linguistic matter than knowing the conditions under which it would be appropriate to wink at him. Both should be treated within the study of human behaviour, rather than within the study of linguistic knowledge. We would also maintain that register variation is irrelevant to linguistic theory even when what appears to be a single word changes its meaning from one register to another. Thus in normal, non-medical speech, a woman who loses her baby prematurely has a *miscarriage* if the event is accidental, but an *abortion* if the event is medically contrived. In medical language, however, the former occurrence is described as *abortion*, and the latter as *termination* of the pregnancy. That is, the word *abortion* has two separable, though largely overlapping senses, which are used by different groups of speakers, and may also be register variants for a single individual. Within the framework we are proposing, the grammar of such an individual should treat the word *abortion* as ambiguous, but it will be his encyclopedic knowledge which tells him which sense is appropriate to which occasion.

Choice of vocabulary, then, is often a good indication of the register being used, and a potential signal of the degree of formality of the occasion as well as the area of specialization. Thus the use of compound forms including *there* and *where*, such as *thereof*, *whereat*, *thereby*, *wherein*, is typical of very formal styles, and the use of slang and colloquialisms of informal style. An extreme example of register difference is provided by those communities in which different situations demand the use of different dialects, or even different languages. An educated Indian, for instance, typically discusses his work in English but his family affairs in Hindi or some other native language of India.

Such cases raise the whole question of how variation in the linguistic community affects the individual and his grammar. So far in this book we have assumed that each individual has at his disposal at any one time only a single grammar. In this section, in discussing free variation, stylistic variation and register variation, we have tacitly maintained this assumption. However, in the case of an individual who has mastered two dialects, or of a bilingual with command of more than one language, it looks as if the claim that the linguistic knowledge of an individual forms a single, homogeneous grammar must at least to some extent be abandoned. In the next section we examine the effects of variation in the linguistic community on the grammars of individual speakers.

Variation in the Community

1977 in Great Britain was the Queen's Silver Jubilee year. The last Silver Jubilee was in 1935, and between these two dates younger speakers of English had acquired a phonological rule of stress-shift which applied to *jubilee*. In 1935, the standard pronunciation was *júbilee*, with stress on the first syllable. (This is still the only pronunciation recorded in the O.E.D.) However, in the earliest B.B.C. broadcasts of 1977, the jubilee was largely referred to as the *jubilée*, with stress on the last syllable. Over the next few months, possibly as the result of protests from older listeners, it was noticeable that the B.B.C., followed by many speakers of English, reverted to the older pronunciation. What had gone on in individual grammars during these few months?

Clearly, not everyone had the same initial pronunciation of *jubilee*, and not everyone had the same final pronunciation.

Presumably, many older speakers started and ended with the form *júbilee*, while many younger speakers started with the form *jubilée* and ended with the form *júbilee*. Others might have started with a single form and ended with two free variants; still others might have ended up with register-variants, the one used with older people or on more formal occasions, the other used with younger people, or on more informal occasions. The problem here is not with providing a number of frameworks within which each individual *could* be fitted – rather it is providing a method for deciding which framework fits which individual. How do we tell which speakers have free variants in their grammars; how do we decide which speakers have no entry for *júbilee*, or which have none for *jubilée*? The claim that grammars are psychologically real, and that there is a strict separation between linguistic and non-linguistic knowledge, means that there should at least in principle be some way of answering these questions.

To approach the same problem from a slightly different point of view, consider dialect variation. A *dialect* is usually defined as a geographically or socially based variant of a language, having particular linguistic idiosyncrasies. For example, (8) is fairly recognizable as a sentence of British English, while its paraphrase in (9) is fairly recognizably American:

(8) The girl dived off the pavement into the river.
(9) The girl dove off of the sidewalk into the river.

(9) differs from (8) phonologically, for example in the pronunciation of the *r* in *girl*; morphologically, in the form *dove* for *dived*; lexically, in the use of *sidewalk* for *pavement*, and syntactically, in the occurrence of *off of* for *off*. On the basis of such differences, we might feel justified in dividing English into two broad dialects: one that includes the rules which generate (8), and another that includes the rules which generate (9). Notice that in the framework we are adopting, because of the endless possibilities of variation in individual grammars, it is no more accurate to talk of 'the Yorkshire dialect' or 'the Cornish dialect' than it is to talk of 'the English language'. There will be individual idiosyn-

crasies among Yorkshire speakers, just as there are among speakers of English. Strictly speaking, then, both *dialect* and *language* are relative terms, based on grouping together speakers with broadly similar grammars.

Given this, it still makes sense to ask what goes on when a speaker of British English understands the American sentence (9); or when a speaker of American English understands the British sentence (8). Does the possibility of understanding sentences from another dialect indicate that the hearer who can do this knows the grammar of that dialect too? At first sight it might seem that the answer is obviously *yes*. If it is grammars that enable us to produce and understand sentences, then surely a speaker who can understand a sentence must know the relevant grammar? In fact, this argument would lead very speedily to absurd conclusions. For example, most speakers are capable of understanding utterances which are completely ungrammatical for them: whether the utterances of children or of foreigners, whether accidental or intended. If every time a speaker understood an utterance, however ungrammatical it was for him, we were forced to assume that he nonetheless possessed an appropriate grammar, then there would be no limit on the psychologically real grammars that speakers would have to know. We might just as well drop the claim that there were psychologically real grammars at all as claim that every success (or indeed failure) in understanding was a direct exercise of linguistic competence.

In fact, we have repeatedly emphasized that there is an important difference between knowing a language and speaking or understanding it; and in particular between the strategies used in sentence-comprehension and the rules embodied in a grammar. It seems to us that it is comprehension strategies rather than rules of grammar that are generally involved in understanding the sentences of unfamiliar dialects, just as it is comprehension strategies that are involved in understanding the ungrammatical utterances of foreigners and children. Comprehension strategies may make particular reference to contextual and pragmatic cues: *what would be a plausible message here?*, *what would it be relevant for the speaker to tell me?* are both questions that might play a part in sentence-comprehension, though not in grammatical analysis. Comprehension strategies may also make reference to imputed syntactic and phonological structure: for example, what words does the utterance contain; what does its stress pattern indicate; what is its surface syntactic structure? In answering these questions, we suggest that hearers might well make use of analogies between unfamiliar utterances and sentences of the language they already know: in other words, the notion of *analogy*, which we have argued could never be an adequate substitute for a grammar, might well be an excellent supplement to it.

Given an unfamiliar word – say *dove* in (9) – a hearer might work out its meaning by comparing it to the familiar pair *strive – strove*. On this analogy, and presumably helped by considerations of contextual plausibility, he might well arrive at the correct conclusion that *dove* is a past tense form of *dive*. Similarly, given the ungrammatical (10a), he should be able to work out its meaning on the analogy of (10b) and (11):

(10) a. *The baby is probable to cry.
     b. The baby is likely to cry.
(11) a. It is probable that the baby will cry.
     b. It is likely that the baby will cry.

The ability to draw analogies is not a specifically linguistic one. If we are right in claiming that analogy plays a part in the comprehension of utterances from unfamiliar dialects, then many such acts of comprehension are not purely linguistic either. However, they do presuppose some linguistic knowledge – knowledge of the sentences and structures of the hearer's own grammar, on which the analogies are based. Moreover, such analogical arguments will in general only be needed where the hearer initially perceives the utterance in question as ungrammatical, or has difficulty working out what it means. We have already argued in Chapter 1 that the notion of analogy cannot form the sole basis for all human linguistic behaviour: for example, although the analogy between (10a) and (10b) might be a valid one for a hearer to draw in understanding the ungrammatical utterance of a foreigner, it is *not* a valid one for a native speaker to draw in his own sentence-production. (10a) is ungrammatical for most speakers of English, in spite of its similarity to (10b).

However, it would be a gross oversimplification to suggest that there are no cases in which a given speaker has mastery of alternative grammars, or that arguments from analogy are only used in understanding sentences from unfamiliar dialects. There *are* clear cases where a speaker knows more than one grammar; and there are also cases where arguments from analogy are used in sentence production as well as sentence comprehension.

In cases of true bilingualism, where a speaker is equally fluent in speaking and understanding two distinct languages, the only possible conclusion to draw is that he has two distinct grammars. Use of one grammar rather than the other on any given occasion would then fall under the heading of register variation, and would be a matter for explanation in a performance model. Since the distinction between bilingualism and bidialectalism is only a matter of degree, it should follow that there are certain cases where a speaker has two distinct grammars, this time associated with two distinct dialects rather than distinct languages. Again, the obvious criterion for deciding whether a given speaker fell into this category would be his ability to produce and understand, on the appropriate occasion, sentences from either dialect. Little is known about the psychological make-up of such speakers – in particular how they organize and store their distinct sets of rules: however, it seems clear in principle that mastery of two or more distinct grammars does actually occur.

A genuine problem arises when, as often happens, the speaker's ability to understand a certain range of utterances is considerably greater than his ability to produce them. Most British English speakers are much better able to understand utterances in American English than they are to produce them, or reproduce them, for themselves. In the next chapter we shall argue that in the same way the child's ability to understand the utterances of adults is considerably in advance of his ability to produce them for himself. Now competence grammars are designed to be neutral between speakers and hearers – in other words, to combine with certain principles of performance to account for both the ability to produce and the ability to understand. How, then, can the discrepancies between production and comprehension be explained?

We would like to suggest that there is not necessarily, or not always, a unitary explanation for such discrepancies. What they mainly indicate is that there are distinct *performance* principles for sentence-production and sentence-comprehension, and that the principles for comprehension are rather more efficient and wide-ranging than those for production. Thus, as we have repeatedly seen, ungrammatical utterances may be perfectly comprehensible to a speaker who would not himself produce them, or would correct himself if he did. We have suggested that the notion of *analogy* to the sentences of the speaker's own dialect is relevant here. In the case where a speaker of one dialect is in frequent contact with speakers of another, but would not himself produce sentences from this alien dialect, we might suggest that he constructs a *code* which relates utterances of the alien dialect to sentences of his own. Thus, speakers who frequently encounter the word *dove*, as in (9), might not incorporate it into their own vocabularies, but might rather construct a decoding principle which related it to their own form *dived*. We would not then need to say that someone who understood (9) but would never produce it had *competence* in American English: merely that he was capable of relating utterances in that dialect to utterances in his own. In both these types of case, the ability to understand unfamiliar sentences would be parasitic on the speaker's competence in his own dialect.

However, there are also clear cases where the fact that a speaker never produces a given sentence does *not* count as evidence that it is not in his dialect. For example, stylistic or other performance factors might influence his unwillingness to produce certain types of sentence. It would not necessarily follow that they were ungrammatical for him. Many speakers avoid using archaic, pedantic or obscene vocabulary for completely non-linguistic reasons; it is possible that there are optional semantic, syntactic or phonological rules that certain speakers never use, also for non-linguistic reasons. Thus we could not erect the speaker's unwillingness to produce a certain sentence into a criterion for deciding whether it was in his dialect or not: as we have seen, even his actual *inability* to produce such a sentence might be due to performance factors rather than matters of competence.

As a final complicating factor, consider the relation between analogy and rules of grammar in sentence production. We have argued that analogy plays a considerable role in the comprehension of utterances that are both unfamiliar to the hearer and ill-formed according to the rules of his own grammar. Thus we have suggested that analogy forms one of many comprehension strategies, but one that is generally invoked for utterances that are strictly speaking ungrammatical for the hearer: certain metaphorical utterances might be a case in point. We have also suggested that many unfamiliar words – e.g. *dove* – may be understood by analogy to more familiar words. If this is so, it is surely also possible that new or unfamiliar words or constructions are actually *produced* by analogy to words or constructions that already exist. This is certainly true in the case of children, but it also seems to be true in the case of creative use of language by adults.

Turning to the domain of word-formation, we have argued that the lexicon should contain not only a list of actual words that the speaker has encountered and stored, but also a set of rules for forming new words (or defining the notion *possible word*). Thus, for most English speakers, *un-English, un-American* and *unhappy* will be stored ready made, whereas such words as *un-Hawaiian, un-Mesopotamian* or *unstiff* would not be listed as such, but covered by the word-formation rules. Similarly, most English speakers today will have ready-stored such words as *sit-in, love-in* and *teach-in*, but *fry-in, hate-in* or *learn-in*, if they form part of the vocabulary at all, would be covered by the productive rules of word-formation, rather than listed as they stand. In such cases, variation among speakers consists in the number of items which can occur in such constructions, and the instability of informants' judgements of well-formedness concerning them on different occasions. It is sometimes argued that if there are examples such as *hate-in*, of whose acceptability people are unsure, then the set of well-formed sentences of the language is itself undecidable. And if what constitutes a sentence of the language is itself vague, then language cannot be a rule-governed system in Chomsky's sense.

This is not the problem that we ourselves feel is raised by such cases. The problem lies in distinguishing the words which are constructed by the application of genuine rules of word-formation, and those that are constructed merely by analogy. We feel that there is a real distinction here, and that words formed by rule are 'in the language', whereas words formed by analogy are not – although of course they may become so. It seems fairly clear that the original *sit-in* was a new coinage, and that forms such as *love-in* and *teach-in* were formed by analogy – just as *beatnik* and *no-goodnik* were formed by analogy to the newly acquired *sputnik*. However, once enough words formed on a similar pattern are in existence, we would argue that speakers may construct actual rules of word-formation which are then applicable in a much wider range of cases. Just where a rule replaces an analogy is a matter for detailed psychological and linguistic investigation, and is likely to vary from speaker to speaker. However, it does not, as far as we can see, destroy the distinction between analogical creations and rule-governed creations. Analogical creations do not become part of linguistic competence until they are explicitly incorporated into a grammar: some such creations succeed, and others do not.

What we have been arguing in this section is that there is a genuine role for arguments from analogy in linguistic performance: both in sentence production and sentence comprehension. However, it does not follow that the notion of analogy has any direct role to play in competence grammar. In fact, we have argued that analogies are best seen as complements to rules of grammar, so that a given construction is formed *either* by rule of grammar, *or* by analogy, but not by both simultaneously. It is clear that analogy has a role to play in language change, and in sentence production and comprehension. It is also clear that the perception of analogies may blur speakers' judgements about purely linguistic well-formedness. However, as far as we can see, this merely lends support to the claim that rules of competence and principles of performance are closely interconnected. It reinforces, rather than undermines, the claim that they are distinct.

Language variation of the kind we have been describing is of interest not only because it raises questions about the relation between competence and performance, but also because it gives some insight into the range of facts that any linguistic theory must be able to describe. On the assumption that our theory must be able to account for the structures found in all languages, it follows that it must be able to handle all facts found in the varying dialects of speakers of any one language. Often it turns out that syntactic or phonological facts normally thought of as exotic in fact turn up in certain dialects of English or French: we gave an example from relative-clause formation in Hebrew, English and French in Chapter 1. For this reason, studying variation in the dialects of English or French is often a good introduction to studying the full range of variation among the languages of the world. In the next section, we survey briefly some of the ways in which languages themselves may vary.

Language Typology

In 1963, Joseph Greenberg published his 'Some Universals of Grammar with Particular Reference to the Order of Meaningful Elements'. This work was based on a sample of relatively transparent surface syntactic and morphological characteristics of thirty languages from various language families in different parts of the world. Greenberg's intentions were modest: to provide data for a future theory of linguistic universals by classifying languages of different syntactic and morphological types. His results were rather puzzling for someone familiar with Chomsky's linguistic framework: even the thirty languages sampled gave little support to the idea of absolute, unconstrained linguistic universals, which would be obeyed with no exceptions.

Many of Greenberg's universals provide statistical correlations between the basic word-order of a language and other features of its grammar. The three most common types of word-order for languages are *subject–verb–object*, as in English, *subject–object–verb*, as in Japanese, and *verb–subject–object*, as in Classical Arabic. To these must be added the *object–verb–subject* order found in Hixkaryana, the *object – subject – verb* order of Apurinã and the *verb – object – subject* order of Malagasy. Examples of sentence-types from such languages are given in (12):[1]

> (12) a. Borg served an ace. [English: SVO]
>   b. Borg an ace served. [Japanese: SOV]
>   c. Served Borg an ace. [Classical Arabic: VSO]
>   d. An ace served Borg. [Hixkaryana: OVS]
>   e. An ace Borg served. [Apurinã: OSV]
>   f. Served an ace Borg. [Malagasy: VOS]

Each of these basic word-orders seems to determine a preference for further types of rule or construction. Greenberg simply lists these preferences, in statements like the following:

> (13) With overwhelmingly greater than chance frequency, languages with normal subject–object–verb order are postpositional.
> (14) In languages with dominant order verb–subject–object, an inflected auxiliary always precedes the main verb. In languages with dominant order subject–object–verb, an inflected auxiliary always follows the main verb.
> (15) Question particles or affixes, when specified in position by

---

1. We should emphasize that it is normal or natural word-order, rather than occasional instances of unusual word-order, that we are using as the criterion for classification here.

reference to a particular word in the sentence, almost always follow that word. Such particles do not occur in languages with dominant order verb–subject–object.

(13) claims that languages like Japanese, which place the verb at the end of the sentence, generally use postpositions rather than prepositions: *by bus* would translate in the order *bus by*. (14) claims that languages in which the verb comes first in the sentence will always place an auxiliary which agrees with the subject in number or gender, or which carries a tense-marker or other inflection, before the main verb. In such languages, *John has left* would translate in the order *Has left John*. (15) claims that where a language inserts a word into a sentence to mark it as interrogative, and where the position of that word is fixed by reference to another word in the sentence, it will generally be inserted after that word, rather than before it. Certain French dialects, for example, mark an interrogative by inserting the particle *ti* into a sentence: this particle always bears a fixed position to the verb and in fact, as Greenberg's universal claims, always follows the verb:

(16) a. Tu veux-ti partir?   (Do you want to leave?)
     b. Il peut-ti marcher?   (Can he walk?)

Within the framework we have outlined, such statements are puzzling for at least two reasons. First, nothing in Chomskyan theory leads us to expect that choice of one feature by a language should influence its other choices. Second, such phrases as 'with overwhelmingly greater than chance frequency' make it clear that there is nothing absolute about these universals. They are in general probability statements, saying what one may expect from a language of a given type, but leaving room for the possibility that these expectations will not always be borne out.

Greenberg's investigations provide detailed evidence about the nature of language variation, which cannot be ignored by anyone who wants to make universal claims about the nature of language itself. There seems to be strong evidence for the claim that certain bundles of linguistic properties go together, so that a language with one property from a given bundle will be likely to possess the rest. An adequate linguistic theory should be able to provide an explanation for this fact. The claim that all languages are basically similar does not absolve linguistic theorists from trying to explain the obvious differences among them.

Nor are the correlations among linguistic properties always dependent on the basic word-order of a language, as many of Greenberg's were. As a final case of language-variation, consider the following. Many languages have a rule of question-formation which moves a constituent containing a *wh*-word unboundedly far to the left. As we have seen, English is one of them: application of question-formation in English sentences yields the following results:

(17) Which pickles did the rajah ask the servant to get his wife to put on the curry?

(18) Who do you think Eliot believed he had seen in the rose-garden?

In a few languages, such as Navajo and Circassian, the equivalent rule of question-formation moves a *wh*-word unboundedly far to the right, so that it could finish up at the very end of the sentence. This difference in the rules for question-formation in two types of language correlates with a difference in the rules for interpreting pronouns as co-referring with other noun-phrases in a sentence. In languages like English, with unbounded leftward movement rules for question-formation, the noun-phrase *John* and the pronoun *he* may be interpreted as referring to the same person in sentences like (19), but not in those like (20):

(19) John admitted he was a dope-fiend.

(20) He admitted John was a dope-fiend.

By contrast, in those languages like Navajo which have unbounded rightward movement rules for question formation, the noun-phrase *John* and the pronoun *he* could be interpreted as referring to the same person in sentences equivalent to (20). In other words, there seems to be a correlation between the direction of movement rules and the possibilities of interpretation of pronouns. No theory of language which is unable to explain such correlations will be entirely adequate.

In this chapter, we have argued that language variation may be explained in a number of different ways. In the simplest case, the language of a single individual permits him alternative ways of saying the same thing: performance factors may dictate the most appropriate way, but the claim that there are competence grammars is not assailed. In other cases, there may be variation among the grammars of individuals belonging to the same linguistic community. Such variation in the data to which each individual is exposed may lead him to make false judgements of well-formedness, and to construct comprehension strategies for the sentences which are not dealt with by his grammar. Furthermore, they may lead him to construct sentences by analogy to others he has heard, rather than by direct use of the rules of his own grammar. Again, the distinction between linguistic and non-linguistic knowledge can be maintained. Finally, there are linguistic differences among the languages of the world, and certain properties of language seem to co-vary rather than being independent of each other. In this case, the explanation must lie not in the grammar constructed by the individual speaker, but in the putatively innate linguistic knowledge possessed by all speakers at birth, which determines the form of language in general. We shall return to this topic in our last chapter. In the meantime, it seems that differences among speakers may sometimes conceal similarities among their grammars; but that there are certain similarities among speakers, and similarities among grammars, which have still to be explained.

10. Language Change

In the last chapter we looked at language variation as a function of social and regional differences. In this chapter we look at how languages change through time, and the implications of such change for a theory of linguistic competence.

Grammars are never static, if only because speakers go on adding new lexical items to their vocabulary for as long as they live. Such changes in grammar are trivial: the finite list of n lexical items which constituted one's vocabulary on August the first is simply extended to a list of $n + 1$ items when one learns the meaning, pronunciation and syntactic properties of, say, *chalaza* on August the second. During childhood the learning of new items may have far-reaching effects. For example, there are many pairs of syntactically and semantically related words in English which show a regular alternation between particular vowels: /i:/ and /e/ in (1a), and /ei/ and /a/ in (1b):

(1) a. obscene – obscenity   b. profane – profanity
      replete   – replenish   vapour   – vapid
      steer   – sterile   rabies   – rabid
      extreme – extremity   declaim – declamatory
      keep   – kept   fail   – fallible

The vast majority of such items do not belong to the everyday vocabulary, and it may not be until the early teens that both members of a given pair are learned. When the child knows only one member of such a pair, he clearly has no basis for associating it with the other member, or even for classifying the vowel as one that occurs in phonological alternation. When the child has learned both members of enough such pairs, however, his grammar is changed not only by the addition of one new item, but by the addition of a new relationship between that item and another item as well. That is, the learning of one form leads to the restructuring of other parts of the total grammar, even if only in extremely minor ways. In the terms of the last chapter, an analogical relationship develops to the point at which it becomes rule-governed.

Change in the lexicon can be largely accounted for by simple addition of items and relationships, or, less frequently, by the desuetude and loss of particular words: by hypothesis no examples of loss should spring to mind, but words like *skylon*, *frug* or teenage slang of the 30s might be candidates. The issue is not so clear-cut, however, with syntactic or morphological change. Take for instance the case of the person who, after moving to America, modifies his speech from British to American English. That is, from producing and understanding sentences such as (2a), he changes to producing and accepting sentences such as (2b):

(2) a. The girl dived off the pavement into the river.
　　b. The girl dove off of the sidewalk into the river.

We cannot talk of him simply expanding his grammar in such cases, because the rules which characterize (2a) are incompatible with those that characterize (2b). We can, however, regard the speaker concerned as gradually acquiring a new dialect, with many rules in common with the old dialect, and this new grammar gradually ousting the old one through time. That is, before moving to America he would have had grammar G1, at some time after moving to America he would have had both G1 and a new G2, and some time later he might have lost, or partially lost, G1. In fact, because of the almost unlimited powers of recognition of the human memory, G1 is unlikely ever to be completely forgotten. However, the children of this hypothetical speaker will learn exclusively G2. The net result is that over a period of time the language used in that speaker's family will have undergone a change: speakers of two successive generations will have knowledge of somewhat different sets of rules.

The process of rule addition and consequent restructuring of the language described by the grammar can be generalized to account for the much more radical changes which a young child's developing language undergoes as he first learns his mother tongue. In this case, however, there is the crucial difference that children *do* forget earlier stages of their developing grammars in ways which adults cannot. That is, while an adult who changes from dialect A to dialect B will retain at least some knowledge of A, a young child who changes his word-order over time from *what that was?* to *what was that?* will retain no knowledge at all of the earlier set of rules. Many children may in fact be fully bilingual in their early years, but if they do not use both their languages continuously they turn into monolingual adults.

In the rest of this chapter we shall look at language change first in the individual as he learns his language, second in the patient who suffers language loss, and finally at language change in a wider and more traditional sense, as when Latin is said to have changed historically into the Romance languages.

Language Acquisition in Children

We look first at an example from the acquisition of phonology which illustrates how children handle natural classes, thus lending support to the claim that natural classes have psychological reality for the child. The early speech of children is characterized by regular, i.e. rule-governed, deviations from the norms of the adult language they are learning. One of the more striking cases of such deviation is provided by *consonant harmony*. A word in the adult language may contain two consonants with differing points of articulation: for example, *duck* contains an alveolar /d/ and a velar /k/. In certain cases, in the child's language, these two consonants assimilate or 'harmonize' to the same point of articulation: thus a typical rendering of *duck* by a two-year-old child would be [gʌk], with the initial *d* replaced by a velar *g* in harmony with the final velar *k*. In the speech of one two-year-old we observed there were dozens of such examples:

(3) dark   pronounced as [gaːk]   stuck pronounced as [gʌk]
    drink   „   [gik]   cheek   „   [giːk]
    leg   „   [gek]   taxi   „   [gegiː]
    ring   „   [giŋ]   jug   „   [gʌk]
    singing   „   [giŋiŋ]   thick   „   [gik]
    snake   „   [ŋeik]   neck   „   [ŋek] etc.

Crucially, however, not all words ending in a velar (/k, g, ŋ/) exhibit harmony. Beside the examples in (3), there are many cases where no harmony was ever shown:

(4) walk   pronounced as [wɔːk]   pink   pronounced as [bik]
    back   „   [bek]   hook   „   [uk]
    big   „   [bik]   mark   „   [maːk]
    pig   „   [bik]   Mike   „   [maik], etc.

If we look carefully at the initial consonants in these sets of words, the basis for the difference in their treatment by the child becomes apparent. Those in (3) all begin with a consonant whose articulation involves the front of the tongue: /t, d, s, θ, tʃ, dʒ, r, l, n/, whereas none of those in (4) does: /p, b, m, w, h/. In terms of distinctive features, these sets of consonants are defined as the classes [+coronal] and [−coronal] respectively, and given that the child is obviously grouping his consonants into two mutually exclusive sets, harmonizing and non-harmonizing, the simplest assumption is that he is doing it by reference to the linguist's feature [coronal], or something equivalent to that feature. This hypothesis has the advantage of making further predictions. No example of words ending in a velar with /z/ as the initial consonant had appeared in the child's vocabulary, but as /z/ is the voiced equivalent of /s/, and hence [+coronal], any such word should belong to the harmonizing set. Accordingly the child was taught the word *zinc*, and he pronounced it, as predicted, as [gik] (the absence of the *n* was also predictable, cf. *drink* in (3)). Further, although the definition of [coronal] within phonology is clear with respect to all the examples above, there is disagreement about whether *y* ([j]) should be [+coronal] or [−coronal]: in articulatory terms it seems to come half-way between the two classes we have been illustrating. For the child, there was no doubt: his treatment of words with initial /j/ and a final velar showed unambiguously that they belonged, for him, to the [+coronal] class. For instance *young* was pronounced as [gʌŋ], *yucca* as [gʌgə], and so on. The naturalness of this class to the child (and hence its psychological reality) is further shown by his treatment of words beginning with /(s)n/ and ending in a velar. The child invariably omitted pre-consonantal /s/, and his pronunciation regularly involved an initial [ŋ], as in the last two examples in (3): that is, it included a configuration which is impossible in the adult language but is predicted by the hypothesis just given. The lack of models for direct imitation is no bar to the child once he has unconsciously hypothesized what the state of affairs is.

Although the young child regularly deforms words of the adult language, it can be shown that he correctly perceives the forms in the adult sound system, even if he does not produce them on the appropriate occasion. First, children can easily recognize contrasts they are unable to make: for instance, they correctly differentiate *sip* from *ship* in perception tests, even if they pronounce them identically as [sip]. Second, the child's failure to pronounce a particular sequence correctly in one situation is not proof that he is unable to pronounce it correctly in another: *puddle* may be regularly 'mispronounced' as [pʌgəl], while *puzzle* is regularly mispronounced as [pʌdəl]. Thus, despite his bizarre pronunciation, the main difference between the child's phonological system, and those of other children, lies in the particular form in which he applies the general process of consonant harmony. While the child described above harmonized *duck* to [gʌk], and treated all *coronal* initial words similarly, another child may harmonize *duck* to [dʌt], changing the velar to an alveolar rather than vice versa, and treat all *anterior* initial words similarly.

In the case of the acquisition of syntax, however, it is clear that the child does not have the same degree of mastery of the adult system as he does with phonology. Here too, though, there seem to be certain clearly definable limits within which individual variation is possible. We shall illustrate with reference to negation.

Apart from the simple use of *no* as a sign of wilful disobedience. we have seen that the child's first use of negation consists in pre-fixing or adding *no* or *not* to a one-or-two-word utterance. In the examples given here, the child always puts the negative at the front:

(5) a. No sit there.
   b. Not will break.
   c. No fall.

Other children put the negative at the end: *Sit there no*, etc. What never happens in this first stage is that the child embeds *no* or *not* into the middle of the sentence: **sit no there*, **will not break*, etc. That this behaviour is rule-governed seems obvious from its consistent regularity. It becomes even more obvious when we see that children will deform rhymes that they have apparently learnt by rote in order to conform to the structures of their own gram-mars. Consider, for example, the following version of Humpty-Dumpty provided by the same two-and-a-half-year-old discussed above:

(6) . . . an' all the king horses an' all the king men
   not put Humpty-Dumpty together again.

Here *couldn't* has been reduced to *not*, despite the fact that in the adult version *not* (*n't*) is unstressed and hence physically non-salient, because in the child's productive grammar all negatives are initial.

At the second stage of learning, one finds both utterances of the earlier form, with a negative at the beginning or the end of the sentence, and also some utterances in which the negative is in-corporated into the sentence:

(7) a. Why it not squeaks?
   b. There no birdie.

    c. Me can't see.
    d. He don't know.

As children often show no use of *can* or *do* without the *n't* at this stage, it is probable that for the child *can't* and *don't* are simply negative units, rather than complexes of a modal verb plus a negative. With normal children the transition from stage one to stage two lasts about four months, with some individual variation on either side of this figure. This contrasts markedly with the case of Genie, discussed in Chapter 2, where the 'negative initial' stage lasted more than one and a half years.

By stage three – anything from one month to one year later – the negative is regularly incorporated into the sentence rather than left at the periphery, but there are still problems with the incorporation of negatives into noun-phrases. This results in the frequent appearance of double-negatives, as in (8):

(8) I didn't see no one.

There is also generally a failure to use *any* for *some*, as in the use of (9) to express the meaning of (10):

    (9) I didn't see something.
    (10) I didn't see anything.

Once *any* has been learnt, it is often overgeneralized to contexts before the negative constituent, where it is not permitted in the adult language: for example, (11) is used with the meaning of (12):

    (11) Anybody can't go in there.
    (12) Nobody can go in there.

Reports on children learning Italian, German and Japanese indicate that they go through similar stages in these languages as well, though with obvious differences when it comes to such idiosyncratic phenomena as the use of *any* and double negatives. The implications of such uniformity both across children and across languages, and its bearing on innateness and universals of language, will be discussed in Chapter 12.

Language Loss

Insight into the nature of linguistic knowledge can be found not only in language learning, but also in an area where the language faculty undergoes even more rapid change: *aphasia*, or language loss, caused by strokes, tumours or accidental damage to the brain. At its most severe, aphasia is linguistically uninteresting, as it results in silence. However, there are less extreme cases in which speech is retained, but with marked deviations from the normal. These cases should allow us, in principle, both to isolate individual linguistic rules or groups of rules, and to correlate them with specific forms of neurological damage, showing which parts of the brain control which parts of language. We are unfortunately rather far from being able to do this yet, but one of the most provocative and stimulating hypotheses in this area, first put forward by Roman Jakobson, is that loss of language in aphasia mirrors language acquisition in childhood. It is true that no case has ever been reported in which a patient reverted step by step through the stages seen in language acquisition. However, it does seem to be true that brain damage of differing severity gives rise to conditions reminiscent of the states we have just looked at in language acquisition.

For example, compare the following three brain-damaged patients. The first used negative utterances where the negative was always in initial or final position, just as for stage one children:

(13) a. No New York.
     b. Money no.

The remaining two used negative utterances both of this type and of the type where *can't* and *don't* were correctly positioned in the middle of the sentence:

(14) Mommy don't have them.

As these two patients did not use *can* or *do* without the negative, the parallelism with the stage two children is striking. Moreover, the patient whose speech corresponded to that of stage one children was considerably more seriously impaired in general than the others, again indicating regression to an earlier stage. Although it is tempting to see such cases as supporting Jakobson's hypothesis, the breakdown of language found in aphasia is usually so unpredictable and so irregular that it is rarely possible to make the kind of explanatory statement we can make for language acquisition. We can define aphasia as the breakdown of the rule system governing normal use of language; however, this breakdown does not proceed in a simple sequence of subtracting rules, but seems rather to involve reference to the general organizing principles of grammar. To the extent that language loss is predictable at all, it seems to indicate that our view of language is over-compartmentalized. What we need to look at is not so much the individual rules of grammar as the organizing principles used to group these rules into a grammar. Just as the transition from pre-Chomskyan to Chomskyan linguistics was marked by a shift from emphasis on data to emphasis on the rules that organize those data, so it seems that further progress in the study of language will have to involve a shift from emphasis on rules to emphasis on the principles used in learning and storing such rules.

Historical Change

We have argued that language change is best described in terms of alterations in grammars: either the grammar of a single individual or in those of groups of individuals – say from one generation to the next. If we are right, what is traditionally called historical linguistic change may provide valuable insight into the nature of individual grammars and the organizing principles which underlie them. We shall take as an example the vowel system of Classical Latin and, by showing how it developed in the various Romance languages, draw some conclusions about the psychological reality of linguistic knowledge.

Classical Latin had the following vowel system (ignoring diphthongs):

(15) i e a o u   ī ē ā ō ū

The dash over a letter indicates a long vowel as opposed to a short one: thus the difference between *malum* 'evil' and *mālum* 'apple' was that the *a* was longer in the latter. In English there is also a distinction between long and short vowels, but it is a phonologically conditioned one: so, for example, the *a* in *bad* is much longer than the *a* in *bat*, but this difference depends on whether the following consonant is voiced or voiceless. In Latin there was no such phonological conditioning, and the difference between *a* and *ā* was phonemic, so that appearance of a long rather than a short vowel could alter the meaning of a word.

Within the framework outlined in Chapter 6, this vowel system would be uncontroversially represented by the following distinctive feature matrix:

(16)	ī	i	ē	e	ā	a	ō	o	ū	u
high	+	+	−	−	−	−	−	−	+	+
back	−	−	−	−	+	+	+	+	+	+
low	−	−	−	−	+	+	−	−	−	−
long	+	−	+	−	+	−	+	−	+	−

The analysis of phonemes in terms of distinctive features allows us to refer to a large number of different natural classes of phonemes. For example, (16) claims that /i/ and /u/ form a natural class of [+high] vowels, in a way that /i/ and /a/ do not. The class of [+long] vowels contains /ī, ē, ā, ō, ū/; the class of [+high] vowels contains /ī, i, ū, u/; the class of [−low] vowels contains /ī, i, ē, e, ō, o, ū, u/; the class of $\begin{bmatrix} -\text{high} \\ -\text{back} \end{bmatrix}$ vowels contains /ē, e/; and so on. The trouble is that too many such 'natural' classes are definable, and we need some way of deciding which of them are psychologically real, and permit significant generalizations to be drawn. Historical change goes some way to helping us with this decision.

The most obvious characteristic of the Latin vowel system as we have described it is the existence of paired long and short vowels. That this is indeed the right way to describe the contrasts involved is shown by the development of the system in Sardinian, where the contrast between long and short vowels disappears, and the result is a simple five-vowel system /i, e, a, o, u/, which corresponds to the Latin system in the obvious way diagrammed in (17):

(17) Latin: ī i ē e ā a ō o ū u
                       ∨   ∨   ∨   ∨   ∨
    Sardinian: i   e   a   o   u

The long vowels /ā/ and /a/ fell together before the rest, but otherwise all of these pairs coalesced roughly simultaneously. That is, the grammars of speakers of the form of Latin used in Sardinia were changed by the addition of a simple rule which made all vowels short. We can explain the fact that all these changes happened simultaneously by claiming that only a single rule was involved; but this in turn entails that the set of vowels affected was correctly described in terms of the feature [+long], and that this feature was therefore psychologically real. In fact, if we want to take account of the slightly earlier disappearance of the contrast between short and long /a/, we need to assume that there was first added to the grammar a rule of the following form:

(18) $\begin{bmatrix} V \\ +low \end{bmatrix} \rightarrow [-long]$

This rule would convert all low vowels to short ones; it was then simplified or generalized by the omission of the feature [+low], so that its revised version was as follows:

(19) [V] $\rightarrow$ [−long]

This rule would convert *all* vowels to short ones. It is important to notice that by eliminating the feature [+low] between (18) and (19), we have increased the number of cases in which the rule applies: in other words, the class of vowels is more natural than the class of low vowels.

The simple development in Sardinian was not the commonest change undergone by the Latin vowel system. The most widespread change is the one characteristic of Vulgar Latin, which has persisted in essence into modern Portuguese. The relationship between the Classical Latin and Vulgar Latin systems might be shown as follows:

(20) Classical Latin: ī i ē e ā a o ō u ū
                 | \/ | \/ | \/ |
    Vulgar Latin: i e ɛ a ɔ o u

Here, there is not just a loss of the contrast between short and long vowels, although the Vulgar Latin system does end up with no long vowels. In addition, it gained a contrast between half-open (/ɛ, ɔ/) and open (/a/) vowels. There are two points to notice about this change. First, it is symmetrical: that is, whatever changes affected the front vowels /ī, i, ē, e/ also affected the back vowels /ū, u, ō, o/ in exactly the same way. We thus have further justification for the claim implicit in distinctive feature analysis that these vowels are the same except for the difference between front and back (and characteristics such as rounding which are predictable from this). Again, the simplest hypothesis is that this parallelism reflects an underlying psychological identity, and the kind of analysis embodied in (16) is vindicated.

Second, it is not at all clear how this symmetrical change can be represented in the system of generative phonology, in spite of the fact that there is a very simple way of describing it verbally. What happened was that short vowels were lowered, and that after this the loss of vowel length described in (19) took place. That is, the short vowels /i, u, e, o/ became /e, o, ɛ, ɔ/, and then /e, o/ fell together with the long vowels of the same quality /ē, ō/. Unfortunately, there is no way in standard generative phonology of representing this lowering in a uniform way, because the natural class of short vowels includes both [+high] and [−high] members, and all undergo lowering equally. Hence we cannot collapse the two putative rules (21) and (22), because they have too little in common:

(21) $\begin{bmatrix} V \\ +\text{high} \\ -\text{long} \end{bmatrix} \rightarrow [-\text{high}]$

(22) $\begin{bmatrix} V \\ -\text{high} \\ -\text{long} \end{bmatrix} \rightarrow [+\text{low}]$

If our arguments about the psychological reality of the other processes discussed were at all valid, then it is clear that we have here historical evidence that linguistic theory should include a simple means of describing vowel-lowering. There is a simple, though radical, way to do this: namely replacing the two binary features [high] and [low] by a single 'n-ary' feature representing height. That is, vowel height would now be described in terms of a single scalar feature [1, 2, 3, 4 high], where n is used to subsume all the relevant integers. The kind of lowering process we have just seen would then be one that changed 1 to 2: /i/ and /u/ to /e/ and /o/; 2 to 3: /e/ and /o/ to /ɛ/ and /ɔ/; and (if it had existed) 3 to 4: /*ɛ/ and /*ɔ/ to /a/. More simply, this would be expressed as follows in the new notation:

(23) [n high] → [n + 1 high]

So far, we have seen evidence for the correctness of an analysis which uses the feature [long] (or some equivalent which defines the same natural class), the feature [back], and an n-ary height feature, to account respectively for the symmetry of the lowering process as between back and front vowels, and the generality of the lowering process as between high and non-high vowels. There is some further evidence that illustrates both the symmetry of historical processes and the individual points on the n-ary height scale. The seven-vowel Vulgar Latin system has been modified in

Spanish and Italian by the diphthongization of the two half-open vowels, both front and back. That is, the Italian system is (in some environments):

(24) Vulgar Latin: i e ɛ a ɔ o u
               | | | | | | |
     Italian: i e ié a uó o u

and the Spanish system is similar:

(25) Vulgar Latin: i e ɛ a ɔ o u
               | | | | | | |
     Spanish: i e ié a ué o u

It is striking that despite the rather radical nature of these changes they have taken place in parallel, underlining the existence of a class of 'half-open' vowels: a class that is very hard to define in standard generative phonology, but is simply 'n = 3' with an n-ary height feature. This same kind of symmetric change took place in Sicilian as well, where the Classical Latin system became the following:

(26) Classical Latin: ī i ē e ā a o ō u ū
                  \|/ | \/ | \|/
     Sicilian: i e a o u

In this case the long mid vowels /ē/ and /ō/ (front and back together) were raised to the quality of /i/ and /u/ so that, on the disappearance of the length contrast, we again have a five-vowel system. Although this looks superficially like the Sardinian system, notice that the five vowels have been arrived at quite differently, with consequent differences in the correspondence among the vowels of Latin, Sardinian and Sicilian in different lexical items with a common root.

Changes of the sort described above provide evidence for the psychological reality of distinctive features, because use of distinctive feature notation enables us to define the natural classes which were the domain of unified historical changes. However, it is probably also true that some changes applied to unique items rather than to natural classes. For instance, in Romanian the vowel system is as follows:

(27) Classical Latin: ī i ē e ā a ō o ū u

Romanian: i   e   ɛ   a   o   u

ie

That is, there have been changes similar to those of Vulgar Latin, Portuguese, Spanish and Italian, but in this case the lowering of the short vowels has been restricted to front vowels: /i/ and /e/ are lowered, but /u/ and /o/ are not. The lowering rule involved still refers to a class of items: the class $\begin{bmatrix} -\text{back} \\ -\text{low} \end{bmatrix}$; hence it still justifies the use of features. However, the later diphthongization of /ɛ/ to /ie/ applies uniquely to this vowel, and thus seems at first sight to be a counterexample to the claim that phonological processes apply to natural classes. In fact, the process of diphthongization here *does* refer to a natural class, but because of the asymmetry of the vowel system – an asymmetry which arose because of the application of another rule – this class contains only one member. Accordingly, although we claimed in Chapter 6 that it was necessary to use phonemes as well as distinctive features, the changes just mentioned do *not* count as further evidence for the phoneme. Given the kind of constraint we tried to place on the use of phonemes, namely that rules referring to phonemes are of a particular functional type such as metathesis, we would not expect phonemes to be necessary in describing the change that took place in (27). What would constitute a counter-example to the claim that phonological changes range over natural classes defined by distinctive features, and simultaneously what would be support for the claim that they range over groups not definable in distinctive feature terms, would be a change applying to (or in the environment of) a pair or more of phonemes which could not be reduced to a natural class: for instance, a case of diphthongization applying not to /ɛ/ and /ɔ/, a natural

class, but to /i/ and /a/, an impossible class. Such instances are
vanishingly rare.

A second example of historical change which illustrates clearly
the psychological reality of rule change is the development of
certain agreement phenomena in French. French nouns are of
either masculine or feminine gender, and an adjective or past
participle modifying a noun has to agree with it in gender. Thus
couteau 'knife' is masculine, and 'small knife' would translate as
petit couteau [pǝti kuto], with the word for *small* pronounced
[pǝti]. *Fourchette* 'fork' is feminine, and 'small fork' would be
translated as *petite fourchette* [pǝtit furʃɛt], with the word for
'small' pronounced [pǝtit], with a final *t*. Similar cases where the
adjective or participle changes its forms can be multiplied at will:
consider the following masculine/feminine pairs with their respective pronunciations:

(28)	masculine		gloss	feminine	
étroit	[etrwa]	narrow	étroite	[etrwat]
gros	[gro]	coarse	grosse	[grɔs]
droit	[drwa]	right	droite	[drwat]
assis	[asi]	seated	assise	[asiz]
tout	[tu]	all	toute	[tut]
bon	[bɔ̃]	good	bonne	[bɔn]
court	[kur]	short	courte	[kurt]
grand	[grã]	tall	grande	[grãd]
fort	[fɔr]	strong	forte	[fɔrt]
gentil	[ʒãti]	kind	gentille	[ʒãtij]
maudit	[modi]	cursed	maudite	[modit]

Historically, it is known that, as is reflected in the spelling, both
masculine and feminine forms were once pronounced with the
final consonant intact, as in the present-day feminine, but that as
the result of a general phonological change deleting final consonants except before a word beginning with a vowel, the consonant
in the masculine form was eventually lost.

On the assumption that the French words for *little, narrow*, etc.
are unitary lexical items in spite of their variant forms, it is clear

that the simplest description of modern French is one in which the basic form is equivalent to the feminine adjective and the masculine form is derived from it by a process of deletion described in (29):

(29) A consonant at the end of a word is deleted before a word beginning with a consonant.

Such an analysis needs to make no reference to the nature of the final consonant – almost any consonant may be deleted – whereas the alternative analysis deriving the feminine form from the masculine by *adding* a consonant would have to specify *ad hoc* for each lexical item what the correct consonant was: /t/ for *petit*, /d/ for *grand*, /j/ for *gentil*, and so on.

Despite the elegance of this standard analysis, and despite the fact that it reflects the historical development just described, we think there is good evidence that, at least for some speakers of French, the psychologically real grammar is one in which the inverse of the historical process takes place. That is, rather than having a rule such as (29) we actually have (30):

(30) In feminine adjectives (participles, etc.) a consonant is inserted at the end of the word.

Thus rather than storing the French for *small* as [pətit] and deleting /t/ to get the masculine form, we are claiming that the speaker of French stores it as [pəti] and adds a /t/ to get the feminine form.

What evidence is there that this superficially implausible analysis might in fact be psychologically correct, with the consequent implication that French has undergone a historical change of a rather striking type? First, note that any process which takes the feminine rather than the masculine as basic, as this one does, is linguistically extremely unusual. In French, for example, whenever it is unclear whether a masculine or a feminine form should be used, as for instance when both a masculine and a feminine noun are modified by the same adjective, it is the masculine form which invariably appears:

(31) Le couteau et la fourchette sont petits (*petites).

In those dialects of both French and other languages where gender distinctions are being lost, the forms preserved for pronouns, adjectives, demonstratives and so on, are in each case masculine and not feminine. To take a striking example, consider (32):

(32) Celui qui a un mari, il peut pas aller se promener.
The one who has a husband can't go out.
[Literally: *He* who has a husband, *he* can't go for a walk.]

Here the masculine *celui* and *il* are used in place of the feminine forms *celle* and *elle*.

This preferred status of the masculine is merely a reason to look for evidence that the masculine form of adjectives is more basic: it does not constitute evidence itself. The second point to notice is that the most frequent consonant to appear in feminine forms is /t/. That is, rather than being faced with the truly formidable task of memorizing which is the relevant consonant to be added for every feminine form in the language, the speaker can make the generalization that in the typical case he adds /t/, but in a listed set of exceptions he has to remember a different consonant as a special fact about the lexical item concerned. It should be noted in passing that most of the exceptional items are fairly common, and would provide no problems of memorization for a normal human being.

Initial evidence for the claim that /t/ is inserted to form the feminine comes from the appearance of words where the /t/ is unetymological: i.e. cases of adjectives (or nouns) where the masculine form historically had no final consonant, and accordingly where it could clearly not have been deleted, but where it might well have been inserted into the feminine form. Examples include the following:

(33) *masculine*   *gloss*   *feminine*
     favori   favourite   favorite
     coi   quiet   coite
     chouchou   pet   chouchoute

Such examples are even more frequent as provincial, cant or juvenile forms:

(34) *masculine*   *gloss*   *feminine* (non-standard)
     gentil   kind   gentite
     guéri   healed   guérite
     fini   finished   finite

The process of /t/ insertion in French is in fact much more general than the examples given up to now would suggest. Thus, agent nouns derived from other nouns typically have an ending -*ier* after a consonant, but contain an unetymological /t/ after a vowel:

(35) pompe – pump   pompier – pump-maker
     laine – wool   lainier – wool-comber
     gaz   – gas   gazier – gas-fitter

but:
     blé   – corn   blatier   – corn-chandler
     clou – nail   cloutier – nail-smith
     tissu – fabric   tissutier – weaver
     bijou – jewel   bijoutier – jeweller

A similar situation occurs when the *ier* suffix is used to form plant-names: a historically unjustified /t/ appears when this suffix is added to a word which ends with a vowel:

(36) cerise   – cherry   cerisier   – cherry tree
     pomme   – apple   pommier – apple tree
     framboise – raspberry   framboisier– raspberry cane

but:
     coco   – coconut   cocotier   – coconut palm
     sagou – sago   sagoutier – sago-palm (also:
                                   sagouier)
     bambou – bamboo   bamboutier – bamboo cane

There is also a productive process of verb formation which inserts /t/ in newly created verbs, under the same conditions:

(37) piano	– piano	pianoter	– tap on a piano
ergo	– therefore	ergoter	– cavil
sirop	– syrup	siroter	– tipple
mafia	– mafia	mafiater	– infiltrate

Finally, consider the well-known phenomenon of liaison, in which certain word-final consonants are pronounced before a following vowel, although they are deleted elsewhere:

(38) a. Mon petit ami [mɔ̃ pətit ami] – my little friend
   b. Mon ami est petit [mɔn ami e pəti] – my friend is little

In standard French there are a number of cases where an excrescent, historically unjustified /t/ appears, for instance the following:

(39) aime-t-il, a-t-il, etc.

In colloquial spoken French the phenomenon is even more widespread:

(40) a. Malbrough s'en va-t-en guerre [. . . sãva*t*ãgɛr]
   b. Il n'est pas a vous [inepa*t*avu] etc.

These examples of speech errors, which are so common as to have been institutionalized under the name of *cuirs*, are most easily accounted for on the assumption that there is a productive rule of /t/ insertion in the language, but a rule whose domain of application is still in a state of flux, leading to the rather irregular pattern of its appearance both in gender agreement and elsewhere.

If we have interpreted them correctly, these rather disparate kinds of evidence indicate that the rules defining a speaker's competence can be rather drastically restructured from generation to generation. At one stage in French there was a rule deleting /t/ and other consonants in one set of environments; at a later stage there was the precise inverse of this rule, inserting a /t/ (and sometimes another consonant) in the complementary set of environments. Although this change has probably been going on sporadically for some centuries, there must exist transitional groups where parent and child have learned different grammars on the basis of largely comparable facts. The reason for the change taking place at all is presumably the strenuous unconscious desire of the language-learning brain to capture a generalization, however marginal, to save itself the bother of memorizing lists. All change is probably due to simplification – the simplification here being one which led to the masculine form being basic, and where there is the most general possible sequence of alternating consonants and vowels, with no clusters of either. However, simplification in one area can lead to complication elsewhere, with the result that languages rarely gain or lose in overall complexity. From this it should follow that no language is significantly more complex than any other, and that the human language faculty is in some sense static. We return to the more general question of universals of language, the nature of the human language faculty and its innate equipment, in the last two chapters of the book.

In this chapter, we have tried to show how various types of linguistic change can give some insight into the nature of linguistic knowledge and its organization in grammar. We have argued that the child learning his language groups phonological units together into natural classes, and that the classes used by the child may shed light on the psychological reality of distinctive features. We have argued that loss of language through brain damage may also provide evidence about how linguistic knowledge is stored, and which parts of the brain are involved in such storage. Finally, we have argued that historical changes in language may provide evidence about the psychological reality of linguistic units and rules, and confirm or refute hypotheses made by linguists on the basis of non-historical studies. What makes such evidence relevant is, in each case, the assumption that human beings know grammars which describe their languages. From this assumption it follows that change in language is ultimately based on, and reflected in, changes in grammars. Without this assumption, the study of language learning would have no more in common with historical change than it would with the study of a given language at a given moment in time. Given this assumption, however, it is possible to use a much wider range of evidence than is available at first sight, in determining the form of human linguistic knowledge.

11. Evaluation of Grammars.

Our main concerns in this book have been with the form of grammars in general and with the contents of English grammar in particular. The reader is likely to have agreed with some of our arguments and disagreed with others. Someone who wants to dispute a particular linguistic argument has a number of different tools at his disposal: he may quarrel with the data, feeling that certain sentences claimed to be grammatical are not grammatical at all; he may refute a generalization by showing that it makes false predictions; he may argue that though a proposed generalization seems to work, it relates phenomena which really should not be related; or he may disagree with the basic framework in which the argument was conducted, from a conviction that the goals of linguistics should not be what they were claimed to be. The problem of evaluating linguistic arguments is thus a wide-ranging one, and one that can be formulated on many different levels. In this chapter we attempt to provide a framework within which arguments about the adequacy of grammars, and of the linguistic theories that underlie them, can be conducted.

Observational Adequacy

Chomsky has himself made a number of interesting points about the evaluation of grammars, and the different levels of adequacy that grammars can attain. He argues that the minimum level a grammar should aim for is that of *observational adequacy*, which is attained by any grammar that gives 'a correct account of the primary linguistic data'. There are two ways of interpreting 'primary linguistic data'. For a child learning its first language, they would be the finite set of utterances he has actually heard. These would include both grammatical and ungrammatical utterances, and giving a correct account of them would involve some means of distinguishing the grammatical from the ungrammatical, indicating how they are pronounced and what they mean. An alternative, and ultimately rather more interesting, view of the primary linguistic data is that they are the full set of well-formed sentences of a language – whether the child's or the adult's – and that giving a correct account of them will involve some means of indicating that they are grammatical, as well as how they are pronounced and what they mean. The reason why this alternative is rather more interesting is that if an observationally adequate grammar has to deal merely with finite sets of observed utterances, there is no reason why it should not achieve its aim merely by listing the finite set of grammatical sentences involved, together with a representation of their pronunciation and their meaning. It is possible that the child does start out in this way, but as we have seen, he quickly moves on to a level where he is formulating rules and making generalizations that go far beyond the observed data. At this stage there would be no interest at all in a level of adequacy which could still in principle be attained by mere listing of observed utterances. When observational adequacy is defined over larger sets of sentences than those observed, however, a grammar which attains this level will have to incorporate rules and generalizations, so that even this lowest level of adequacy will be a significant one to reach. Since our ultimate aim in constructing grammars is to give an account of human linguistic knowledge and its organization, and since we have seen that such knowledge seems to involve rules, we shall interpret observational adequacy as applying mainly to grammars which incorporate rules generating infinite sets of well-formed sentences and relating their pronunciation to their meaning.

An observationally adequate grammar for most speakers of English would record the following sorts of information:

(1a–c) are items of the vocabulary; (1d–e) are not:

(1) a. *brook, crook, look*
   b. *phótograph, photográphic, photógraphy*
   c. *grócer, grotésque, cópper, Copérnicus*
   d. **blook, *clook, *slook*
   e. **bnook, *lrook, *dlook*

(2a–c) are grammatical sentences: (2d–f) are not:

(2) a. Which men did you see Bill with?
   b. The girl I like is clever.
   c. Did that surprise you?
   d. *Which men did you see Bill and?
   e. *The girl likes me is clever.
   f. *Did that he left surprise you?

(3a–c) are meaningful sentences; (3d–f) are not:

(3) a. On the table, I found a letter.
   b. John stands up for himself and others.
   c. I understand why you left.
   d. *Between the table, I found a letter.
   e. *John behaves himself and others.
   f. *I understand whether you left.

The most elementary type of disagreement about whether a grammar is observationally adequate or not is disagreement about the data it attempts to describe. For example, someone might claim that he possesses one of the vocabulary items in (1d–e), or considers one of the sentences in (2d–f) grammatical, or understands one of the sentences in (3d–f). Once it is realized that there is an enormous amount of linguistic variation among speakers of English, many such disagreements will be seen as essentially trivial. To point out that a grammar designed to cover a given set of data fails to work for a different set is of no particular interest, as long as a grammar which *does* cover this new set can be constructed.

Supposing that there is agreement on the initial set of data to be described, one can show that a grammar fails to reach the level of observational adequacy for those data by showing that it fails to give a correct account of them in one way or another. For example, if the data in (1)–(3) above are correct, a grammar which fails to rule out (2d) as ungrammatical, or (3d) as meaningless, will be observationally inadequate. Similarly, a grammar which fails to generate (2a), or to assign (3a) a meaning, will also be observationally inadequate. At this point, a new type of disagreement can arise: for example, consider a grammar which correctly accounts for all the data in (1)–(3) in terms of a simple set of rules, but which also happens to mark (2f) as grammatical. For the linguist, it is very tempting at this stage to alter his judgement about (2f). If this otherwise adequate grammar predicts (2f) as well-formed, perhaps it *is* grammatical after all; perhaps there are non-linguistic factors which are affecting our grammaticality judgements, and perhaps we should revise these judgements in the light of the grammar. This is the well-known phenomenon of 'letting the grammar decide': if a grammar makes correct predictions in all the clear-cut cases, maybe we should accept these predictions in the unclear cases too. If informants still persist in regarding (2f) as ungrammatical, then their judgements should be ignored or dismissed, at least for the time being.

This sounds a dangerously authoritarian way of proceeding, and it could be disapproved of for a number of different reasons. First, someone might feel that allowing the grammar to treat certain marginal cases as clearly grammatical would debase the language in some way. But since grammars as we conceive of them are not prescriptive models of correct style or usage, nor models for teaching people how to talk well, there is no reason for suspecting that the decision of the grammar in certain marginal cases would have any effect at all on the set of utterances actually produced. Moreover, since a grammar is only a model of one particular person's linguistic knowledge, what is marked well-formed in his grammar will not necessarily be found to be well-formed in the next person's. Nothing necessary will follow from the facts of one person's grammar about how people in general should speak.

Second, someone might feel that marking certain sentences which are by hypothesis of doubtful grammatical status as *either* clearly grammatical *or* clearly ungrammatical would be falsifying the facts on which grammars are supposedly based. Chomskyan grammars aim to give a correct account of the *psychologically real* linguistic knowledge of speakers and hearers, as reflected in their intuitions about the sentences of their language. But if the person who *knows* the grammar is incapable of deciding whether a given sentence is grammatical or ungrammatical, how can we impute to him a grammar which makes a clear judgement about its grammatical status? One might go on from there to reject the whole Chomskyan approach to grammar for being inconsistent: for claiming to account for psychological data – intuitions – which do not exist, or which, if they do, are ignored by the linguist whenever it suits his purpose.

In deciding whether this sort of objection – either to the particular proposal for handling unclear cases or to the foundations of Chomskyan grammar itself – is justified, we might look at one or two cases of marginality which have actually arisen over the last few years, and at how they have been dealt with. For example, consider the following sentences. There is something wrong with (4b) and (5b), although the related (4a) and (5a) have nothing wrong with them:

(4) a. A man came in who was smiling.
   b. ?A man picked up an umbrella who was smiling.
(5) a. I saw a girl last Tuesday who was wearing a red hat.
   b. ?I gave a girl a bookmark who was wearing a red hat.

By standard syntactic arguments, (4a) and (5a) should be related to (4c) and (5c):

(4) c. A man who was smiling came in.
(5) c. I saw a girl who was wearing a red hat last Tuesday.

By the same arguments, (4b) and (5b), if grammatical, would relate to (4d) and (5d):

(4) d. A man who was smiling picked up an umbrella.

(5) d. I gave a girl who was wearing a red hat a bookmark.

The question that arises is whether (4b) and (5b) are actually ungrammatical. If they are, any rule which derives (4a) and (5a) from (4c) and (5c) would have to be prevented from deriving (4b) and (5b) from (4d) and (5d); and a grammar which allowed this latter derivation to go through would be observationally inadequate. There is, of course, an alternative possibility: perhaps (4b) and (5b) *are* grammatical after all, but some non-linguistic factors are affecting the judgements of speakers, causing them to make wrong pronouncements on these sentences. Neither of these alternatives is incoherent: given that grammars exist as psychologically real entities, there is nothing which says they cannot be overridden on occasion by purely non-linguistic factors. This is a subject we touched on briefly in Chapter 2: in the terms we used there, the question is whether (4b) and (5b) belong to the class of ungrammatical, unacceptable utterances, or to the class of grammatical, unacceptable sentences.

One way of seeing how best to answer this question is to look at how the alternative answers would actually be formulated. If (4b) and (5b) are really ungrammatical, then it must be possible to formulate some linguistic condition which would prevent these two sentences being derived from the grammatical (4d) and (5d) by the same rule – Extraposition from NP – which derives (4a) and (5a) from (4c) and (5c). A little consideration will show that formulating such a rule would not be easy. For example, by looking at the difference between (4a) and (4b), one might decide to forbid a relative clause to extrapose across a following NP. (4b) would then be ungrammatical because the relative clause *who was smiling* has extraposed across the NP *an umbrella*. However, this condition would be violated by the grammatical (5a), in which the relative clause *who was wearing a red hat* has extraposed across the NP *last Tuesday*. Notice too that (4e), which contains a reflexive pronoun *himself*, sounds much better than (4b):

(4) e. A man picked up my umbrella who was smiling secretively to himself.

Furthermore, changing the tense of (4b) from past to future makes it sound distinctly better:

(4) f. The way you will recognize our Agent will be as follows: you go into the airport, a man will be standing near a telephone booth who will offer to buy you a drink.

It is quite clear that any attempt to formulate a purely linguistic condition governing the application of Extraposition from NP will have to be very complex indeed. Moreover, it seems that the application of this rule has to be sensitive to a number of stylistic and contextual factors which by definition fall outside the scope of a grammar, but which affect the acceptability in context of the various sentences in (4) and (5) above. In other words, unless we are prepared to let these marginal and delicate cases alter our whole conception of grammar, we will be forced to treat all the sentences in (4) and (5) as equally grammatical, and invoke some non-linguistic explanation for their variations in acceptability. This is in no way to reject informants' judgements that there is something wrong with (4b) and (5b) in particular: it is merely to note that a judgement does not come ready-labelled with an indication of its source.

An account of (4) and (5) would not be complete unless we could indicate what non-linguistic factors *do* give rise to their variations in acceptability. The major factor is clearly a processing one. It seems that hearers automatically interpret sentences so as to minimize the amount of discontinuity they involve. Each of the sentences in (4) and (5) involves some discontinuity between the extraposed relative clause and the NP with which it formed a constituent in underlying structure. The discontinuity in (4a) is not great, and in any case, since *a man* is the only NP in the sentence with which the relative clause could possibly be associated, there is no alternative analysis which would reduce the discontinuity. In the case of (4b) and (5b), however, there is a possible syntactic analysis which eliminates the discontinuity altogether, by associating the extraposed relative clauses with the NPs *an umbrella* and *a bookmark* respectively. Of course, the resulting semantic interpretations would be bizarre: (4b) would imply that umbrellas can smile, and (5b) that bookmarks can wear red hats. People's judgements about (4b) and (5b) might thus be affected by the oddness in meaning of the syntactically preferred sentences. The processing principle involved seems to have some support from psycholinguistic work on the interpretation of utterances; it would ultimately be explained in turn by constraints on short-term memory capacity – a hearer who has to wait too long for the second half of a discontinuous item will have forgotten the first half by the time he reaches it. Much subtler principles would have to be invoked to explain how much discontinuity hearers *were* prepared to tolerate, and how the various syntactic and semantic considerations mentioned above affect their tolerance. However, it seems in principle possible to explain the acceptability judgements on (4b) and (5b) along these lines, without invoking a linguistic source for them at all.

In short, the grammaticality judgements of speaker-hearers must be explained in some terms by a linguist who is concerned with the psychological reality of linguistic knowledge. However, he is not committed to accepting every judgement at face-value; he may choose to ignore some of them in writing a grammar, and he is likely to make this choice for one of two reasons. Either there is a clear non-linguistic explanation for them, and he has no need to account for them in the grammar; or there is no clear non-linguistic explanation, but it is impossible to account for them within the type of grammar he believes to be correct. Enough such cases might, of course, force him to revise his conception of grammar. But a linguist who abandoned all hope of ever writing a grammar simply because of uncertainty about the grammatical status of (4b) would be a rather irrational individual.

Though a grammar which reached the level of observational adequacy would be of considerable interest for the linguistic data it would provide, it might be of rather less interest to those concerned with the connection between grammar and mind. It seems clear that there could in principle be many different observationally adequate grammars of a language, each generating all and only the set of well-formed sentences and providing them with phonological and semantic representations, but each operating with different rules and different theoretical constructs. If the ultimate aim in writing grammars is to reconstruct the linguistic knowledge of the native speaker-hearer, clearly not just *any* observationally adequate grammar will do.

Descriptive Adequacy

Chomsky argues that grammars should attempt to reach the higher level of *descriptive adequacy*, at which a correct account is given, not just of the primary linguistic data, but also of the native speaker-hearer's intrinsic competence: that is, his linguistic knowledge. A grammar attaining this level would provide a model of the speaker-hearer's own internalized grammar. In terms we used in Chapter 1, such a grammar would record the significant linguistic generalizations about a language, and thus give an insight not only into the language under investigation, but also into the minds of those who spoke it.

We saw in (1) above that an observationally adequate grammar of English would merely record the existing vocabulary items and reject all non-existent ones. A descriptively adequate grammar would have to distinguish among the non-existent ones, recording the fact that certain of these are merely missing by accident, and could be called into use if the vocabulary expanded, whereas others are necessarily absent, because they violate the underlying principles of the language. The items in (1d) and (6a) fall into the first class, and those in (1e) and (6b) into the second:

(6) a. **clook*, **lom*, **marp*, **ager*
    b. **bnook*, **hlom*, **msarp*, **aaaaager*

We saw in Chapter 3 that a grammar which can distinguish examples like (6a) and (6b) correctly would have to possess rules specifying the phonological content of possible, as well as actual, words. To go beyond the level of observational adequacy, the grammar of English would have to incorporate some such rules. Another case in which speakers of English seem to know more than the mere correct pronunciation of actual words is where there is a predictable relationship among the pronunciations of related words. For example, there is a predictable relationship among the items of (1b) above, but *not* among the pairs in (1c). To take another example, consider the stress patterns on the following pairs, of which the first member is a noun and the second a related adjective:

(7) a. télegraph   telegráphic
    b. télescope   telescópic
    c. aútomat   automátic
    d. aésthete   aesthétic
    e. átom   atómic

An observationally adequate grammar of English would merely have to state the correct stress-pattern for each of the words in (7). Moreover, since the vocabulary of any speaker is finite, this could be done by simple listing of the correct stress for each word in the lexicon. However, a grammar which merely used listing, although it would be observationally adequate, would be able to give no account of the fact that there is a clear relationship between the stress patterns in (7a–e). Stress in the adjective is regularly attracted towards the syllable immediately preceding the adjective-forming suffix -*ic*. Moreover, speakers treat this attraction as rule-governed: given a noun and told that it has an adjective formed in -*ic*, they would automatically assign the correct stress-pattern to this newly constructed adjective:

(8) a. phótoscope   photoscópic
    b. métronome   metronómic
    c. ágronome   agronómic

As is implied by the use of the terms *adjective* and *noun*, achieving descriptive adequacy here involves providing an explanation for facts at one level of analysis, phonology, by reference to constructs at a different level, syntax. We argued in Chapter 3 that syntax is descriptively prior to both phonology and semantics, in the sense that phonological and semantic rules need access to syntactic information, but not vice versa. Given this, it should quite often be possible to account for phenomena at the semantic and phonological levels by appealing to syntactic facts. The rule involved in (8) seems to be a case in point, and a fairly complex one. It distinguishes between the adjective-forming suffix *-ic*, to which it applies, and other occurrences of *-ic*, to which it does not. Thus the noun *aríthmetic* does not have stress on the pre-final syllable, but the adjective *arithmétic* does; the noun *bíshopric*, although it ends in *-ic*, does not stress its pre-final syllable; nor does the noun *héretic*. It seems clear that there is a significant linguistic generalization to be made here, and a grammar concerned with descriptive adequacy would be required to make it.

In the case of the syntactic component, we have seen that even a grammar which achieves observational adequacy will have to incorporate rules, since the syntax of an infinite set of sentences can only be described in rule-governed terms. The difference between observational and descriptive adequacy in this area would lie in a difference between the constraints imposed on setting up the rules involved. An observationally adequate grammar could use any arbitrary set of rules which produced the correct output; a descriptively adequate grammar would have to use rules which produced the same set of sentences, but also captured the significant relationships among them.

For example, there is a significant relationship among the constraints that have to be placed on certain syntactic rules of English to prevent them from generating ungrammatical sentences. The rule of Topicalization optionally moves an NP to the front of its sentence, relating (9a) and (9b):

(9) a. I want to invite that boy to my party.
   b. That boy, I want to invite to my party.

This rule must be prevented from moving an NP out of a co-ordinate *NP and NP* structure: otherwise it will relate (10a) to the ungrammatical (10b):

(10) a. I want to invite this girl and that boy to my party.
     b. *That boy, I want to invite this girl and to my party.

An observationally adequate grammar of English would merely have to constrain the rule of Topicalization so that it could not extract an NP from such a co-ordinate structure. In fact, exactly the same constraint would have to be placed on other rules: on the rule of Wh-Movement, for example, which relates (11a) to (11b):

(11) a. Mary met some tourist in the street.
     b. Which tourist did Mary meet in the street?

Without this constraint, *Wh*-movement would relate (12a) to the ungrammatical (12b):

(12) a. Mary met a policeman and some tourist in the street.
     b. *Which tourist did Mary meet a policeman and in the street?

In fact, this same constraint on extraction of an NP from within a co-ordinate structure would have to be placed on a wide range of movement rules in English if the grammar is to achieve observational adequacy.

There is surely something significant about the fact that the same constraint is appearing in the statement of a number of different rules. An observationally adequate grammar could ignore any significant generalization there was to be drawn, but a descriptively adequate grammar would be required to take account of it. This could be done by stating once and for all in the grammar of English that *no* rule may extract an NP from within a co-ordinate structure. This would go well beyond the mere listing of the same condition on any rule which happened to obey it. It would also make the claim that there is no *possible* rule of English which could perform such an extraction. Thus, if we made up a hypothetical rule of Right Topicalization, which moved NPs to the end of a sentence, relating (13a) and (13b), we would automatically predict that it would have to be constrained so as to make (14b) ungrammatical:

(13) a. Mary heard the nightingale.
b. Heard the nightingale, Mary.
(14) a. James and Mary heard the nightingale.
b. *James and heard the nightingale, Mary.

If such hypothetical claims are valid, as many linguists feel they are, the grammar of English will have to go beyond the level of observational adequacy, in order to account for them correctly.

In the course of this book, we have proposed a number of generalizations about English which we have taken to be significant. In some cases, the reader may have been able to formulate an alternative generalization which seems to fit the facts equally well, or better. This raises a problem: how do we choose between two grammars which both achieve observational adequacy? How do we know which of them, if either, is making significant generalizations and which only accidental ones? What are the criteria used to judge how descriptively adequate a grammar actually is?

It might be worth pointing out here that in a vast number of cases where alternative treatments of the same set of facts have actually been proposed, the choice between them can be made on grounds of observational adequacy alone. In Chapter 1 we gave an example of this type to do with the occurrence of reflexive pronouns in English. It turned out that our original generalization – that reflexive pronouns only occur in direct object position with a co-referent subject – simply collapsed when exposed to a further range of facts. In fact, at the end of Chapter 5, we argued that one reason for dealing with reflexivization by rules of semantic interpretation rather than by syntactic transformation was simply that no one had ever been able to formulate an observationally adequate syntactic transformation. If this sort of result happened often enough, it might well indicate that there was only one set of consistent generalizations which could be made about a given set of sentences: in this case, a grammar which embodied these generalizations would be the single descriptively adequate grammar for that set.

Another way of arguing for one possible analysis of a set of facts over another, this time assuming that they are both observationally adequate, is to introduce evidence from other languages. Suppose, for example, that someone is still hesitating about how best to describe the facts in (9)–(12) above. We can assume he was not convinced by the hypothetical argument put forward in (13) and (14), designed to show that one of the available alternatives was more descriptively adequate than the other; it is quite possible that someone might find this type of argument suspect. It will be recalled that the two available observationally adequate accounts were as follows:

(15) a. For each rule like *Wh*-Movement or Topicalization, which moves NPs to positions they did not occupy in underlying structure, there must be a particular constraint which forbids it to extract an NP from within a co-ordinate structure.

   b. The grammar of English simply contains a general constraint to the effect that *no* rule, whether possible or actual, may extract an NP from within a co-ordinate structure.

(15a) is essentially a list; (15b) is a generalization about both possible and actual rules of English. We are disallowing the construction of hypothetical rules and the attempt to judge whether they would or would not obey the constraint in (15b). It seems clear that no amount of further evidence from English will adjudicate between the two alternative treatments.

It turns out that the facts of English illustrated in (9)–(12) also occur in large numbers of other languages, both related and unrelated to English. Thus, parallel to (10) and (12) are the following sentences of French:

(16) a. J'aime beaucoup ton frère et ta sœur.

   b. *Ta sœur, j'aime beaucoup ton frère et.

(17) a. Marie a rencontré un gendarme et quelques étudiants dans la rue.
   b. *Quels étudiants Marie a-t-elle rencontrés un gendarme et dans la rue?

Clearly, (16b) and (17b) are outrageous. Nor is it only European languages which exhibit such behaviour: the following examples are taken from the African language Nupe:

(18) a.   egi-zì   gí   yïkã   tò   nãkã̀
         children eat fish   and meat
      [the children ate fish and meat]
   b. *nãkã̀   kíci   egi-zì   gí   yïkã   tò   o?
         meat which children eat fish   and
      [*which meat did the children eat fish and?]

In the face of such widespread occurrence of the same phenomenon, it is hard to remain convinced that simple listing of the same constraint on every extraction rule in every language is adequate to the facts. If there are any significant generalizations to be drawn at all, this is clearly one of them. If it could be shown that *every* language possessed such a constraint, we would obviously want to formulate a universal ban on extraction from a co-ordinate structure, which could be stated at the level of a universal theory of language, and which would then be automatically obeyed by extraction rules in every language, and would not have to be mentioned in the grammars of particular languages at all.

Thus, even where two analyses are equally adequate to the facts of the language they were designed to describe, one analysis might be preferred to the other on universal grounds. To make such a universal argument work, one would have to show that a general theory of language provides reasons for this preference. Given that such a thing as a general theory of language exists, it is clear that it should make some generalization about the possibility of extraction rules of the type we have just seen. In certain other cases, it is possible to show that of two alternatives that seem equally adequate for handling the same phenomenon in many languages, only one is observationally adequate for some further language. In these cases, again given the assumption that there *is* a general theory of language, it should follow that the analysis which is preferable for one language is preferable for all.

The justification of particular analyses and particular grammars has thus been shifted back a step, and turned into the question of how to justify a general theory of language, a universal linguistic theory, itself. We have argued that a particular grammar is to be judged adequate if it fits in with significant generalizations we can make about the grammars of *all* languages; but how do we judge these higher-level generalizations themselves? As we have seen, some of them may be justified by showing that only they permit an observationally adequate grammar of some particular language to be constructed. In other cases, though, we may find that two alternative universal generalizations may be made, and we have no way of choosing between them. It may turn out, however, that only one of these generalizations is consistent with other generalizations which are independently motivated by considerations of observational adequacy of the sort we have just mentioned. In that case, this generalization is clearly to be retained. Failing this, the only further resort would be to nonlinguistic considerations: perceptual, functional, neurological, psychological and so on. We shall have some further remarks to make on this subject in the next chapter.

Towards Explanatory Adequacy

In concluding this chapter, we would like to raise a separate, though related issue. Suppose that we have managed to produce a universal linguistic theory which incorporates all the significant generalizations about language that there are to be made. What happens if there is more than one grammar available for a given language, which is both observationally adequate *and* consistent with the general theory of language? By definition, all such grammars will be descriptively adequate, and Chomsky allows for the possibility that there could be more than one descriptively adequate grammar for a single language. In fact, he argues that in addition to a series of generalizations about the nature of language and grammar, a universal theory of language must also contain an *evaluation measure* which is precisely designed to select one out of the series of alternative descriptively adequate grammars for a particular language, and evaluate it as the best grammar for that language. A universal linguistic theory which contains such an evaluation measure he calls *explanatorily adequate*, because it would explain why the grammars that children construct are as they are.

Sceptics have often felt that the notion of explanatory adequacy, with its dependence on an evaluation measure, is one of the weakest parts of Chomsky's theory. There are a number of reasons why one might feel dissatisfied with it. For example, it would only be needed if more than one descriptively adequate grammar could be constructed for each language. But recalling the definition of a descriptively adequate grammar as one that gives a *correct* account of the native speaker's intrinsic competence, it is rather hard to see how there could be more than one such correct account. In that case, the evaluation measure and the level of explanatory adequacy seem to have no real function within the theory.

While Chomsky allows that it is logically possible that only one descriptively adequate grammar for a language might be available – that only one such grammar might be consistent with the descriptively adequate universal theory of language – he has always insisted on the importance of an evaluation measure, and he has always insisted that the attainment of explanatory adequacy was the highest goal which a linguistic theory could achieve. He has also suggested that the range of alternative descriptively adequate grammars are *notational variants* of each other: devices for saying the same thing in different ways, rather as (19a) and (19b) do:

(19) a. John kissed his sister.

b. John pressed his lips to those of his female sibling in token of affection.

And of course the difference in length between (19a) and (19b) suggests an obvious ground for choosing between notational variants: that of simplicity. In some intuitive sense, (19a) is a simpler way of expressing a particular claim than (19b) is. If we regarded the evaluation measure as some measure of the simplicity or complexity of grammars, we could make sense both of the idea that there was more than one descriptively adequate grammar, and of the idea that it is possible for both the child and the linguist to choose among them.

Chomsky has also repeatedly emphasized that there is no antecedently given notion of simplicity which linguists can merely adapt to their own purposes. How could one choose between two grammars, one of which contained more but shorter rules, the other of which contained fewer but longer rules; one of which had a small syntactic component and a large set of semantic and phonological rules, others organized in different ways; one of which had few rules but many conditions on rules, others of which had large numbers of rules but no conditions on rules, and so on? Quite apart from this, it is standard practice for linguists to work on fragments of grammar rather than whole grammars; and it would clearly be nonsensical to claim greater simplicity for one fragment of a grammar over an alternative without being able to see what repercussions these alternative fragments have on the remainder of rules still to be formulated.

It seems, then, that Chomsky is placing an enormous amount of emphasis on constructing an evaluation measure for grammars. This evaluation measure is to be added to a universal linguistic theory which already captures all the significant, empirically motivated generalizations to be made about the nature of language and grammar. It thus seems that it cannot be motivated by any facts of language; nor can it be justified on independent, non-linguistic grounds. It is for this sort of reason that the whole notion of explanatory adequacy, and the aim of achieving it, have been challenged on many occasions, by both linguists and others. In the next chapter we turn to a more detailed look at the contents of a universal theory of language, in an attempt to see whether these criticisms cannot be overcome.

12. What is Language?

In the past twenty years, two distinct strands have been visible in the search for linguistic universals. On the one hand, there has been the intensely theoretical interest of Chomsky, with his emphasis on providing explanatory frameworks for every level of linguistic generalization. On the other hand there has been the largely factual concern of Greenberg and his followers, who have provided a mass of statistical data about correlations between the rules to be expected in languages of different types. In this chapter, we want to show how Greenberg's data can be accommodated within Chomsky's framework, incidentally providing some genuine content to the notion of an evaluation measure, and thus giving linguistic theory a level of explanatory adequacy.

Universals and the Language Acquisition Device

One of Chomsky's main contributions to the study of linguistic universals has been to make the search for a universal theory of language respectable. Within Chomsky's framework, linguistic universals are expected to exist. As we have seen, this expectation is in turn based on arguments for an innate language acquisition device: a series of concepts and principles which the child brings to first-language learning, and which we have discussed briefly in Chapters 1, 2 and 6.

The language acquisition device plays two roles in Chomskyan theory: first, it accounts for the striking similarities among human languages, even those which, as far as is known, are historically and geographically unrelated. We gave an example of such a similarity in Chapter 1, using relative clause constructions from English, Hebrew and French. Another example can be found in interrogative constructions. Every known language has a linguistic means of distinguishing interrogatives from declaratives; furthermore, most languages use one or more of three basic devices for marking yes-no questions. Either they preserve the syntactic form of the declarative and change the intonation, as in (1b), or they perform some syntactic operation such as inverting the subject and verb, as in (1c), or they add an extra word or phrase to the basic declarative form, as in (1d). English exploits all three possibilities:

(1) a. You want to buy a new pencil.

    b. You want to buy a new pencil?

    c. Do you want to buy a new pencil?

    d. You want to buy a new pencil, $\left\{ \begin{array}{l} \text{don't you?} \\ \text{right?} \\ \text{what?} \end{array} \right\}$

French has analogous forms to (1b–d), and, as we saw in Chapter 9, in certain dialects possesses an additional variant of (d) in which the inserted word occurs in a fixed position in the middle of the sentence, immediately after the first verb, as in (2e):

(2) a. Tu veux acheter un nouveau crayon.

    b. Tu veux acheter un nouveau crayon?

    c. Veux-tu acheter un nouveau crayon?

    d. Tu veux acheter un nouveau crayon, n'est-ce pas?

    e. Tu veux-ti acheter un nouveau crayon?

Most other languages use one or other of these basic forms. If the form of questions were dictated by the language acquisition device, so that only certain types of question could be learned or used by humans who possessed it, the similarities among languages could be traced back to the innate linguistic equipment of those who learn and speak the languages concerned.

The second role of the language acquisition device is in accounting for the speed, ease and regularity with which children learn their first language – a speed and ease which, as we have seen, decreases rapidly after the child reaches adolescence. Certain critics have argued that appeals to language-learning skills are unconvincing: that it makes no sense to marvel at how quickly and easily children learn language unless there is some standard of comparison according to which children really *do* learn quickly. One answer here is to compare normal children with Genie, the child mentioned in Chapter 2 who came to first-language learning long after most normal children. Genie's progress has been extremely slow compared with that of much younger children. Another standard for comparison is that of second-language learning on the basis of mere exposure to the language rather than conscious teaching, where again the young child far outstrips the adult in both speed and accuracy of acquisition. If we assume that the child is born with a series of principles he can use in grammar construction, so that on the basis of a fairly small sample of utterances he can construct a working model of the language, this speed and ease of acquisition would begin to have an explanation. Moreover, the fact that all the children learning a given language seem to pass through the same regular stages in their acquisition might also be explained on the assumption that children possess an innate theory of language of the form Chomsky outlines. As we saw in Chapter 10, children learning English regularly pass through a stage of deforming standard negative sentences into double negations (*He don't know nothing*). If the language acquisition device contained an evaluation measure which marked certain constructions as linguistically more complex than others, and if the double negative in English turned out to be simpler than the standard form according to this measure, then we would precisely expect children to pass through the simpler, double negative stage on their way to acquiring the final, more complex form.

Within this framework, then, it is natural to look for language universals. The language acquisition device would guarantee their existence, by ensuring that the only learnable languages would conform to innately determined principles. Moreover, the language acquisition device would itself *be* a theory of language universals, equipping the child with information about the form and content of grammars in terms of which he could organize the linguistic data he encountered. Thus for Chomsky, just as the study of individual grammars is linked to the search for psychologically significant generalizations, so the study of universal grammar has its roots in the organization of the mind. At both levels, the question is not what interesting patterns linguists *can* find in a language or languages, but what patterns human beings actually *do* find in them – and indeed put into them.

What should a universal grammar actually contain? In general, we can expect it to incorporate all the linguistic information a child must bring to the language-learning process. If learning a language involves learning a grammar, then the universal linguistic theory must specify the form grammars must take, the types of rules they contain, the way in which these rules must be formulated, and the possible interactions among them. Given these, we can see how the child, on exposure to the data from a particular language, will construct a grammar consistent both with the data and with the universal principles of language. Such a grammar would be descriptively adequate. If in addition the language acquisition device contained an evaluation measure, choosing one among a range of possible descriptively adequate grammars which were all consistent with the data and the universal principles, the language acquisition device would not only constrain, but actually explain the choice of grammar that the child eventually made.

Consider again the examples we gave in Chapter 10, of regular deviations in children's pronunciation of words of the adult language, and the rules which we suggested might account for them. Looking at the effects of such rules, when formulated in terms of distinctive features, we can say that they are invariably special cases of one of the following four learning strategies used in the acquisition of phonology. First, to maximize harmonic or assimilatory processes of the sort seen in the rendering of *duck* as [gʌk]; second, to minimize sequences of consonants such as the *bl* in *blue* or the *br* in *brush,* by deleting one of them or inserting another vowel between them; third, to decrease the number of phonological contrasts made in the adult language, as in the neutralization of *s* and *sh* in *bus* and *brush*; and finally to simplify the rest of the grammar by eliminating morphological contrasts such as that between singular and plural. Ultimately these strategies may have their own physiological and neurological explanation in terms of the innate perceptual and articulatory capacity of the child; but as yet, they stand in their own right as constraints on a theory of linguistic innateness, limiting the ways in which pronunciation may vary from child to child and language to language. *Very* occasionally there appear data on child language which fall outside these universal constraints, but their rarity and the fact that they are not incorporated into the rest of the system is a clear indication of their non-preferred status when judged by the evaluation measure.

Following Chomsky's most recent work, we might divide linguistic universals into two types: *formal* and *functional.*[1] As their name indicates, formal universals specify the form of rules in a grammar, the vocabulary in which they are stated and the way in which they interact; functional universals specify the way in which the rules apply to the actual linguistic data they are designed to describe. The formal universals, for example, might define a class of phonological distinctive features, such as [±nasal], [±voice], [±coronal], which the phonological rules may refer to. In defining this class, the universal linguistic theory would be making the claim that all possible human languages may be described in terms of a finite set of distinctive features. Notice that, as we have already emphasized, it is not being claimed that every language uses every member of the set: the implication is rather that languages may pick and choose among the members, and that every language will make a possible choice.

1. The notion of *formal universal* now subsumes the earlier contrast between formal and substantive universals.

In the case of syntax, the universal theory might define a class of syntactic categories, such as N, V, Adj, NP, VP, which may be used in the formulation of syntactic rules. Again, it is not claimed that every language will use every possible syntactic category; rather, it is claimed that every language will select a subset from this universal set. Thus a language like Japanese, which has no adjectives, will not falsify the claim that there is a universal class of syntactic categories available both to the linguist and to the child constructing his grammar. In the case of semantics too, it is possible that there is a finite set of semantic features, such as [±Animate], [±Human], [±Male], available for the formulation of semantic rules. The plausibility of this claim will ultimately depend on how many such features are necessary for semantic description. Since universal features are claimed to be innate, the more universal semantic features are needed for the description of a language, the more innate knowledge has to be imputed to the child. One is naturally reluctant to go beyond the evidence. In fact, it is quite consistent with Chomsky's theory that no innate semantic features exist at all; one could imagine a universal theory which prescribed the form of semantic rules, but left their vocabulary to be constructed by the child in the course of his cognitive development: the more concepts he acquired, the more semantic rules he would be able to construct, all of a pre-determined form.

Apart from the vocabulary of the various types of rule contained in a grammar, the universal theory would also be concerned with the formal properties of rules. For example, if grammars contain phrase-structure rules defining underlying syntactic structures, and transformational rules relating these to surface structures, the child must have a definition of 'phrase-structure rule' and 'transformation', and a series of constraints on their formulation. The examples in (3) are all permissible phrase-structure rules; those in (4) are not:

(3) a. NP → (Det) N
    b. VP → V NP

   c. S → NP VP
(4) a. *NP + VP → N
   b. *NP → NP
   c. *VP → V → Adj

The formal properties of phrase-structure rules and transformations are fairly well known, and there would be no difficulty in formulating a linguistic theory incorporating them. The form of phonological and semantic rules would also have to be taken account of: the context-dependence of phonological rules and the ordering properties of semantic rules would have to be built explicitly into the theory.

The interaction between the various components of a grammar might also be dealt with under the heading of formal universals. For example, we saw in Chapter 6 that the stress rules of the phonological component must have access to syntactic and morphological information, so that the contrasting stresses on the noun *aríthmetic* and the adjective *arithmétic* can be related by phonological rule. The universal theory would have to specify which types of phonological rule could have access to which type of syntactic information. Similarly, we saw in Chapter 7 that the semantic rules of English must have access to information about stress-contours, so that the different semantic and pragmatic properties of (5a) and (5b) may be correctly predicted:

(5) a. I *dropped* the book on purpose.
   b. I dropped the *book* on purpose.

Again, the possible points of interaction between stress placement and semantic interpretation must be defined by the universal theory of language. Similar remarks apply to the interaction between syntactic and semantic rules, and to the relation between all three components on the one hand and the lexicon on the other.

At various times, it has been suggested that the theory of language can go beyond this in its account of the organization of grammars. For example, it has been suggested that, parallel to the pool of phonological features and syntactic categories from which each language may draw a subset, there might be a pool of phonological and syntactic rules on which each language might draw. Thus the similarities among imperatives, interrogatives, relative clauses and passives across languages of widely differing types might be accounted for on the assumption that there is a schematic imperative, interrogative, relative or passive transformation included in the child's innate linguistic equipment. Universal phonological processes of assimilation and contraction, for example, might also be handled in this way.

In the last few pages we have been deliberately hypothetical. While we can say fairly clearly what framework the theory of formal universals fits into, and what general properties it must have, there is no possible way of knowing what its exact contents will be until the detailed investigation of many more languages has been undertaken. It might be worth clearing up a misconception here. One sometimes sees remarks such as 'Transformational grammar is only suitable for the study of English', or 'All the conclusions of transformational grammar are based on a superficial study of a handful of languages'. Such remarks are certainly not true. Many detailed studies have been done over the last twenty years, by many students and other research workers, on large numbers of widely differing languages. On the basis of these studies, it would be perfectly possible to make detailed claims about the contents of universal grammar: however, the fact that many other languages remain totally unstudied and undocumented means that most interesting claims that have been made, or could be made at this stage, will probably turn out tomorrow to be false.

Actually, one of the criticisms that could be made of certain formal universals as we have outlined them is that there is no possible way of falsifying them. This is a criticism because they set out to make empirical, testable claims. If they turn out to be unfalsifiable, then they are not making testable claims at all. For example, it sounds as if a great deal is being claimed by someone who proposes that all languages can be described in terms of a fixed set of syntactic categories, from which each language draws a subset. However, suppose that a new language which turns up tomorrow contains a class of words which seem to fit into no syntactic category previously encountered. Strictly speaking, of course, this language would refute any universal theory we had formulated. However, we could easily construct a new theory which *was* adequate, simply by adding a new syntactic category to the universal 'fixed' set from which all languages may draw. The fixed set of phonological features has expanded in just this way as new languages were discovered, so that, for example, a special innate feature had to be postulated merely to account for the click sounds encountered only in a small area of Africa. Similar remarks apply to the claim that there is a universal set of phrase-structure rules from which every language may draw a subset. It can be shown that from *any* arbitrary set of phrase structure rules, provided that a relatively unconstrained set of transformations is used, any language which is describable at all can be generated. Again, this means that there is little point in claiming that the theory of universals must specify a fixed set of phrase structure rules: such a claim is uninteresting because it is unfalsifiable.

The functional universals proposed within the Chomskyan framework have occasionally seemed to succumb to the opposite temptation: they are not only falsifiable, but false. It will be recalled that the functional universals are those that state how the grammar fits the data: how the particular rules of the grammar apply in the analysis of any given sentence. So, for example, we might know how to formulate the rule of passive for English, but be in doubt about whether, how or where to apply it in the derivation of a particular transitive sentence. Any universal which prescribed the functioning of grammatical rules in the analysis of a given sentence would be a functional universal in Chomsky's sense.

In the last chapter, we saw an example of one such universal. A ban on the extraction of NPs from within co-ordinate structures of the type *NP and NP*, or *VP and VP* would be a functional universal. It would constrain the application of any rule extracting NPs, by forbidding them to operate in certain environments. Particular applications of such rules in the analysis of a given sentence would be subject to this universal constraint, and any application which violated the constraint would be predicted to result in an ungrammatical sentence. A large number of constraints of the same general type have been proposed by Chomsky and others over the last ten years or so.

The reason why such universals often prove to be not only falsifiable but actually false is an interesting one. For virtually any functional universal that has been proposed, it is generally possible to find some rule in some language that disobeys it. This is interesting because it disproves one natural sceptical claim that could be made about the whole Chomskyan framework of linguistic universals. Someone reading the last chapter in a critical spirit might have argued in the following way. The supposed linguistic constraint on extraction of NPs from co-ordinate structures is not really a linguistic constraint at all, but a psychological one. Just as we have argued that certain unnatural-sounding sentences are really grammatical, but disallowed by language-*users* for processing or perceptual reasons, so sentences in which an NP has been extracted from a co-ordinate structure are perfectly grammatical, but hard for language-users to produce and understand. The distinction between linguistic and non-linguistic knowledge cuts both ways. The fact that there actually exist languages, like Fe'Fe', which permit the extraction of NPs from co-ordinate structures, while it might seem to raise problems for the theory of linguistic universals, does at least show that appeals to processing or perceptual difficulties will not provide an adequate explanation for the cases in which such universals are obeyed. An example from Fe'Fe' is given in (6):

(6) wa	tá	a	lá	cwée	mbáa	m-ben
who	topic	be	past	cut	meat	and-thank

This presumably comes from an underlying co-ordinate structure like the one associated with the English (7a) and (7b):

(7) a. He cut meat and thanked *who*?
   b. *Who did he cut meat and thank?

In (6), unlike (7b), the *wh*-word can be extracted from its underlying position in a co-ordinate structure and moved to the front
of the whole sentence – a clear violation of the supposedly universal ban on such extractions. Now (6) presumably presents no
processing or perceptual difficulties to speakers of Fe'Fe'.
Presumably also, if one group of humans has no difficulty in
producing and understanding a certain type of construction, one
cannot account for the failure of another group to produce an
exactly analogous construction by saying merely that they would
find it too hard to understand. It thus seems that whatever explanation can be found for the fact that the majority of languages do
not permit extraction from co-ordinate structures, it must be a
genuinely linguistic one.

The problem here is that functional universals have generally
been construed as absolute universals, and the existence of even
one rule in one language which disobeys an absolute universal
automatically refutes it. It would, of course, be possible to retreat
to the position we outlined in our account of formal universals:
we might argue simply that the universal theory contains a fixed
list of functional universals from which any language may draw
a subset. Then the fact that a certain language disobeyed some
universal need not come as any surprise. Even this much weaker
position would be refuted by languages with a majority of rules
which obey a certain constraint, but one or two rules which
violate it – which seems to be a perfectly possible state of affairs.
But the most serious problem about all 'fixed list' universals is
that they give no account of two closely related types of fact. First,
for most functional universals, the majority of constructions in
the majority of languages do obey them: we should thus *expect*
them to be obeyed, and be surprised when they are not obeyed.
But the 'fixed list' treatment merely says that each rule in each
language is free to obey or disobey each proposed constraint – not
a very interesting claim. Second, among the 'fixed lists' of

phonological features and syntactic categories, we will find certain items which are almost always chosen by a given language, and certain others which are chosen very rarely indeed. The feature [+nasal], for example, is almost always chosen; the feature used in analysing clicks almost never. The mere postulation of a fixed list of phonological features or syntactic categories, all of equal status, will provide no explanation of the fact that the probabilities of a particular language selecting a particular feature or category vary greatly, and predictably.

It seems that this line of investigation has reached an impasse. Chomsky has provided an elegant framework for the study of linguistic universals, but the facts of language do not fit with the framework. We know that we must look for universals of form and function; no such universals seem to exist. At this point, it might be worth investigating a quite separate approach to the study of universals, which has co-existed with Chomsky's, but which seems to provide data which have no place within Chomsky's framework.

The Evaluation Measure and Linguistic Complexity

In Chapter 9 we mentioned the work of Joseph Greenberg, which provides evidence that universals of language are not absolute but rather probabilistic, in the sense that the majority of languages will observe them, but no language is likely to observe them all. Furthermore, Greenberg showed how certain linguistic properties correlate with others, for example that the basic word order of a language may be used to predict a number of other processes in its grammar. We have already seen that nothing in Chomsky's theory of language has so far led us to expect universals of this kind. However, as the study of universals has progressed, more and more of these seemingly inexplicable generalizations have come to light. Greenberg, apart from some remarks about 'harmony' and 'disharmony' among various constructions and categories, made no attempt to explain them. Clearly, though, since generalizations of this type are among the few universal linguistic statements that are both testable and not actually false, we must reject any theory of language which provides no natural account of them.

Chomsky's reaction to the sort of universal data brought to light by his own and Greenberg's work has been seen by some as a retreat. What he has increasingly done is reformulate the falsified 'absolute' universals as relative universals. That is, instead of claiming that the theory of language should place an absolute ban on, say, extracting NPs from within co-ordinate structures, he has argued that it should really contain principles of the following form: No rule may extract an NP from within a co-ordinate structure, *unless otherwise stated*. A large number of similar functional universals, to which much of Chomsky's recent work has been devoted, have been reformulated along similar lines, so as to allow for exceptions. It is easy to see why this reaction has been regarded as a retreat. Chomsky is one of those who have most insisted on the need for linguistic generalizations to be testable. But how does one go about testing the claim that a given generalization is true of all languages except for those in which it is not true?

In fact, what Chomsky has apparently succeeded in doing with this reformulation is to provide some genuine insights into the nature of the evaluation measure. It will be recalled from the last chapter that this is the device which, according to Chomsky, guides the child towards the best available grammar: the grammar that is consistent both with the facts of the particular language and the generalizations of universal linguistic theory. According to Chomsky, the only way in which we can explain the child's final choice of a grammar is by constructing an adequate evaluation measure. We also saw that if all universals are absolute, and if there is no antecedently given measure of simplicity which linguists can adapt to their own purposes, it seems to be in principle impossible to give any interesting account of what the evaluation measure might contain.

Now suppose that the relative universals are construed as part of an evaluation measure for grammars. Suppose that a rule which conforms to a relative universal is automatically evaluated as simpler and better than one which does not. It follows that each relative universal will provide a measure of the linguistic complexity of a particular construction or rule. For example, a rule of English which extracts NPs from co-ordinate structures, although it must be admitted as a possible rule, will also be predicted as more complex than one which does not. We could imagine this complexity reflected in the formulation of the rule itself. A rule which makes no explicit reference to co-ordinate structure might be interpreted as unable to apply into such structures; any rule required to apply into co-ordinate structures would then have to make explicit reference to all the types of co-ordinate structure into which it *could* apply. Such a rule would automatically have a much more complex and lengthy formulation than a rule which obeyed the relative universal.

This new notion of linguistic complexity makes a number of testable claims. In particular, since it is construed as part of a language acquisition device, it will make predictions about the order of acquisition of certain rules and constructions by the child. Rules which violate linguistic universals, since they will be more complex and less expected, should be learned later than those which conform to them. Such a claim would be fairly easy to test. Furthermore, a child who has been exposed only to data which conform to the universals at a time when he is formulating a particular rule, should not spontaneously produce new sentences which violate them. It will be recalled that a rule must now be treated as conforming to the universals unless it contains explicit indication to the contrary: a child who has no evidence to the contrary in formulating the rule, then, must treat that rule as conforming to the universal. Again, these predictions are fairly easy to test. Children learning English, which obeys the co-ordinate structure constraint, should not normally produce sentences which violate it: we are invoking here the notion 'impossible mistake for a child learning language X to make'. We might also predict that a child will find it harder to learn a rule which violates a universal, not just because it will be less expected, but also because its exact formulation will not follow from universal principles, and the child will have to use a considerable amount of trial and error before he gets it to cover exactly the right range of cases.

Another type of correlation between linguistic complexity and observable facts might be found in the direction of dialect variation and language change. For example, we might find that any language which violates a universal will have a related series of dialects which do not; we might predict that the direction of language change would be towards conformity to universals rather than away from it – bearing in mind our claim in Chapter 10 that simplification in one area of a grammar may lead to added complexity elsewhere. All these areas might provide both empirical evidence for the particular contents of the evaluation measure, and a range of cases against which it might be tested.

Interestingly, Greenberg's statistical universals would not in themselves provide the most direct evidence either for or against the evaluation measure. It is possible that there are accidental correlations in these data. It is also possible that in certain cases the majority of languages have chosen a particular rule or construction which violates a universal – one might imagine this happening by sheer accident, or because there are non-linguistic reasons making this construction particularly desirable. It is important, then, to find a number of independent pointers to linguistic complexity, beyond mere likelihood of occurrence in any given language. If all these pointers lead in the same direction, then one could be fairly confident that the results were genuine.

It is also possible to see how the evaluation measure could be used to predict the choices that languages make among the members of 'fixed list' universals. For example, we could mark certain members of such lists as more complex, less likely to be selected, than others. Again, any attempt to do this would have to rely on evidence not just from likelihood of occurrence across languages, but also on evidence about the language acquisition process, 'natural' mistakes of the child learning the language, and the direction of historical change. Others of Greenberg's generalizations are rather easier to explain. For example, one of his claims is that there is a correlation between the position of the auxiliary and that of the verb: if the verb comes at the end of the clause, so does the auxiliary. If, as we argued in Chapter 4, auxiliaries really *are* verbs, then this fact is not surprising. Similarly, the fact that the position of prepositions/postpositions correlates with that of the verb would be explained on the assumption, sometimes put forward, that prepositions/postpositions in underlying structure really are verbs, or at least occupy the same positions as verbs. Any grammar which gave prepositions/postpositions different surface structure positions from verbs would therefore have to incorporate an extra rule, and hence would be more complex.

It seems, then, that the existence of relative universals can be accommodated naturally within Chomsky's framework, as part of the evaluation measure for grammars. The evaluation measure, far from being a pointless and untestable article of dogma, becomes quite central to the theory of language as a whole. It provides a measure of how natural a specific process in natural language is.

Conclusion

Chomsky's writings have been enormously influential in disciplines that are more or less closely related to linguistics. Often, they have been influential for the wrong reasons, and in the wrong way. If human linguistic knowledge is different in kind from other types of knowledge, requiring special programming and special principles, it is unlikely that the study of the non-linguistic systems constructed by humans can draw in any direct way on what we know about human languages. In particular, to liken social systems to languages, and look for deep structures, transformations, semantic rules and so on, in these social systems is not likely to provide revealing results. It is quite possible that linguistic knowledge is not the only type of innate knowledge, but there is no particular reason to expect any further innate knowledge discovered to resemble linguistic knowledge at all closely.

What Chomsky has done is to provide a coherent account of how testable and interesting claims can be made about linguistic knowledge, both innate and acquired. At every point where scepticism might arise about the validity of these claims, he has pointed to a further level of argument which could be used to confirm some claims and disprove others. There is no level in Chomsky's framework which cannot be supported by some independent factual observation.

Part of Chomsky's success must be attributed to his willingness to ask interesting questions. Suppose, for example, he had set off from the assumption that language was above all a social system. He might then have been led to ask such questions as 'What makes Old English and Modern English both English?' This is a question to which the only coherent answer is a historical one. Historical questions can rarely be answered within any homogeneous scientific theory; indeed, it is quite possible that they cannot be answered scientifically at all. Or suppose he had set off from the assumption that language was above all a communicative system. He might then have been led to believe that any sentence with no known communicative function would be ungrammatical, or that the universals of language should be determined by the requirements of any well-functioning communicative system. Throughout this book, we have attempted to show that this correlation breaks down. Chomsky's concern with the child's ability to learn a language, and with the knowledge of language that can be ascribed to the individual, has made it possible to provide a coherent account of language itself.

The picture of language that emerges from Chomsky's writings, though complex, is generally clear. Language is a reflection of the human mind, not just in the sense that humans have produced it, can learn it, and do speak it, but in the much more specific sense that language is as it is because the human mind is as it is. Nor is it just that humans are intelligent enough to construct and learn languages; rather, they are specially designed to construct and learn the sort of languages they do, and this ability is not a reflection of general intelligence at all. The human language faculty is unique and innate. Chomsky's achievement has been to make this clear.

Glossary

Absolute neutralization In phonology, the device of assigning arbitrary features to particular lexical items (or phonemes within lexical items) so that they undergo a rule which other apparently similar lexical items do not undergo. The feature assigned has no distinct phonetic realization.

Acceptable An utterance is acceptable if it is readily comprehensible and appropriate to context. Normally, but not always, acceptable utterances correspond to grammatical sentences, and unacceptable utterances to ungrammatical sentences. Acceptability is a feature of performance or language use, grammaticality is a feature of competence.

Acoustic phonetics The branch of phonetics dealing with the physical properties of speech, as e.g. the shapes of the formants characteristic of vowels.

Adequacy (levels of) Levels of success attained by grammars and theories. A grammar is *observationally adequate* if it recapitulates the observed data explicitly: i.e. it is essentially a representation of facts. A grammar is *descriptively adequate* if it attains observational adequacy and gives a characterization of the data in psychologically valid terms. A theory is *explanatorily adequate* if it allows a reasoned choice among competing descriptively adequate grammars.

Adverbial A cover term for various classes of adverb and phrases containing adverbs. In some cases it also subsumes prepositional phrases. e.g. *happily, extremely stupidly, with obvious malice.*

Agree, Agreement Two grammatical elements are said to *agree* if they are both marked for the same category: e.g. *the boy* (singular) *runs* vs. *the boys* (plural) *run*. Here the verb agrees with its subject NP in number. In many languages articles and adjectives must agree with the noun they modify in *gender*, e.g. French:

| *un* | *bon* | *vin* | *blanc* | – | *une* | *bonne* | *viande* | *blanche* |
| a | good | wine | white | | a | good | meat | white |

where *vin* is masculine and *viande* is feminine.

Allophone Allophones of a phoneme (q.v.) are sounds which are the same for the users of a language and whose slight phonetic differences are predictable in terms of their position in the word. e.g. in English, the phoneme /l/ is pronounced 'clear' before a vowel as in *leaf*, /liːf/, [liːf], but 'dark' (i.e. velarized) elsewhere, as in *feel*, /fiːl/, [fiːɫ]. [l] and [ɫ] are allophones of /l/.

Alveolar Any sound articulated with the tip or front of the tongue against the *alveolar ridge*, the ridge behind the upper teeth. e.g. English /t/, /n/.

Ambiguous, Ambiguity A word or sentence is ambiguous if it has two or more linguistically determined meanings.

e.g. *plane*, meaning 'aeroplane' or 'flat surface'.

   We aren't using this example because it is ambiguous.

The possibility of giving a sentence two interpretations does not entail that it is ambiguous: there is nothing linguistic in the fact that:

   John's ear is bleeding

refers to two possible situations depending on whether his left or his right ear is hurt. Such sentences are merely *vague*.

Analogy A process of comparison whereby features of one construction are ascribed to another on the basis of perceived similarity between them without the intervention of a general rule. Thus:

   It's both our donkey

is formed from: *It's the donkey of both of us* on analogy with:

It's the donkey of both the children ∼ *It's both the children's donkey*

Analyse (a tree) To segment or factorize a tree (q.v.) so that each part of the structural description of a transformation corresponds to some part of that tree. For instance, the tree:

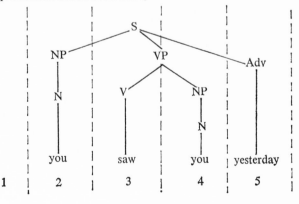

has been analysed, as indicated by the vertical lines, to meet the structural description for the transformation of reflexivization:

viz.: SD X – NP – X – NP – X
      1   2   3   4   5

(SC converts term 4 to a reflexive pronoun).

Analytic sentence Sentences which are true in virtue of their meaning are analytically true.
e.g. *All gorillas are animals.*

Anomalous, Anomaly Any sentence which is semantically incoherent or nonsensical:
e.g. *This woman is the father of three pins.*
Anomaly is often extended to purely pragmatic peculiarity: i.e. to sentences which merely describe unusual situations such as:
   My brother trickled into the inkwell.

Anterior A distinctive feature describing sounds whose major point of articulation is further forward in the mouth than that of /ʃ/ (in *sh*op) or /tʃ/ (in *ch*urch). e.g. /p, t, θ, f, s/ in English.

Aphasia The loss of the ability to use and/or understand language because of damage to the brain.

Articulation (point of) The point of major contact or constriction in the vocal tract in the pronunciation of a speech sound. The point of articulation of /p/ is the lips, of /t/ the alveolar ridge, etc.

Articulatory phonetics The branch of phonetics dealing with the production of speech: specifically the manner of pronunciation, or *articulation*, of the various speech sounds.

Aspiration A puff of air produced immediately after the release of a consonant such as /p/, /t/ or /k/. In initial position before a stressed vowel in English these are pronounced as: [pʰ], [tʰ] and [kʰ].

Assimilation A process whereby two dissimilar sounds become more similar when close to each other. e.g. /n/ in *sane* assimilates to the /p/ at the beginning of *people*, in the sequence *sane people*, by becoming [m]: i.e. the alveolar [n] becomes a bilabial because of the bilabial [p] following it.

Auditory phonetics The branch of phonetics dealing with the perception of speech: e.g. the relative perceived quality of /iː/ and /i/ in *beat* and *bit*.

Auxiliary (verb)   A member of a class of verbs whose syntactic behaviour is irregular in some respects: e.g. in failure to form questions with *do*, in being able to permute with the subject, etc. *May* is an auxiliary verb, *say* is a main verb, cf.:

John may come.	*John says nothing.*
May John come?	**Says John nothing?*
*Does John may come?	*Does John say nothing?*

Back   A distinctive feature characterizing sounds (mainly, but not exclusively, vowels) which are articulated with the back part of the tongue raised. e.g. /u, o/ in English.

Background entailment   The entailment obtained by replacing the focus (q.v.) of a sentence by an indefinite phrase.
e.g. **Karpov** *checkmated his opponent* has someone checkmated his opponent as its background entailment, whereas *Karpov checkmated* **his opponent** has Karpov checkmated someone as its background entailment.

Bilabial   Sounds produced with closure or approximation of the lips are bilabial. e.g. /p, b, m/ in English.

Bidialectalism/Bilingualism   Mastery of two linguistic systems, e.g. English and French (bilingualism) or British English and American English (bidialectalism). The distinction between language and dialect is a matter of degree and is usually determined on non-linguistic – e.g. political or cultural – grounds. Accordingly the difference between bidialectalism and bilingualism is itself a matter of degree.

Binary (features)   Distinctive features when used phonologically, i.e. to distinguish lexical items from each other rather than to specify minute details of pronunciation, are *binary* in that each feature must be specified as plus (+) or minus (−) with no third value possible.

Bracketing (labelled)   A linear representation of tree structure such that each labelled bracket corresponds to a node in the tree. The following are exactly equivalent:

s[NP[N[John]] VP[V[saw] NP[Art[the] N[fish]]]]

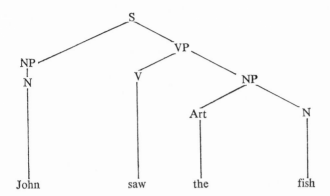

Clause A syntactic constituent containing a single main verb. Technically, any part of a tree exhaustively dominated by an S node.

Click A speech sound typical of a small number of South African languages (e.g. Xhosa) whose articulation involves making a velar closure which causes a partial vacuum when the back of the tongue is lowered, and abruptly releasing a closure further forward in the mouth. Clicks occur in English only as signs of disapproval (*tut tut*), or to encourage horses.

Code A relationship between items in different dialects inferred by speakers in their attempt to produce or understand sentences from dialects other than their own. e.g. a speaker of British English listening to American English might encode a correlation between the American sequence of 'vowel + r + consonant' and his own 'long vowel + consonant': for instance, *bird* with the pronunciation [bərd] would be interpreted as [bəːd].

Competence Knowledge of language. That part of our knowledge which is exclusively linguistic. It includes knowledge of the vocabulary, of phonology, of syntax and of semantics. The part of such knowledge which is different from language to language is learned; the part which is universal, e.g. the presence of categories such as V, is innate.

Complement (sentential) When the subject, direct object or other NP constituent of a sentence is itself a sentence, as in:
That he kissed her *made Mary think* **she was beautiful**

it is referred to as a sentential *complement*. A non-sentential complement is an NP, Adjective or prepositional phrase dependent on a verb but not functioning as a direct object:

e.g. *John became* **king**   *John turned* **purple**

Complementary distribution   Two or more items which occur in consistently different environments are said to be in complementary distribution. The allophones of a phoneme are in complementary distribution, as, for instance, the phoneme /l/ in English has two allophones [l] and [ɫ], the first of which occurs only before vowels and the second of which occurs only before consonants and finally. Thus [l] and [ɫ] are in complementary distribution. Complementary distribution and phonetic similarity are the criteria used for assigning different sounds to the same phoneme.

Complementizer   A syntactic class of words which introduce a subordinate clause such as *that, for, whether*, in:
I know **that** *he is coming.*
I wonder **whether** *he is coming.*
I want desperately **for** *him to come.*

Component   Our knowledge of language can be divided into semantic, syntactic and phonological parts. The grammar which describes this knowledge is then itself divided into three corresponding *components*: semantics, syntax and phonology.

Compound noun   An item whose internal structure may consist of a sequence of nouns, adjective and noun, etc., but whose syntactic behaviour is the same as that of a simple noun. e.g. *telephone bell, paper-knife, bluebird*.

Comprehension strategy   A procedure used in the attempt to understand sentences which lie outside one's own internalized grammar, either because they are the output of a different dialect or because they contain performance errors. Comprehension strategies have recourse to contextual and pragmatic cues, to linguistic structure inferred on the basis of analogies with one's own dialect, etc.

Conjunction   (1) Traditionally, any word linking one clause to another. e.g. *and* in: *I did it and I regret it.*
       (2) An alternative term for *coordination* (q.v.).

Consonant harmony An assimilatory process whereby consonants with different features become more similar. For instance, children often pronounce words of the adult language which contain consonants of differing points of articulation with the same point of articulation. e.g. *duck* may be pronounced [gʌk].

Constituent Any sequence of elements which form a syntactic unit, as in the **bold** parts of:

> **The three musketeers** *attacked* **the fort.**

Technically any sequence which can be traced back exhaustively to a single node in a tree is a constituent.

Continuant A distinctive feature used to characterize sounds whose articulation involves no complete obstruction of the air-flow from the lungs: e.g. all vowels and consonants such as /s, f, θ/ in English.

Contraction A phonological process which reduces the form of a word generally by the omission of a vowel.
e.g. *He is coming*   contracts to: *He's coming*
     I am here   contracts to: *I'm here*

Contradiction Any sentence which simultaneously asserts the truth and the falsity of a proposition is a contradiction.
e.g. *I have a mute brother who is always chattering.*

Contrastive stress Extra strong emphasis on a particular word or syllable in a sentence to contrast it with some other part of the sentence.
e.g. **John** *swallowed the walnuts, not Fred.*
     *I said be*nign *rather than* ma*lign.*

Conversational implicature The pragmatic implication of an apparently irrelevant utterance which follows only if it is construed as being relevant. For instance, the reply: *He's very good at spelling* to the question: *Is Charles a suitable candidate for the chair in mathematics?* would conversationally implicate that Charles was not a very good candidate, although it clearly does not entail this.

Coordinate (clause), Coordination A clause linked to another by *and, or*, etc., such that each clause is of equal status is termed a coordinate clause. A sequence of such clauses is a coordination or conjunction of clauses.
e.g. *Harriet resigned* **and** *Michael took over.*

Coreference, Coreferential   Two NPs which refer to (designate) the same individual or set of individuals are said to be coreferential. A number of transformations have been claimed to depend for their application on coreference: e.g. Reflexivization.

Coronal   A distinctive feature characterizing consonants pronounced with the tip or front part of the tongue as the active articulator: e.g. /t, d, s, tʃ/ in English.

Declarative   The sentence structure standardly used to make statements: e.g. *John is a fool*. It contrasts with *interrogative* sentences, standardly used to ask questions, and *imperative* sentences, standardly used to give orders.

Deep structure   The output of the phrase structure rules and lexicon, and the input to the transformations and the semantic component of the 'standard theory' of transformational generative grammar.

Dental   A consonant articulated with the tip of the tongue in contact with the teeth. In French /t, d, n/ are dental – [t̪, d̪, n̪] – whereas in English they are alveolar.

Derive, Derivation, Derived structure   (1) The process whereby a sentence is generated through the use of different rules is a *derivation*. Thus: *Stanley was seduced by a mermaid* is derived via the PS rules S → NP VP, VP → V NP, etc. and the transformation of Passivization. *Derived structure* is used to describe the output of any transformation: i.e. anything other than deep structure.

(2) In etymological statements one word is said to be derived from another if it represents a recognizable phonological and semantic development. e.g. *flaw* is derived from the Old Norse *flaga*.

Dialect   A variety of language typical of a particular region or class. The standard language is merely one dialect among many.

Directionality   The claim that phonological and semantic rules may have access to syntactic information, but that syntactic rules never have access to phonological or semantic information.

Dissimilation   The change of one of two similar sounds to a different sound to avoid the repetition of identical elements.
e.g. Latin *peregrinus*, *pilgrim*, with two occurrences of *r*, became French *pélerin* with the first *r* dissimilated to *l* because of the second *r*.

Distinctive features A set of universal, putatively innate, phonetic and phonological properties by reference to which the speech sounds of the world's languages are described. e.g. [voiced], [nasal], [coronal].

Dominate In a tree, A dominates B if A is higher in the tree than B and it is possible to trace a downward path from A to B (cf. (i) and (ii)). A *immediately dominates* B if no node intervenes between A and B (cf. (iii)).

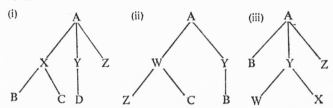

Dummy A meaningless element which has syntactic but no semantic function. e.g. *It* in: *It upsets me that he left.*

Echo question A question which seeks specific information about a mis-heard or incredible part of a preceding utterance by repeating everything except the constituent queried.
e.g. *You said that John and* **who** *were coming?*

Embed, Embedding Where a sentence has another sentence as one of its constituents, this smaller (subordinate) sentence is said to be embedded inside the larger (superordinate) one. For instance, the sentence *all cows are purple* is embedded into the sentence *John thinks that the claim is silly* in:
John thinks that the claim that all cows are purple is silly.

Entail, Entailment A sentence A entails a sentence B if the truth of B follows logically from the truth of A.
e.g. *Colin ate all the kippers* entails Someone ate something.

Evaluation measure A theoretical device to compare alternative grammars for the same language and decide, on universal grounds, which is preferred. The evaluation measure is a necessary part of a theory which aims for explanatory adequacy.

Expand, Expansion A phrase-structure rule which specifies the constituent make-up of a particular category is said to *expand* into those constituents. Thus, in 'S → NP VP (Adv)' S is said to expand into NP followed by VP optionally followed by Adv, and 'NP VP' is one of the expansions of S. *Re-write* is used with the same sense.

Extrapose, Extraposition   A transformation which moves a constituent rightwards over intervening material is said to *extrapose* that constituent. In the structure:
[*That Cuthbert dabbles in necromancy*] *fills me with foreboding*
the bracketed string may be extraposed to produce:
It fills me with foreboding [*that Cuthbert dabbles in necromancy*].

Feature (syntactic)   Any property of lexical items which affects their morphological shape or syntactic distribution is called a syntactic feature. e.g. the property of being a common noun rather than a proper noun: *boy* is [+common], *John* is [−common], the property of being a transitive verb: *castigate* is [+ —— NP], etc.

Filter   A device for marking as ungrammatical certain sequences of items which have been generated by phrase structure or transformational rules. e.g. a sequence of *being + V-ing* is excluded by means of a filter.

Focal scale   The logically ordered series of entailments produced by substitution of an indefinite phrase (e.g. *someone*) for each surface structure syntactic constituent which contains the most heavily stressed word.

Focus   The surface structure syntactic constituent selected for emphasis by placement of heavy stress: one of the surface constituents which contains the most heavily stressed item.
e.g. *kicked the bucket* could be the focus of: *Bill's kicked the* **bucket**.

Free variation   Where either of two (or any of three or more) items may occur indiscriminately, they are in free variation.
e.g. *John picked up the baby* ∼ *John picked the baby up*
The term is most frequently used in phonology where, e.g., the pronunciations *défect* and *deféct* are in free variation for many speakers; and in phonetics where, e.g., [t] and [tʼ] are in free variation in final position in English.

Gender   The grammatical difference among *masculine – he; feminine – she;* and *neuter – it.*

Generate A set of rules whose output is a particular language (or set of sentences) is said to *generate* that language or those sentences. An alternative term is *enumerate*.

Grammar, Grammatical, Ungrammatical The grammar of a language consists of a set (or sets) of rules which generate a set of sentences: in the case of all natural languages, an infinite set of sentences. Any sentence generated by the rules is, by definition, *grammatical*; any sentence not generated by the rules is, by definition, *ungrammatical*. Writing a grammar then consists in large part of formulating rules which stipulate the correct grammatical and ungrammatical sets.

Grammatically specified entailment The set of entailments obtained from a surface structure by substituting indefinite phrases such as *someone* for each constituent of the surface structure.
e.g. *Horace fried an egg* has as two of the set of grammatically specified entailments: someone fried an egg and Horace did something.

Grammatically unspecified entailment All the entailments of a sentence except the grammatically specified ones. e.g. John exists is a grammatically unspecified entailment of *John is tall*.

Half-open (vowel) A vowel, such as [ɛ], [ɔ] – similar to those in *get;* *got* – intermediate in quality between [e] and [a], and between [o] and [ɑ].

High (vowel) A vowel articulated with the tongue raised as far to the roof of the mouth as is possible without causing friction. An alternative term is *close* vowel.

Imperative The sentence structure standardly used to give orders.
e.g. *Give me that egg-cup. Put your hands on your head.*

Indirect question, Indirect statement A question or statement which is embedded as the complement of a superordinate verb.
e.g. *Mavis will guess* **that you are here.**
Mavis will guess **why you are here.**

Inflection Modifications to the form of words to indicate their syntactic relationships are *inflections.* e.g. the contrast *who : whom* for subject : object, or *write : writes* for first and second person singular : third person singular, in English.

Informant   A native speaker of a language whom one uses to gain judgements of well-formedness, ambiguity, etc. about his language. Linguists frequently use themselves as informants.

Input   (1) The input to a component of the grammar is the set of structures which are operated on by the rules of that component: e.g. the input to the phonological component is the infinite set of surface structures.

(2) The input to a rule is the class of elements or structures which the rule affects: e.g. the input or structural description of a transformation defines the class of structures to which it applies. Thus Passive applies to any structure of the form: NP V NP.

Interdental   A sound articulated with the tip of the tongue between the teeth, as *th* – /θ/ – in *teeth*.

Internalize   To learn unconsciously, as the rules of one's native language.

Interpret, Interpretation   (1) In transformational generative grammar the syntactic component is taken to be descriptively prior to the phonological and semantic components, because the rules of the latter need to refer to syntactic information, but syntactic rules never need to refer to semantic or phonological information. The rules which associate a syntactic representation with a phonological representation and a semantic representation are said to *interpret* that syntactic structure, or to give it a phonological or semantic *interpretation*.

(2) When speakers associate a particular meaning with an utterance they hear, they are said to interpret it. This usage is particularly common in the case of ambiguous sentences where one of two or more possible readings is chosen.

Interrogative   The sentence structure standardly used to ask questions. e.g. *Can you dance the watusi?* It contrasts with declarative and imperative sentences.

Intonation   Variation in pitch which has the sentence rather than the word as its domain. For instance, *cats are friendly* may be uttered with a falling pitch as a statement, with a rising pitch as a question and so on. All languages, including tone languages (q.v.), have intonation.

Intransitive (verb)   A verb which cannot occur with a direct object is *intransitive*. e.g. *The spoons vanished* but **Sophie vanished the spoons.*

By extension, a sentence containing such a verb is also called intransitive.

Intuitions   Every native speaker is able to give judgements abou putative sentences of his language: e.g. for English, that *This is a crocus* is acceptable, that *It is too hot to eat* has several meanings (at least four), that *I prevented him to do it* is unacceptable, and so on. Such judgements are referred to as the native speaker's *intuitions.* Note that these intuitions are usually not conscious, and are never about how to *analyse* the sentences of his language.

Labio-dental   A sound produced with the top teeth in contact with the tower lip, as /f/ and /v/ in English, is labio-dental.

Language acquisition device   The set of innate constructs which are necessary and sufficient for learning a first language. Children are thought to be born with a predisposition to learn language, specifically any human language, and this predisposition is specific to language rather than general to all learning. For instance, human infants are born with the ability to discriminate phonologically relevant differences in voicing; are assumed to have an innate knowledge of possible linguistic rule, and so on.

Lateral   A distinctive feature used to characterize sounds pronounced with passage of air along the sides of the tongue, as /l/ in English.

Learning strategy   Part of the language acquisition device consists of general strategies that children bring to bear on the task of learning their language. One such strategy is the harmonization of consonant and vowel sounds in words of the adult language to facilitate the child's production task.

Level of analysis   Linguistic knowledge is of various kinds: phonological, syntactic and semantic. Each of these kinds of knowledge is dealt with in a different component (q.v.) of the grammar. Any component defines at least one level of analysis: e.g. semantics and phonology. Within syntax there are claimed to be two levels necessary: deep structure and surface structure. Formally a level is defined as the output of sets of rules having particular formal properties: phrase structure rules, transformational rules and so on.

Lexical entry, Lexicon   The lexicon contains information about every word of the language in the form of lexical entries. Each lexical entry has to provide phonological, syntactic and semantic data, so *weasel*, for example, will be entered in a distinctive feature representation corresponding to the phonemic /wiːzəl/, as a common, count noun, as an animal, etc. Properties common to many lexical items which are not accounted for by transformational or semantic rules are listed in the form of lexical *redundancy rules* (q.v.).

Liaison   The phenomenon in French whereby a word-final consonant is pronounced only in specific environments: e.g. before another word beginning with a vowel where the two words are not in separate major constituents. Thus the final *t* of *petit* (*little*) is pronounced in *mon petit ami* (*my little friend*) but not in *mon ami est petit* (*my friend is little*).

Logical truth   A logical truth is a statement that is true under all conceivable circumstances: e.g. *An animal is an animal.*

Long (vowel)   A distinctive feature characterizing sounds which are of greater duration than some other phonetically similar element: e.g. Latin *mālum – apple; malum – evil.* In English, length differences correlate with quality differences so that /iː/ in *beat* is both longer and higher than the /i/ in *bit.*

Low (vowel)   A distinctive feature characterizing sounds (especially vowels) articulated with the tongue retracted and low in the mouth: e.g. /a/ in *cat* and /ɑː/ in *father.*

Major syntactic category   The categories N, V, Adj and Adv and any category dominating any of these: e.g. VP, NP, PP.

Matrix   A two-dimensional display of the values taken by particular phonemes for specific distinctive features. The names of the features are put in rows on the left, and the columns correspond to particular speech sounds. e.g.

	p	ı	n
consonantal	+	−	+
coronal	−	−	+
anterior	+	−	+
voiced	−	+	+

Metathesis   A phonological process in which two segments are transposed: e.g. the pronunciation [wɔps] for *wasp*. Spoonerisms are a kind of metathesis across word boundaries.

Modal (verb)   A class of irregular (defective) verb whose usual function is to specify such concepts as possibility and necessity: e.g. *can, may, must*. Modal verbs are a sub-class of auxiliary verb.

Morpheme   The minimal syntactic unit. Words consist of one or more morphemes, so in *cats*, *cat* is a morpheme, *s* is a morpheme, and the whole word consists of two morphemes of which the first happens also to be a word, but the second is unable to occur except in conjunction with such a word.

Morphology   The study of the internal structure of words in terms of morphemes (q.v.).

Morphophonemic rule   Any rule which effects a change in the phonemic make-up of words or their constituent morphemes. e.g. the addition of the past tense marker to *see* – /siː/ – triggers a morphophonemic change of the vowel to /ɔː/: hence, *saw* – /sɔː/.

n-ary features   Distinctive features when used for specifying points of fine phonetic detail are given a scale of possible values: 1, 2, 3 ... n in place of their phonological binary values. In some cases n-ary specification may be needed at the phonological level as well.

Nasal   A distinctive feature characterizing sounds pronounced with passage of air through the nose as well as or instead of through the mouth, e.g. /m, n/ in English.

Natural class   A class of phonemes which can be more economically specified than any subset of that class. The class [+strident] is natural in English because it defines the set of phonemes /s, z, ʃ, ʒ, tʃ, dʒ/, where to define any subset, e.g. /s, z/ alone, would require the specification of further features, in this case [+continuant] as well as [+strident].

Node   Any point in a tree from which one or more branches emanate.

Notational variant   When two sets of rules (grammars) have exactly the same output, i.e. they generate the same set of sentences, they are said to be notational variants.

Number   The grammatical contrast between singular and plural: e.g. *rabbit* (sing.), *rabbits* (plur.). This contrast is marked in both the noun and the verb: *the* **boy** **is** *laughing*, *the* **boys** **are** *laughing*.

Output   (1) The output of a component is the set of structures generated by the rules of that component or subcomponent. Thus the output of the transformational component is the infinite set of surface structures.

(2) The output of a rule is the structure obtained by applying that rule to a prior element or structure. Thus the output of the transformational rule of Reflexivization is a structure containing an NP marked with the syntactic feature [+reflexive].

Paradigm, Gap in paradigm   A paradigm is a set of forms or sentences illustrating a particular grammatical phenomenon. A gap occurs in such a paradigm if one sentence is ungrammatical although, if the rules of the grammar had been maximally general, it would have been grammatical. Illustrative sentences preceded by an * are typically examples of a gap in a paradigm.

Paraphrase   A sentence which expresses the same proposition (has the same meaning) as another sentence is a paraphrase of that sentence. e.g. *Heath sold a book to the queen* and *The queen bought a book from Heath*. Paraphrase is to sentences as synonymy is to lexical items.

Participial clause   A clause based on the present or past participial form of a verb. e.g. given a verb *detect* one can form the participles *detecting* and *detected* and use them as the basis of such clauses as:
Detecting a certain lack of sympathy, *John retired.*
Detected in his foul crime, *the miscreant surrendered.*

Particle   A word such as *up, back, down* which combines with a verb to form a separate lexical item: e.g. *look up, give back, put down.* Particles differ syntactically from prepositions among other ways in being separable from their associated verb. Compare:
He looked up the address $\sim$ *He looked the address up*
where *up* is a particle, with:
He looked up the stairs $\sim$ **He looked the stairs up*
where *up* is a preposition.

Passive, Passivization   A grammatical process which relates sentences of the active form 'NP$_1$ V NP$_2$' such as:
Harry admired the beautiful rainbow
to (passive) sentences of the form 'NP$_2$ was Ved by NP$_1$' such as:
The beautiful rainbow was admired by Harry.

The process involved is called the Passive transformation or Passivization.

Perceptual strategy When processing speech, people have recourse not only to the rules of their internalized grammar, but also to 'short cuts' which enable them to by-pass some of the complexity of the formal rules. Such short cuts are called *perceptual strategies* and can be illustrated by the example: 'Treat any sequence of *NP V (NP)* as a main clause'. This usually works, cf. *clear examples improve the style*, but when the strategy fails, as in: *Businessmen like secretaries are hard to find*, one has to have recourse to the rules of the grammar, and processing takes correspondingly longer.

Perfective have The verb *have* as used in *I have seen the Aga Khan*. The implication of the perfective is that the state or action described by the immediately following main verb is complete but still of current relevance.

Performance The use of language in speaking and understanding utterances is linguistic performance. Performance is dependent in part on one's linguistic knowledge (competence) and in part on non-linguistic knowledge of an encyclopedic or cultural kind, as well as on extraneous factors such as mood, tiredness, the ambient noise, and so on.

Person The grammatical contrast among first person – *I, we;* second person – *you;* and third person – *he, she, it, they*.

Phoneme, Phonemic representation Sounds which can signal the difference between possible pairs of lexical items in a language are phonemically distinct in, or phonemes of, that language. e.g. in English, /t/ and /k/ are phonemically distinct because of the minimal pair *toffee, coffee*. The same phoneme may have slightly different pronunciations in different environments: e.g. the *s*'s at the beginning and end of *sacks*, but such *allophonic* differences can never signal a difference in lexical item and hence are not phonemic.

A representation of pronunciation which includes only such distinctive information, without finer phonetic (allophonic) detail, is termed a *phonemic representation*.

Phonetic representation A representation of pronunciation which includes all the phonetic detail audible to the phonetician irrespective of whether the contrasts transcribed are phonemically distinctive or not.

Phonology The linguistic level which deals with the sound structure of the language and its relation to the syntax. The phonology or phonological component deals with all aspects of the sound system including the finest phonetic detail. However, 'phonological' is often used as a synonym for 'phonemic' (i.e. distinctive) representation in contrast to phonetic representation.

Phrase-structure rule (PS rule) A rule which specifies the constituency or internal make-up of a syntactic category. The statement that 'a sentence consists of a noun phrase followed by a verb phrase optionally followed by an adverb' would be formalized as the PS rule: S $\rightarrow$ NP VP (Adv).

A grammar consisting only of PS rules is a phrase structure grammar. Transformational grammarians claim that a PSG is a necessary but not sufficient component of an adequate grammar, and that transformations as well as phonological and semantic rules are needed as well.

Plosive Any sound articulated with an abruptly released closure, e.g. /p, t, k/ in English.

Post-alveolar Any consonant articulated with the tip of the tongue immediately behind the alveolar ridge or at the extreme back of the alveolar ridge. In English, /t/ has a post-alveolar allophone when immediately before /r/ as in *try*.

Postposition The equivalent of a preposition occurring after the NP rather than before it. e.g. the Hindi equivalent of *from Delhi* is *dilli se*, where *se* is a postposition meaning *from*. English uses postpositions in some temporal expressions: e.g. *a week* **ago**, *three days* **hence**.

Pragmatics Conditions affecting the appropriate use of language in communication. Pragmatics is one part of the field of linguistic performance.

Pragmatic implication Pragmatic implications are contrasted with semantic entailments. A semantic entailment follows logically from a sentence in isolation from any context; a pragmatic implication follows logically from an utterance together with the background knowledge shared by speaker and hearer in context.

Prepositional phrase A phrase consisting of an NP preceded by a preposition. e.g. in *the house*, at *the races*.

Presupposition The presupposition of a sentence is standardly defined as a necessary condition on that sentence's being either true or false. For example, he has been a smoker is said to be a presupposition of *he has given up smoking*, in the sense that one would not be inclined to assert *or* deny the latter unless the former were true.

Processing In language use the understanding of utterances which takes place by reference to rules of grammar and to performance strategies.

Progressive be The forms of the verb *be* as in *John is playing with his toes* are called progressive. The implication of the progressive is that the state or action described by the immediately following main verb is in progress at the time specified.

Proposition The semantic content of a sentence.

Q-Floating A transformation which removes a quantifier from its basic position in an NP and puts it elsewhere in a sentence. It thus relates *All the tentacles have dropped off* and *The tentacles have all dropped off*.

Quality (of a vowel) Vowels may be open (e.g. [a]) or close (e.g. [i, u]) or intermediate between these (e.g. [e, o]). They may be back (e.g. [u, o]) or front (e.g. [i, e]); pronounced with the lips spread (e.g. [i, e]) or rounded (e.g. [u, o]) etc. All such differences are referred to as differences of *quality*.

Quantifier Any element such as *all* (the universal quantifier), *some* (the existential quantifier), numerals, and so on, which specify the quantity of the rest of the NP modified by them.

Quantifier-floating, see **Q-Floating.**

Raise To take a constituent (usually an NP) from an embedded clause and insert it inside a higher clause in the same tree: e.g. *Tough-movement, Raising* (q.v.).

Raising A transformation which, in the context of a small number of predicates including *seem, appear*, raises the subject of an embedded clause to be the subject of the higher (superordinate) clause. The deep structure of *John seems to like pickles* is (i) which is transformed into the derived structure (ii):

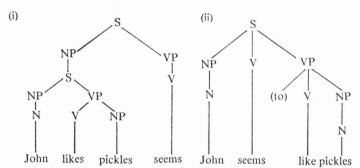

Redundancy rule   A lexical rule which states a generalization about a class of lexical items. e.g. all nouns which are [+human] – *boy, protestant, misogynist*, etc. – are also [+animate], so this latter feature can be omitted from individual lexical entries, provided a general statement is made that '[+human] → [+animate]', i.e. the presence in a lexical entry of the former feature entails the presence of the latter.

Reflexive pronoun, Reflexivization   A pronoun marked by *-self* or *-selves* which is coreferential with some antecedent NP in the same sentence is a reflexive pronoun. Reflexivization is a transformation which introduces such reflexive pronouns on the basis of their co-referentiality.

Register   A variety of speech characteristic of a particular occupational or social group: e.g. the language of law or the church. Register variation may consist of differences in vocabulary, pronunciation or choice of syntax.

Relevance   A remark P is relevant to a remark Q if P and Q, together with background knowledge, yield new information not derivable from either P or Q, together with background knowledge, alone.

Retroflex   A sound articulated with the tip of the tongue curled back towards or to touch the roof of the mouth. Retroflex sounds occur distinctively in many Indian languages and Indian speakers of English frequently replace English alveolar consonants with them.

Selectional restrictions Constraints on the combination of lexical items, designed to obviate the construction of anomalous sentences. e.g. *condescend* must have a human subject, as witness:
John condescended to see me. ∼ *?The bucket condescended to see me.*
Terrify must have an animate object, as witness:
I terrified my parents. ∼ *?I terrified my overcoat.*

Semantics The study of meaning.

Sentence The basic unit of grammar, taken to be a theoretical primitive. The sentence is a construct of competence, whereas the utterance is a construct of performance.

Standard language A dialect of a language which, for social or cultural – but not linguistic – reasons, has become institutionalized as the official medium for education, broadcasting, etc.

Strategy see (1) Learning strategy
(2) Perceptual strategy
(3) Comprehension strategy

Stress Greater loudness in the articulation of a syllable or word. Stress may be of varying degrees. The most heavily stressed syllable is said to have *primary* stress, except where the even louder contrastive stress is involved.

Strident A distinctive feature characterizing a class of sounds whose pronunciation involves more acoustic noise than non-strident sounds: e.g. /s, z, ʃ, ʒ, tʃ, dʒ/ in English.

String Any sequence of words.

Structural description, Structural change The input to a transformation defines the class of trees to which that transformation can apply. This input is called the *structural description*. The modification to the tree by the transformation is the *structural change*. Structural description and structural change are given in terms of syntactic categories and variables, marked off by hyphens and numbered from left to right. e.g. the transformation of Particle movement which relates such sentences as: *John gave back the book* and *John gave the book back* is formalized as:
S.D. X – V – Prt – NP – X
    1   2   3   4   5 → (S.C.) 1 2 4 3 5

Structure dependence   All grammatical rules operate on structures rather than simply on unstructured strings of words. Thus the rule of Passive permutes two NPs rather than, say, the first and third words of a sentence. No rule of any language could be of this latter form.

Subject   (1) *Surface subject*: that NP which controls such morphological processes as subject verb agreement, which normally occurs first in the sentence, etc.

(2) *Underlying* or *logical subject*: that NP immediately dominated by S in the underlying structure (of English). It normally has the semantic function of agent or instigator of a state or action.

Subordinate clause   Clauses embedded inside another S, either under the domination of NP or an adverbial, are subordinate to the main clause. e.g. the bracketed sections of:
I want [*John to go*].
I like her [*because she sings sweetly*].

Substantive universal   Any feature or category, phonological, syntactic or semantic, which is part of the vocabulary necessary and sufficient for the description of the world's languages.
e.g. the set of distinctive features: [nasal], [voiced], etc.
the set of syntactic features and categories: NP, [+N], [+Reflexive], etc.
the set of semantic features: [human], [physical object], etc.

Surface structure   The output of the transformational sub-component of the syntax, and the input to the phonological component. In some versions of transformational generative grammar, including that discussed here, surface structure is also available to rules of semantic interpretation.

Synonymy   Two words or sentences with the same meaning are synonyms. Two words which share one or more semantic features, or two sentences which share one or more entailments, are *partial synonyms*.

Tautology   Statements which are true in virtue of the laws of logic are tautologous: e.g. *If Bill is tall and fat, he is fat.*

There-insertion   A transformation which, by inserting *there* into specified tree structures, relates such sentences as: *A unicorn is nudging my elbow* and *There is a unicorn nudging my elbow.*

Tone language Any language, such as Chinese or Nupe, in which pitch variation serves to differentiate lexical items. e.g. in Nupe, *kpé* (on a high tone) means *to open*, while *kpe* (on a mid tone) means *to close*.

Topicalization A transformation which moves a constituent indefinitely far to the front of the sentence to produce such examples as: *The Weetabix, I suspect you told me not to eat* from: *I suspect you told me not to eat the Weetabix*.

Tough-movement A transformation which, in the context of a small number of predicates including *tough, hard, easy*, etc., raises the object of an embedded clause to be the subject of a higher clause, thereby relating such sentences as: *It is hard to lasso elephants* and *Elephants are hard to lasso*.

Transformation A grammatical rule which converts one tree into another. The set of transformations of a language convert *deep structures* to *surface structures*, and arguments for transformations can be viewed as arguments for two levels of representation within syntax.

Transitive verb A verb which requires an object: e.g. *scorn* in *I scorned his offer*. ∼ **I scorned*. By extension, a sentence containing such a verb is also called transitive.

Tree A diagrammatic representation of hierarchical constituent structure. Base trees are generated by phrase structure rules and then converted into derived trees by transformations.

Typology The study of the ways in which languages may differ from each other. For instance, in terms of word-order languages may be verb initial (Classical Arabic), verb medial (English) or verb final (Hindi). Typology is complementary to the study of universals.

Unacceptable see **Acceptable**.

Unbounded rule Any rule such as *Wh*-Movement, Topicalization, etc. which moves a constituent over an unlimited number of intervening S nodes: e.g. **The owl** *is believed to have been thought to be easy to catch* — *by the Incas*, where *the owl* has been topicalized from the position indicated by the dash.

Underlying structure An alternative term for *deep structure* (q.v.). It is also sometimes used to refer to any stage in a derivation prior to surface structure.

Ungrammatical see **Grammatical.**

Universal Linguistic theory has to provide mechanisms for the description of all languages. The vocabulary of elements or features used are *substantive* universals (q.v.); the framework of rules and their organization, e.g. that all languages require PS rules and transformations, are *formal* universals. Constraints on such rules, e.g. the impossibility of extracting items from coordinate structures, are *functional* universals. Universals which occur in every human language are *absolute* or strong universals; those which occur in the description of some but not all languages, and so need to be provided for by the theory, are *relative* or weak universals.

Utterance A string of words produced on a particular occasion. The study of utterances belongs to the study of performance. Utterances are acceptable or unacceptable and correspond only indirectly to sentences which are grammatical or ungrammatical.

Uvular Any sound articulated with contact between the uvula and the back of the tongue: e.g. the *r* in Parisian French or Northumberland English; the *q* in Classical Arabic, etc.

Variable In the structural description of a transformation a variable, usually represented by X, is an indication that the rule is applicable irrespective of what occurs in the position indicated by X, whether this be several clauses or nothing at all.

Velar Any sound articulated with contact between the velum (soft palate) and the tongue: e.g. /k, g, ŋ/ in English.

Voice A distinctive feature characterizing sounds articulated with concomitant vocal cord vibration.

Voice onset time (VOT) The moment at which voicing begins in the articulation of a syllable whose initial element may be 'voiced' or 'voiceless'. That is, /pa/ and /ba/ are distinguished not merely by the presence or absence of voice in the first element, but by the time that voicing commences. Given that the vowel is always voiced, even different articulations of /pa/ may have different VOTs. Infants appear to be innately sensitive to VOT.

Vowel harmony A situation in which all the vowels in a word have the same or a similar quality, or a process whereby such similarity is brought about by phonological rule. In Turkish all the vowels in a word must be back or front and all affixes added to such words must agree with the backness of the final vowel: e.g. adam – *man*, adam*lar* – men; dil – tongue, dil*ler* – tongues.

Wh-Movement A transformation which removes a constituent containing a *wh*-word (*who*, *what*, *which*, etc.) and places it at the beginning of a sentence. It thus derives: *Which piglet did the farmer say you were tickling?* from: *The farmer said you were tickling which piglet?*

Wh-question A question including a *wh*-word (*who*, *what*, *which*, *where*, etc): i.e. one which requires an answer providing specific information, so that the answers *yes* or *no* are always inappropriate. e.g. *Who did you see? John.*
Who did you see? * Yes.

Wh-word Any of a group of words which introduce questions and which are (mostly) spelt with an initial *wh*: *who, what, which, when, where, whether, whither, whence, why, how.*

Yes-no question A question which requires *yes* or *no* as an appropriate answer. e.g. *Did John come? – Yes.*
Are you bored? – No.

Abbreviatory Notations and Phonetic Symbols

Abbreviatory Notations

Adj – Adjective.
Adv – Adverb.
Art   – Article.
G   – Grammar.
N   – Noun.
NP – Noun Phrase.
O   – Object.
P   – Preposition.
PP – Prepositional Phrase.
Prt – Particle.
Q   – Quantifier.
S   – Sentence *or* Subject.
V   – Verb.
VP – Verb Phrase.
X   – Variable: used in the formulation of transformations to represent any sequence of categories at all, or nothing.
*   – Ungrammatical sentence.
?   – Semantically or pragmatically unacceptable utterance.
–   – Morpheme boundary *or* constituent boundary.
[ ] – Syntactic features are enclosed within square brackets and preceded by a + or −. These features may represent either inherent properties of the item concerned, as in [+N], or contextual properties as in [+ — NP]. In this latter case the dash indicates where the item concerned must occur: e.g. a verb such as *scorn* must occur *before* an NP.

     Labelled brackets as in : ₐᵣₜ [the] indicate the syntactic category membership – Article – of the item enclosed within them: in this case *the*.
Elements within (. . .) are optional.

Of elements within $\left\{\begin{smallmatrix} \cdot & \cdot & \cdot \\ \cdot & \cdot & \cdot \end{smallmatrix}\right\}$ either one or the other but not both must be selected.

→   – consists of.

Phonetic Symbols Used in the Text

Elements within /.../ represent phonemic sequences of Southern British English. These elements are:

p as in *p*at	l as in *l*et
t as in *t*en	j as in *y*es
k as in *k*in	iː as in b*ea*d
b as in *b*at	i as in b*i*d
d as in *d*en	e as in b*e*d
g as in *g*o	a as in b*a*d
tʃ as in *ch*in	ɑː as in b*ar*d
dʒ as in *g*in	ɔ as in b*o*dy
f as in *f*at	ɔː as in b*aw*dy
θ as in *th*in	u as in b*oo*k
s as in *s*in	uː as in b*oo*t
ʃ as in *sh*in	ʌ as in b*u*d
h as in *h*at	əː as in b*ir*d
v as in *v*at	ə as in *a*bove
ð as in *th*at	ei as in d*ay*
z as in *z*oo	ou as in b*oa*t
ʒ as in mea*s*ure	ai as in b*uy*
m as in *m*at	au as in c*ow*
n as in *n*o	ɔi as in b*oy*
ŋ as in si*ng*	iə as in b*eer*
w as in *w*et	ɛə as in b*ear*
r as in *r*ed	

Stress is indicated by an acute accent as in *abóve* or /əbʌ́v/, or by italicization of a word or phrase.

Rising pitch is indicated by ⟋

Falling pitch is indicated by ⟍

Elements within [...] represent phonetic sequences. In addition to those above, the following phonetic symbols are used:

superscript ʰ to indicate aspiration: pʰ, tʰ, kʰ, bʰ.

subscript ◡ to indicate a dental articulation: t̪, d̪, n̪.

superscript ˃ to indicate an unreleased stop: p̚˃, t̚˃.

superscript ˜ to indicate vowel nasalization: õ, ã.

superscript ⁻ to indicate vowel length: ī, ē, ā, ō, ū.

acute accent ′ to indicate high tone: pá.

grave accent ‵ to indicate low tone: pà.

ɛ to indicate a half-open front unrounded vowel – as in French belle.

ɔ to indicate a half-open back rounded vowel – as in French bonne.

æ to indicate a vowel intermediate between ɛ and a – as in pat.

ɑ to indicate a back fully open vowel – similar to that in father.

x to indicate a voiceless velar fricative – as in Bach.

ɫ to indicate a 'dark' (velarized) l – as in feel.

ɱ to indicate a labio-dental nasal – as in nymph.

V is used as a cover symbol for any vowel.

Further Reading

For full publication details of the works referred to here, see the Bibliography which follows.

Introduction

Noam Chomsky's first published book was Chomsky (1957), *Syntactic Structures*; it was based on a much longer work, published as Chomsky (1975a), *The Logical Structure of Linguistic Theory* (for some historical remarks, see particularly the (1975) Introduction to this work, which was originally written in 1955). The classic statement of Chomsky's views on language is Chomsky (1965), *Aspects of the Theory of Syntax*. Works which are relatively comprehensible to the layman include Chomsky (1968), *Language and Mind* (enlarged edition 1972), and Chomsky (1975b), *Reflections on Language*.

On the relations between language and mind, see Chomsky (1968), and Fodor (1975), *The Language of Thought*. For Locke's views on language, see Locke (1690), *An Essay concerning Human Understanding*, Book III. For Bloomfield's views, see Bloomfield (1933), *Language*. On the relations between linguistics and philosophy, see Hacking (1975), *Why Does Language Matter to Philosophy?*, especially Ch. 6.

For a historical survey of linguistics, see Lyons (1974), 'Linguistics'. For the historical antecedents of Chomsky's approach to language, see Grinder and Elgin (1973), *A Guide to Transformational Grammar*, especially Ch. 3. For the development of Chomsky's thought, see Grinder and Elgin (1973). A good overview of Chomskyan grammar is Huddleston (1976), *An Introduction to English Transformational Syntax*; see also Smith (1978), 'Syntax for Psychologists'.

1: What Is a Language?

p. 13 On communication, see Cherry (1957), *On Human Communication*. On animal communication, see Sebeok (1977), *How Animals Communicate*. On language and social systems, see Ardener (1971), *Social Anthropology and Language*, especially the editor's introduction, and Part III, pp. 209–41. See also Trudgill (1974a), *Sociolinguistics*.

p. 14 On linguistic rules, see Chomsky (1961), 'On the Notion "Rule of Grammar"'; Searle (1969), *Speech Acts*, Ch. 2, section 5; and Cooper (1975), *Knowledge of Language*, Ch. 3.

p. 15 On dialect differences, see Robins (1971), *General Linguistics: an Introductory Survey*, especially for the notion 'standard language'. For sociological implications, see Trudgill (1974a), or Trudgill (1974b), *The Social Differentiation of English*, a more technical account.

Example (5) from Alther (1976), *Kinflicks*.

p. 16 On linguistic habits and customs, see Skinner (1957), *Verbal Behavior*. See also Chomsky (1959), 'Review of Skinner'; Fodor, Bever and Garrett (1974), *The Psychology of Language*, especially pp. 148 ff.

On linguistic and other conventions, see Lewis (1969), *Convention: a Philosophical Study*.

On novelty in language, see Chomsky (1966), *Topics in the Theory of Generative Grammar*, especially p. 11 (for a somewhat exaggerated elaboration).

p. 17 Example (8) and other data in this section (pp. 17–19) from unpublished notes taken by Neil Smith. Any book on language acquisition provides a variety of further examples: see for example Brown (1973), *A First Language* (Penguin edn 1976); Clark and Clark (1977), *Psychology and Language*, especially part 4.

p. 19 Example (18) from Smith (1973), *The Acquisition of Phonology*, p. 172.

On aphasia, see Goodglass and Blumstein (eds.) (1973), *Psycholinguistics and Aphasia*; Lenneberg (1967), *The Biological Foundations of Language*.

p. 20 Example (21) from unpublished research notes taken by Neil Smith.

p. 21 On psychological reality, see Joan Bresnan (1978), 'A Realistic Transformational Grammar'.

On knowledge of language, see Chomsky (1965), *Aspects of the Theory of Syntax*, Ch. 1, section 1; Fodor (1975), *The Language of Thought*.

On unconscious knowledge, see Quine (1972), 'Methodological Reflections on Current Linguistic Theory'. For a reply to Quine, see Chomsky (1975b), *Reflections on Language*, Ch. 4. Cooper (1975), Chs. 4 and 7, contains further critical remarks.

p. 22 On memory and language, see Chafe (1977), 'The Recall and Verbalization of Past Experience', or Chafe (1973), 'Language and Memory'.

On linguistic analogies, see Bloomfield (1933), *Language*, especially p. 275. For a more recent view, see Derwing (1973), *Transformational Grammar as a Theory of Language Acquisition*, especially p. 310. See also Hockett (1968), *The State of the Art*, especially pp. 93ff; and for a reply, Lakoff (1969), 'Empiricism Without Facts' (a critical review of Hockett).

p. 24 On significant linguistic generalizations, see Chomsky (1965), Ch. 1.

For a statistical approach, see Hurford (1977), 'The Significance of Linguistic Generalizations'.

Reflexives have been repeatedly used to exemplify linguistic patterning: see for example Chomsky (1975a), *The Logical Structure of Linguistic Theory*, pp. 528ff, and any of the standard texts such as Huddleston (1976), Grinder and Elgin (1973), or Akmajian and Heny (1975), *An Introduction to the Principles of Transformational Syntax*.

p. 26 On historical change, see King (1969), *Historical Linguistics and Generative Grammar*; Kiparsky (1968), 'Linguistic Universals and Linguistic Change', pp. 171–202.

p. 27 On innateness, see Chomsky (1975b), Chs. 1, 2 and 4; Chomsky (1968) *Language and Mind*; Lenneberg (1967); Fodor (1975); Chomsky (1972a), especially 'Linguistics and Philosophy', pp. 161–94. See also Chomsky *et al.* in J. Searle (ed.) (1971), *The Philosophy of Language*, Ch. 7.

For critical views, see Derwing (1973), especially Ch. 3.5. See also Cooper (1972), 'Innateness: Old and New', and the reply by Chomsky (1975c), 'On Innateness: A Reply to Cooper'.

pp. 27–9 On universal properties of relative clauses, see Keenan and

Comrie (1977), 'Noun Phrase Accessibility and Universal Grammar', and Ross (1974), 'Excerpts from *Constraints on Variables in Syntax*' in Harman (ed.) *On Noam Chomsky: Critical Essays*, pp. 165–200; Peranteau, Levi and Phares (eds.) (1972), *The Chicago Which Hunt*.

p. 29 On language acquisition, see Clark and Clark (1977), especially pp. 348 ff.

p. 30 On the language of chimpanzees, see Aitchison (1976), *The Articulate Mammal*, especially Ch. 2, and Chomsky (1975b), Ch. 2.

2: Knowledge of Language

pp. 32–3 On linguistic versus non-linguistic knowledge, see Chomsky (1965), *Aspects of the Theory of Syntax*, Ch. 1; Chomsky (1975b), *Reflections on Language*, Ch. 1, especially pp. 20 ff, and Ch. 2; Clark and Clark (1977), *Psychology and Language*, Ch. 11.

p. 33 On the species-specificity of language, see Sampson (1975), *The Form of Language*, Ch. 6.

On language learning by observation and generalization, see Derwing (1973), *Transformational Grammar as a Theory of Language Acquisition*, for a recent extreme example. For a detailed refutation of such a view, see Fodor (1975), *The Language of Thought*.

On language learning by conditioning, see Skinner (1957), *Verbal Behavior*, and Chomsky (1959), 'Review of Skinner', for detailed criticism.

On language as a set of dispositions to behave, see Quine (1960), *Word and Object*, especially p. 33 and section 46; Ryle (1949), *The Concept of Mind*, especially Ch. 5; Cooper (1975), *Knowledge of Language*, Ch. 7.

p. 34 On genetic predisposition for language, see Lenneberg (1967), *The Biological Foundations of Language*.

On Genie's case, see Curtiss (1977), *Genie: A Psycholinguistic Study of a Modern-day 'Wild Child'*. See also Curtiss *et al.* (1974), 'The Linguistic Development of Genie'.

p. 35 On separating linguistic from non-linguistic knowledge, see Lakoff (1971a), 'Presuppositions and Relative Well-formedness', and Lakoff (1971b), 'The Role of Deduction in Grammar'. For criticism of Lakoff's views, see Katz and Bever (1976), 'The Fall and Rise of Empiricism'. See also Kempson (1975), *Presupposition and the Delimitation of Semantics*.

pp. 35–6 On human behaviour in general, including some linguistic aspects, see Pike (1954–60), *Language in Relation to a Unified Theory of the Structure of Human Behaviour*. See also Grice (1975), 'Logic and Conversation', for an account of the relation between language use and non-linguistic behaviour.

p. 37 On linguistic cues to social and regional origins, see Trudgill (1974a), *Sociolinguistics*, and Trudgill (1974b), *The Social Differentiation of English*.

On styles of speech, see Crystal and Davy (1969), *Investigating English Style*.

On figurative language, see Sperber (1975), *Rethinking Symbolism*, especially Chs. 4 and 5, and Sperber and Wilson (forthcoming), *The Interpretation of Utterances: Semantics, Pragmatics and Rhetoric*.

p. 38 On linguistic complexity, see Clark and Clark (1977), pp. 337 ff.; Miller and Chomsky (1963), 'Finitary Models of Language Users'; Chomsky (1975b), especially Ch. 3.

On intuitions, see Chomsky (1965), Ch. 1; Chomsky (1964), *Current Issues in Linguistic Theory*, Chs. 1 and 2; Chomsky (1966), *Topics in the Theory of Generative Grammar*, especially pp. 31 f. See also Chomsky (1972a), *Language and Mind*; Cooper (1975), Ch. 5. For a critique, see Derwing (1973), *Transformational Grammar as a Theory of Language Acquisition*, Chs. 7 and 8, and Sampson (1975), Ch. 4. For a general discussion see Harman (1973), review of Noam Chomsky's *Language and Mind*.

p. 39 On co-ordinate versus subordinate clauses, see Corum, Smith-Stark and Weiser (eds.) (1973), *You Take the High Node and I'll Take the Low Node*; Quirk *et al.* (1972), *A Grammar of Contemporary English*, especially Ch. 11.

p. 41 Example (10) is adapted from Bever (1974), 'The Psychology of Language and Structuralist Investigations of Nativism'.

p. 42 The strategy referred to is adapted from Bever (1970), 'The Cognitive Bases for Linguistic Structures'. See also Fodor, Bever and Garrett (1974), *The Psychology of Language*, Ch. 6, especially pp. 344–8. On perceptual strategies in general see

Fodor, Bever and Garrett (1974); Langendoen and Bever (1973), 'Can a not unhappy person be called a not sad one?'; and Grosu (1971), 'On Perceptual and Grammatical Constraints'.

p. 44 On competence and performance, see Chomsky (1965), Ch. 1, sections 1–4; King (1969), *Historical Linguistics and Generative Grammar*, pp. 8–16; Katz (1972), *Semantic Theory*, pp. 24–9; Fodor and Garrett (1966), 'Some Reflections on Competence and Performance'; Harman (1973), review of *Language and Mind*.

For criticisms of the distinction, see Lakoff (1973), 'Fuzzy Grammar and the Competence-performance Terminology Game'; Derwing (1973). For a reply, see Katz and Bever (1976). On grammaticality and acceptability, see Chomsky (1965), Ch. 1, section 2, and pp. 75–9, 148–53; Fillmore (1972), 'On Generativity'; Ruwet (1973), *An Introduction to Generative Grammar*, pp. 18–24.

p. 45 On performance models, see Miller and Chomsky (1963); Fromkin (1968), 'Speculations on Performance Models'; Kaplan (1972), 'ATNs as Psychological Models of Sentence Comprehension'; Miller and Johnson-Laird (1976), *Language and Perception*.

Little is known about production as opposed to perception, but see Clark and Clark (1977), Ch. 6; Fodor, Bever and Garrett (1974), Ch. 7; Forster (1974), 'Linguistic Structure and Sentence Production'; and Straight (1976), 'Comprehension versus Production in Linguistic Theory'.

On the distinction between sentence and utterance, see Lyons (1977), *Semantics*, Vol. 1, pp. 25 ff.; Huddleston (1976), *An Introduction to English Transformational Syntax*, pp. 2 ff.; Lemmon (1966), 'Sentences, Statements and Propositions'.

p. 46 On the complexity of self-embedded structures such as (21), see Fodor, Bever and Garrett (1974), Ch. 6.

p. 48 Those who have argued against the competence-performance distinction include Lakoff (1973); Lakoff and Thompson (1975a), 'Introducing Cognitive Grammar'; Lakoff and Thompson (1975b), 'Dative Questions in Cognitive Grammar'; Kaplan (1972); and Straight (1976).

3: Types of Linguistic Knowledge

p. 51 Good introductions are:
To semantics: Fodor (1977), *Semantics: Theories of Meaning in Generative Grammar*, and Kempson (1977), *Semantic Theory*.
To phonology: Hyman (1975), *Phonology: Theory and Analysis*.
To syntax: Bach (1974), *Syntactic Theory*.
On the lexicon, see Chomsky (1965), *Aspects of the Theory of Syntax*, Ch. 4, section 2; for a less technical account, see Huddleston (1976), *An Introduction to English Transformational Syntax*, Ch. 10; for an interesting critique, see Hudson (1976), 'Lexical Insertion in a Transformational Grammar'.

p. 52 On the pronunciation of British English see Gimson (1962), *An Introduction to the Pronunciation of English*. For the pronunciation of *r* as in (4b) see Gimson (1962), p. 204.

p. 54 On accidental gaps, see Chomsky (1964), *Current Issues in Linguistic Theory*, especially section 2.1, and Chomsky and Halle (1968), *The Sound Pattern of English*, especially Ch. 8, section 8.

p. 55 On word-formation, see Aronoff (1976), *Word Formation in Generative Grammar*; Marchand (1969), *The Categories and Types of Present-day English Word Formation*.

p. 56 For semantic constraints on word-formation, see Chomsky (1965), Ch. 1, especially footnote 15, p. 201. See also McCawley (1971), 'Prelexical Syntax'.

p. 57 On arbitrariness of sound-meaning correlation, see Lyons (1977), *Semantics*. Vol. 1, pp. 70 f.

p. 60 On agreement, see Robins (1971), *General Linguistics*, pp. 235 ff.

p. 61 On sentence-relatedness, see Burt (1971), *From Deep to Surface Structure*, especially p. 4, and Smith (1978), 'Syntax for Psychologists', pp. 16 f.
On paraphrase, see Katz (1972), *Semantic Theory*, examples on p. 5.

p. 63 On ambiguity, see Kempson (1977), *Semantic Theory*, Ch. 8.
On contradiction and anomaly, see Kempson (1975), *Presupposition and the Delimitation of Semantics*, Ch. 7, section 2, and Katz (1972), pp. 5–6.

p. 64 On tautology and analytic truth, see Katz (1972), Ch. 4.
On entailment, see Katz (1972), Ch. 4, section 5, and Fodor

(1977), *Semantics: Theories of Meaning in Generative Grammar*, Ch. 2, sections 4, 6.

On stress variation in English, see Gimson (1962), pp. 265 ff. On contrastive stress, see Ch. 7 below and Wilson and Sperber (1979), 'Ordered Entailments: An Alternative to Presuppositional Theories'.

p. 65　On tone and intonation, see Robins (1971), pp. 104 f. For the Nupe examples see Smith (1969), 'The Nupe Verb'.

p. 66　On interactions between syntax and phonology, see Pullum and Zwicky (forthcoming), *The Syntax-phonology Interface*. An explanation for the constraints on contraction phenomena in sentences similar to (50)–(55) was first suggested in King (1970) 'On Blocking the Rules for Contraction in English'.

p. 68　Counter-examples to the claim that syntactic rules do not need access to phonological information have been suggested by Zwicky (1969), 'Phonological Constraints in Syntactic Description'; Perlmutter (1971), *Deep and Surface Structure Constraints in Syntax*; and Hetzron (1972), 'Phonology in Syntax'. We find none of them very convincing (but see Ch. 6 below).

On the relation between syntax and semantics, see Jackendoff (1972), *Semantic Interpretation in Generative Grammar*, especially Ch. 1, and Seuren (ed.) (1974), *Semantic Syntax*.

p. 69　On the relation between semantics and phonology, see Ch. 7 below, and Wilson and Sperber (1979).

p. 71　On selection restrictions, see Chomsky (1965), pp. 113–15; McCawley (1968), 'The Role of Semantics in a Grammar'; Kempson (1977), Ch. 7, section 2; and Kuroda (1969), 'Remarks on Selectional Restrictions and Presuppositions'.

p. 74　On analytic truth and its putative non-existence, see Quine (1953), 'Two Dogmas of Empiricism' (first dogma). For a defence of the distinction, see Katz (1972), Chs. 4 and 6.

4: Formalizing Linguistic Knowledge

p. 75　The best introduction to the technical machinery of transformational grammar is Bach (1974), *Syntactic Theory*. See also Huddleston (1976), *An Introduction to English Transformational Syntax*; Ruwet (1973), *An Introduction to Generative Grammar*; and Keyser and Postal (1976), *Beginning English Grammar*.

On constituent structure, see Huddleston (1976), Chs. 3 and 4; Kimball (1973), *The Formal Theory of Grammar*, pp. 1–13; and Ruwet (1973), Ch. 3.

On syntactic features, see Chomsky (1965), *Aspects of the Theory of Syntax*, Ch. 2, and Huddleston (1976), Ch. 10.

p. 77 On arguing for constituent structure, see Akmajian and Heny (1975), *An Introduction to the Principles of Transformational Syntax*; and Chomsky (1957), *Syntactic Structures*, Ch. 5.

p. 80 On substantive universals, see Chomsky (1965), pp. 27–30 and 116–18; see also Bach (1974), Ch. 11.

p. 84 On the recursive power of phrase-structure rules, see Chomsky (1970b), 'Reply to Max Black'; Huddleston (1976), Ch. 7; and Keyser and Postal (1976), Ch. 14.

p. 85 On auxiliary verbs and their behaviour, see Pullum and Wilson (1977), 'Autonomous Syntax and the Analysis of Auxiliaries'. Criteria for identifying auxiliaries are given on pp. 742–3; the rest of the article argues that auxiliaries are merely a subclass of verbs.

p. 87 On the status of VP as a constituent, see Akmajian and Heny (1975), Ch. 7; McCawley (1970), 'English as a VSO Language'; and Keyser and Postal (1976), Ch. 27.

p. 89 For further details of this analysis of auxiliaries, see Pullum and Wilson (1977).

On filters, see Chomsky (1965), Ch. 3; Perlmutter (1971), *Deep and Surface Structure Constraints in Syntax*; and Chomsky and Lasnik (1977), 'Filters and Control'.

On transformations see the references at the beginning of this chapter.

p. 93 On quantifier floating, see Keyser and Postal (1976), Chs. 24 and 25.

On variables, see Bach (1974), p. 83.

p. 94 On types of transformation, see the references above, and Stockwell (1977), *Foundations of Syntactic Theory*.

On unbounded rules, see Ross (1967), *Constraints on Variables in Syntax*; Chomsky (1977), 'On Wh-Movement'; and Bresnan (1977), 'Variables in the Theory of Transformations'.

p. 98 On deep structure and surface structure, see Chomsky (1965), pp. 16–18, and any of the standard textbooks referred to above. Recently Chomsky has given up the term 'deep structure' in favour of the term 'initial phrase marker'; see Chomsky (1975b), *Reflections on Language*, pp. 80–81.

5: For and Against Deep Structure

p. 100 On arguments for deep structure, see Keyser and Postal (1976), *Beginning English Grammar*, Part 1; Smith (1978), 'Syntax for Psychologists'; and Huddleston (1976), *An Introduction to English Transformational Syntax*, especially Ch. 6.

On subject and object, both grammatical and logical, see Huddleston (1976), and Chomsky (1965), *Aspects of the Theory of Syntax*, especially p. 23. On traditional definitions of subject, see Jespersen (1924), *The Philosophy of Grammar*, Ch. 11.

p. 101 The claim that subject and object are not necessary 'labels' (theoretical primitives) in syntax is controversial. See the preface to, and the papers in, Cole and Sadock (eds.) (1977), *Syntax and Semantics 8: Grammatical Relations*.

p. 103 Sentences parallel to those in (7) and (8) first appear in Chomsky (1955), *The Logical Structure of Linguistic Theory*.

The notion of deep structure is implicit in Chomsky (1955); it is first made explicit in Chomsky (1965). For the historical antecedents of the term and the concept, see Chomsky (1965), pp. 198–200 (footnote 12 to Ch. 1).

p. 105 The term 'Tough-movement' is from Postal (1971), *Cross-over Phenomena*; see Ch. 3.

p. 106 For Extraposition, see Keyser and Postal (1976), Ch. 19. (The term is due to Jespersen.)

On tag-questions, see Akmajian and Heny (1975), *An Introduction to the Principles of Transformational Syntax*.

p. 107 On There-insertion, see Huddleston (1976), pp. 115 ff.

p. 109 On Raising, see Postal (1974), *On Raising*, pp. 369–74.

p. 112 On the distribution of NPs of the form found in sentences (33)–(46), see Chomsky (1970a), 'Remarks on Nominalization', pp. 202 ff.

p. 113 On the use of reflexives to justify deep structure, see Postal (1964), 'Underlying and Superficial Linguistic Structure'; Huddleston (1976), pp. 58 f.; and Smith (1978). The analysis goes back to Chomsky (1955).

p. 115 'Generative semanticist' refers mainly to Lakoff, Ross, McCawley, Seuren; see references to these authors in the Bibliography.

'Interpretive semanticist' refers to Chomsky (since 1967), Jackendoff, Emonds, etc. (see Bibliography).

p. 116 On lexical decomposition, see McCawley (1971), 'Prelexical Syntax'; Fodor (1970), 'Three reasons for not deriving *kill* from *cause to die*'; Lakoff (1972), 'Linguistics and Natural Logic', section VII; and Fodor, Fodor and Garrett (1975), 'On the Psychological Unreality of Semantic Representations'.

p. 120 On the treatment of passives in the lexicon, see Bresnan (1978), 'A Realistic Transformational Grammar'.

p. 121 On redundancy rules, see Chomsky (1965), pp. 164 ff.

p. 122 On problems with reflexives, see Jackendoff (1972), *Semantic Interpretation in Generative Grammar*, especially pp. 131 ff., and Lasnik (1976), 'Remarks on Coreference'.

6: Phonetics and Phonology

p. 125 The best introduction to phonology is Hyman (1975), *Phonology: Theory and Analysis*. The best introduction to phonetics is O'Connor (1973), *Phonetics*.

p. 126 On regional variation in the pronunciation of English, see Wells (1970), 'Local Accents in England and Wales'.

p. 127 On phonemes, allophones, free variation and complementary distribution, see O'Connor (1973) especially Ch. 6, and Hyman (1975).

p. 128 For the Athabaskan languages, see Hoijer *et al.* (1963), *Studies in the Athapaskan Languages*, especially the article by Howard.

For Dyirbal, see Dixon (1972), *The Dyirbal Language of North Queensland*.

For Hindi, see McGregor (1972), *Outline of Hindi Grammar*.

For the phonetics of French, see Armstrong (1932), *The Phonetics of French*.

p. 129 On distinctive features, see Hyman (1975), Ch. 2; Chomsky and Halle (1968), *The Sound Pattern of English*, Ch. 7. For an earlier, acoustically based version of distinctive feature theory, see Jakobson *et al.* (1951), *Preliminaries to Speech Analysis*. The features we use are taken from Chomsky and Halle (1968).

p. 130 On articulatory, acoustic and auditory phonetics, see O'Connor (1973).

p. 131 On the binary status of phonological distinctive features and the n-ary status of phonetic distinctive features. see Chomsky and Halle (1968), p. 297.

p. 132 On phonological rules, see Anderson (1974), *The Organization of Phonology*, Ch. 4; and Langacker (1972), *Fundamentals of Linguistic Analysis*, Ch. 4, section 3.

p. 133 On assimilation and other processes mentioned here, see Hyman (1975).

On consonant elision, see Gimson (1962), *An Introduction to the Pronunciation of English*.

p. 134 On stress assignment, see Chomsky and Halle (1968), Ch. 3.

p. 135 On metathesis, see Smith (1973), *The Acquisition of Phonology*, pp. 98 ff.

For the abstract /e/, see Chomsky and Halle (1968), pp. 146–8.

The abstractness controversy of which this is a small part is discussed at length in Kenstowicz and Kisseberth (1977), *Topics in Phonological Theory*.

p. 136 On naturalness in phonology, see Hyman (1975), Ch. 5; Hooper (1976), *An Introduction to Natural Generative Phonology*; and Chomsky and Halle (1968), Ch. 9.

p. 137 Languages with voiceless vowels include some of the Uto-Aztecan Languages of North America, see Pinnow (1964), *Die Nordamerikanischen Indianersprachen*, p. 42.

p. 139 On phonological units, see Chomsky and Halle (1968), p. 64; Hyman (1975), Ch. 6; and Smith (1973), Ch. 5, section 1.

The standard argument against the phoneme was given by Halle (1959), *The Sound Pattern of Russian*, and repeated in Chomsky (1964), 'Current Issues in Linguistic Theory', pp. 89 f.

p. 141 On slips of the tongue and their theoretical relevance, see Fromkin (1973), *Speech Errors as Linguistic Evidence*.

On tone and intonation, see Hyman (1975), Ch. 6.

p. 142 For the Nupe examples, see Smith (1969), 'The Nupe Verb'.

p. 143 For the nuclear stress rule, see Chomsky and Halle (1968), p. 17.

Bresnan's proposal is in Bresnan (1971), 'Sentence Stress and Syntactic Transformations'.

p. 145 On the genetic basis of auditory perception, see Cutting and Eimas (1975), 'Phonetic Feature Analyzers and the Processing of Speech in Infants'.

p. 146 On the speculation that the learning of phonology consists in inhibiting innate predispositions, see Stampe (1969), 'The Acquisition of Phonetic Representations'.

7: Semantics and Meaning

p. 149   For the distinction between sentence, statement and proposition, see Lemmon (1966), 'Sentences, Statements and Propositions'; and Katz (1972), *Semantic Theory*, Ch. 4, section 1.

p. 150   For the entailment theory of meaning, see Fodor (1977), *Semantics: Theories of Meaning in Generative Grammar*, Ch. 2, sections 4–6; and Kempson (1977), *Semantic Theory*, Ch. 3. For problems with the definition of synonymy, etc. see Quine (1953), 'Two Dogmas of Empiricism'. For further discussion, see Katz (1972), Chs. 1, 2, 4 and 6.

p. 158   For detailed discussion of ordered entailments, see Wilson and Sperber (1979), 'Ordered Entailments: An Alternative to Presuppositional Theories'.

p. 159   On the substitution of indefinite phrases for surface structure constituents, see Chomsky (1971), 'Deep Structure, Surface Structure and Semantic Interpretation', pp. 199–207.

p. 162   For further discussion of normal and heavy stress, see Schmerling (1974), 'A Re-examination of Normal Stress'.

p. 165   For further discussion of the notion of presupposition, see Wilson (1975), *Presuppositions and Non-truth-conditional Semantics*; Kempson (1975), *Presupposition and the Delimitation of Semantics*; and Gazdar (1976), *Formal Pragmatics for Natural Language: Implicature, Presupposition and Logical Form.*

p. 166   On the analysis of word-meaning, see Clark and Clark (1977), *Psychology and Language*, Chs. 11–14, and Fodor (1977), Ch. 5.

p. 171   On the relation between semantic rules, deep structure and surface structure, see Barbara Hall Partee (1971), 'On the Requirement that Transformations Preserve Meaning'; and Chomsky (1971). See also Jackendoff (1972), *Semantic Interpretation in a Generative Grammar.*

8: Pragmatics and Communication

p. 172   For a general discussion of pragmatic theory, see Sperber and Wilson (forthcoming), *The Interpretation of Utterances: Semantics, Pragmatics and Rhetoric*, on which much of the discussion in this chapter and the last is based. For a slightly different approach, see Gazdar (forthcoming), *Pragmatics*.

p. 175 On Grice's theory of pragmatics, see Grice (1975), 'Logic and Conversation'. For further discussion, see Gazdar (forthcoming); Wilson (1975), *Presuppositions and Non-truth-conditional Semantics*, Ch. 5; Kempson (1975), *Presupposition and the Delimitation of Semantics*, Chs. 7 and 8; and Harnish (1977), 'Logical Form and Implicature'.

p. 176 For a definition of relevance, see Sperber and Wilson (forthcoming).

p. 181 For further discussion of the pragmatic effects of semantic ordering, see Wilson and Sperber (1979), 'Ordered Entailments: An Alternative to Presuppositional Theories' and Sperber and Wilson (forthcoming).

9: Language Variation

On variation in general, see Labov (1972), *Sociolinguistic Patterns*; Trudgill (1974a), *Sociolinguistics*; Trudgill (1974b), *The Social Differentiation of English*; Fillmore (1972), 'On Generativity'; and Carden (1970), 'A Note on Conflicting Idiolects'.

p. 190 On free variation, see Chomsky (1959), review of Skinner; on free variation in phonology, see Hyman (1975), *Phonology: Theory and Analysis*, pp. 65–6.

p. 192 On stylistic variation, see Chomsky (1965), *Aspects of the Theory of Syntax*, pp. 10 f.; Jacobs (1973), *Studies in Language*, pp. 87 ff.

p. 193 On optional transformations, see Bach (1974), *Syntactic Theory*, p. 88.
On register variation, see Trudgill (1974a), p. 104; and Bolinger (1975), *Aspects of Language*, Ch. 11.

p. 196 On dialect, see Bolinger (1975), pp. 345 f.; and Robins (1971), *General Linguistics*, Ch. 2, section 2.

p. 197 On comprehension in general, see Clark and Clark (1977), *Psychology and Language*, part 2.

p. 198 For analogy, see the references to Ch. 1, p. 11, above.

p. 199 On bilingualism, see Bolinger (1975), pp. 419 ff.

p. 201 On metaphor, see Sperber and Wilson (forthcoming), *Pragmatics and Rhetoric: The Interpretation of Utterances*.

On word-formation, see Aronoff (1976), *Word Formation in Generative Grammar*.

p. 202 On the problem for transformational grammar of semi-productive processes, see Matthews (1974), *Morphology*, Ch. 12; and Dik (1967), 'Some Critical Remarks on the Treatment of Morphological Structure in Transformational-generative Grammar', especially pp. 370 ff.

p. 203 On language typology, see Greenberg (1963), 'Some Universals of Grammar with Particular Reference to the Order of Meaningful Elements'; Robins (1971), Ch. 8, section 2.

p. 204 On word-order typologies, see Pullum (1977), 'Word-order Universals and Grammatical Relations'. For Hixkaryana, see Derbyshire (1977), 'Word-order Universals and the Existence of OVS Languages'. For Apurinã, see Derbyshire and Pullum (1978), 'Object-Initial Languages'. For Malagasy, see Keenan (1976), 'Remarkable Subjects in Malagasy'.

p. 205 On French dialects, see Bauche (1951), *Le Langage populaire*.

p. 206 On Wh-Movement, see Chomsky (1977), 'On Wh-Movement'; and Bresnan (1977), 'Variables in the Theory of Transformations'.

For Circassian, see Colarusso (1976), 'An Instance of Unbounded Rightward Movement'. For Navajo, see Kaufman (1974), 'Navajo Spatial Enclitics: A Case for Unbounded Rightward Movement'. In Navajo the movement is of elements only some of which correspond to *wh*-words in English.

10: Language Change

On language change in general, see Bloomfield (1933), *Language*, Chs. 17–24; Bynon (1977), *Historical Linguistics*; and Weinreich *et al.* (1968), *Empirical Foundations for a Theory of Language Change*.

p. 208 On vowel alternations as in *obscene–obscenity*, see Chomsky and Halle (1968), *The Sound Pattern of English*.

p. 210 For consonant harmony, see Smith (1973), *The Acquisition of Phonology*, from which these examples are all taken.

p. 212 The child's perceptual ability is a matter of controversy; see Braine (1976), review of Smith (1973).

p. 213 On the acquisition of negation, see Clark and Clark (1977), *Psychology and Language*, pp. 348 ff., and references therein.

p. 214   For Genie, see Curtiss (1977), *Genie: A Psycholinguistic Study of a Modern-day 'Wild Child'*.

p. 215   On language loss, see Goodglass and Blumstein (1973), *Psycholinguistics and Aphasia*. Jakobson put forward his ideas on aphasia and language acquisition in Jakobson (1941), *Kindersprache, Aphasie und allgemeine Lautgesetze*.

These examples are taken from Meyerson and Goodglass (1972), 'Transformational Grammars of Three Agrammatic Patients'.

p. 217   The facts on Latin and Romance vowel systems are taken from Lausberg (1956), *Romanische Sprachwissenschaft*, Vol. 1. Comparable data can also be found in Elcock (1960), *The Romance Languages*.

On natural classes, see Hyman (1975), *Phonology: Theory and Analysis*, Ch. 5.

p. 220   On binary versus n-ary features, see Hyman (1975), pp. 55–7; Smith (1970), 'Bedik and Binarity'; and Ladefoged (1971), *Preliminaries to Linguistic Phonetics*.

p. 223   Our discussion of agreement in French has drawn heavily on Baxter (1974), *Some Aspects of Naturalness in Phonological Theory*.

p. 224   For rule inversion of the type illustrated in (30), see Vennemann (1972), 'Rule Inversion'.

p. 225   Example (32) is from Durand (1936), *Le genre grammatical en Français parlé à Paris et dans la région Parisienne*.

11: Evaluation of Grammars

On evaluation of grammars in general, see Chomsky (1964), *Current Issues in Linguistic Theory*, Ch. 2; Chomsky (1965), *Aspects of the Theory of Syntax*, Ch. 1, section 7; Postal (1972), 'The Best Theory'; and Chomsky (1957), *Syntactic Structures*, section 6.

p. 230   On primary linguistic data, see Chomsky (1964), section 1. In Chomsky (1965), Chomsky says explicitly that primary linguistic data are finite (p. 31). He was concerned here with the child's ability to construct a grammar on the basis of a finite set of heard utterances; however, there is also an interesting sense in which the primary data for the linguist are infinite sets of sentences. The two notions are distinct, but related.

p. 230 On observationally adequate grammars, see Chomsky (1964), section 2.

p. 233 On 'letting the grammar decide', see Chomsky (1957), p. 14.

p. 234 On objections to using intuitions, see Sampson (1975), *The Form of Language*, Ch. 4.

The examples in (4) and (5) are modified from Grosu (1971), 'On Perceptual and Grammatical Constraints', pp. 423 f.

p. 236 The principle of minimizing discontinuity is from Grosu (1971), p. 423.

p. 238 On descriptive adequacy, see Chomsky (1964), section 2; and Chomsky (1965), pp. 30–38.

p. 239 On the stress pattern of *telegraph – telegraphic*, see Chomsky (1964), p. 31; and Chomsky and Halle (1968), *The Sound Pattern of English*, pp. 11–12.

p. 240 On the relationship between syntax and phonology, see the references for Ch. 3 above.

p. 241 On constraints on rules of the type discussed here, see Ross (1967), *Constraints on Variables in Syntax*; and Chomsky (1973), 'Conditions on Transformations'.

p. 244 Example (18) is taken from Smith (1971), 'Syntactic Universals and African Languages'.

p. 245 On explanatory adequacy, see the references above, and Chomsky (1975b), *Reflections on Language*, Chs. 2 and 4; Chomsky (1972b), 'Some Empirical Issues in the Theory of Transformational Grammar', especially section 2.2.

p. 246 On the evaluation measure, see Chomsky (1965), Ch. 1, sections 6, 7.

Typical sceptics include Derwing (1973), *Transformational Grammar as a Theory of Language Acquisition*, p. 62 for example.

On notational variants, see Chomsky (1972b), section 5.

p. 247 For further remarks on simplicity, see Chomsky (1965), p. 37.

12: What is Language?

On Greenberg and universals, see references for Chs. 9 and 11 above. For universals within transformational grammar, see Bach (1974), *Syntactic Theory*, Ch. 11.

p. 252 These learning strategies are taken from Smith (1973), *The Acquisition of Phonology*, Ch. 4, section 3.

p. 253 For one such rare example, see Priestley (1977), 'One Idio-syncratic Strategy in the Acquisition of Phonology'.

On formal and functional universals, see Chomsky and Lasnik (1977), 'Filters and Control', p. 437, footnote 24.

p. 256 For the notion 'schematic imperative', see Bach (1965), 'On Some Recurrent Types of Transformations'.

p. 257 On the proliferation of 'universal' phonetic features, see Sampson (1974), 'Is There a Universal Phonetic Alphabet?'

On the use of any arbitrary set of PS rules, see Peters and Ritchie (1969), 'A Note on the Universal Base Hypothesis', and Peters and Ritchie (1973), 'On the Generative Power of Transformational Grammars'.

The literature on constraints is vast: the clearest survey is probably Chomsky (1976), 'Conditions on Rules of Grammar'.

p. 258 The example from Fe'Fe' is taken from Smith (1971), 'Syntactic Universals and African Languages'.

p. 260 On harmony and disharmony, see Greenberg (1963), 'Some Universals of Grammar with Particular Reference to the Order of Meaningful Elements', p. 97.

p. 261 On relative universals, see Chomsky (1977), 'On Wh-Movement'.

p. 264 One language which has word-order SOV and prepositions is Persian.

Bibliography

Aitchison, J. (1976), *The Articulate Mammal: An Introduction to Psycholinguistics*, Hutchinson.

Akmajian, A., and Heny, F. (1975), *An Introduction to the Principles of Transformational Syntax*, M.I.T. Press.

Alther, L. (1976), *Kinflicks*, Chatto & Windus.

Anderson, S. (1974), *The Organization of Phonology*, Academic Press.

Anderson, S., and Kiparsky, P. (eds.) (1973), *A Festschrift for Morris Halle*, Holt, Rinehart & Winston.

Ardener, E. (1971), 'Social Anthropology and Language' in Ardener, E. (ed.), *Social Anthropology and Language*, A.S.A. Monograph 10, Tavistock Publications, pp. ix–cii.

Ardener, E. (1971), 'Social Anthropology and the Historicity of Historical Linguistics' in Ardener, E. (ed.), *Social Anthropology and Language*, A.S.A. Monograph 10, Tavistock Publications, pp. 209–241.

Armstrong, L. E. (1932), *The Phonetics of French*, G. Bell & Sons.

Aronoff, M. (1976), *Word Formation in Generative Grammar*, M.I.T. Press.

Bach, E. (1965), 'On Some Recurrent Types of Transformations' in *Georgetown University Monograph Series on Languages and Linguistics*, 18, pp. 3–18.

Bach, E. (1974), *Syntactic Theory*, Holt, Rinehart & Winston.

Bach, E., and Harms, R. (eds.) (1968), *Universals in Linguistic Theory*, Holt, Rinehart & Winston.

Bauche, H. (1951), *Le Langage populaire*, Payot.

Baxter, A. R. W. (1974), *Some Aspects of Naturalness in Phonological Theory*, Oxford University B.Litt. thesis.

Bever, T. (1970), 'The Cognitive Basis for Linguistic Structure' in Hayes (ed.) (1970).

Bever, T. (1974), 'The Psychology of Language and Structuralist Investigations of Nativism' in Harman (ed.) (1974).

Bever, T., Katz, J., and Langendoen, T. (eds.) (1977), *An Integrated Theory of Linguistic Ability*, T. Y. Crowell.

Binnick, R., Davidson, A., Green, G., and Morgan, J. (eds.) (1969), *Papers from the Fifth Regional Meeting*, Chicago Linguistics Society.

Bloomfield, L. (1933), *Language*, Allen & Unwin.

Bolinger, D. (1975), *Aspects of Language* (2nd edn), Harcourt, Brace, Jovanovich.

Borger, R., and Cioffi, F. (eds.) (1970), *Explanation in the Behavioural Sciences*, Cambridge University Press.

Braine, M. D. S. (1976), review of Smith (1973), *Language*, 52, 489–98.

Bresnan, J. (1971), 'Sentence Stress and Syntactic Transformations', *Language*, 47, 257–81.

Bresnan, J. (1977), 'Variables in the Theory of Transformations' in Culicover *et al.* (eds.) (1977), pp. 157–96.

Bresnan, J. (1978), 'A Realistic Transformational Grammar' in Halle, M., Bresnan, J., and Miller, G. (eds.), *Linguistic Theory and Psychological Reality*, M.I.T. Press.

Brown, R. (1973), *A First Language*, Allen & Unwin; Penguin edition, 1976.

Burt, M. K. (1971), *From Deep to Surface Structure: An Introduction to Transformational Syntax*, Harper & Row.

Bynon, T. (1977), *Historical Linguistics*, Cambridge University Press.

Carden, G. (1970), 'A Note on Conflicting Idiolects', *Linguistic Inquiry*, 1, 281–90.

Chafe, W. (1973), 'Language and Memory', *Language*, 49, 261–81.

Chafe, W. (1977), 'The Recall and Verbalization of Past Experience' in Cole (ed.) (1977).

Cherry, C. (1957), *On Human Communication*, Science Editions, M.I.T.

Cherry, C. (ed.) (1974), *Pragmatic Aspects of Human Communication*, D. Reidel.

Chomsky, N. (1955), see Chomsky (1975a).

Chomsky, N. (1957), *Syntactic Structures*, Mouton.

Chomsky, N. (1959), review of Skinner (1957), *Language*, 35, 26–58.

Chomsky, N. (1961), 'On the Notion "Rule of Grammar"' in *Proceedings of XII Symposium in Applied Mathematics*, pp. 6–24. Reprinted in Fodor and Katz (eds.) (1964).

Chomsky, N. (1964), *Current Issues in Linguistic Theory*, Mouton.

Chomsky, N. (1965), *Aspects of the Theory of Syntax*, M.I.T. Press.

Chomsky, N. (1966), *Topics in the Theory of Generative Grammar*, Mouton.

Chomsky, N. (1968), *Language and Mind*, Harcourt, Brace, Jovanovich. Enlarged edition printed 1972.

Chomsky, N. (1970a), 'Remarks on Nominalization' in Jacobs and Rosenbaum (eds.) (1970), pp. 184–221.

Chomsky, N. (1970b), 'Reply' to Max Black, in Borger and Cioffi (eds.) (1970), pp. 462–70.

Chomsky, N. (1971), 'Deep Structure, Surface Structure and Semantic Interpretation' in Steinberg and Jakobovits (eds.) (1971), pp. 199–207.

Chomsky, N. (1972a), see Chomsky (1968).

Chomsky, N. (1972b), 'Some Empirical Issues in the Theory of Transformational Grammar' in Peters (ed.) (1972), pp. 63–130.

Chomsky, N. (1973), 'Conditions on Transformations' in Anderson and Kiparsky (eds.) (1973), pp. 232–86.

Chomsky, N. (1975a), *The Logical Structure of Linguistic Theory*, Plenum. Introduction (1975) to the original written in 1955.

Chomsky, N. (1975b), *Reflections on Language*, Temple Smith.

Chomsky, N. (1975c), 'On Innateness: A Reply to Cooper', *Philosophical Review*, 84, 70–87.

Chomsky, N. (1976), 'Conditions on Rules of Grammar', *Linguistic Analysis*, 2, 303–51. Also in Cole (ed.) (1977).

Chomsky, N. (1977), 'On Wh-Movement' in Culicover *et al.* (eds) (1977), pp. 71–132.

Chomsky, N., and Halle, M. (1968), *The Sound Pattern of English*, Harper & Row.

Chomsky, N., and Lasnik, H. (1977), 'Filters and Control', *Linguistic Inquiry*, 8, 425–504.

Clark, H., and Clark, E. (1977), *Psychology and Language*, Harcourt, Brace, Jovanovich.

Colarusso, J. (1976), 'An Instance of Unbounded Rightward Movement: Wh-Movement in Circassian', unpublished mimeo, University of Vienna.

Cole, P., and Morgan, J. (eds.) (1975), *Syntax and Semantics 3: Speech Acts*, Academic Press.

Cole, P., and Sadock, J. (eds.) (1977), *Syntax and Semantics 8: Grammatical Relations*, Academic Press.

Cole, R. W. (ed.) (1977), *Current Issues in Linguistic Theory*, Indiana University Press.

Cooper, D. E. (1972), 'Innateness: Old and New', *Philosophical Review*, 81, 465–83.

Cooper, D. E. (1975), *Knowledge of Language*, Prism Press.

Corum, C., Smith-Stark, T., and Weiser, A. (eds.) (1973), *You Take the High Node and I'll Take the Low Node*, papers from the Comparative Syntax Festival, Chicago Linguistics Society. The differences between main and subordinate clauses. A paravolume to *Papers from the Ninth Regional Meeting*.

Crystal, D., and Davy, D. (1969), *Investigating English Style*, Longman.

Culicover, P., Wasow, T., and Akmajian, A. (eds.) (1977), *Formal Syntax*, Academic Press.

Curtiss, S. (1977), *Genie: A Psycholinguistic Study of a Modern-day 'Wild Child'*, Academic Press.

Curtiss, S., Fromkin, V., Krashen, S., Rigler, D., and Rigler, M. (1974), 'The Linguistic Development of Genie', *Language*, 50, 528–54.

Cutting, J., and Eimas, P. (1975), 'Phonetic Feature Analyzers and the Processing of Speech in Infants' in Kavanagh and Cutting (eds.) (1975), pp. 127–48.

Davidson, D., and Harman, G. (eds.) (1972), *Semantics of Natural Language*, D. Reidel.

Derbyshire, D. (1977), 'Word Order Universals and the Existence of OVS Languages', *Linguistic Inquiry*, 8, 590–98.

Derbyshire, D., and Pullum, G. (1978), 'Object-Initial Languages'. Paper presented at the fortieth Summer Meeting, Linguistic Society of America.

Derwing, B. (1973), *Transformational Grammar as a Theory of Language Acquisition*, Cambridge University Press.

Dik, S. C. (1967), 'Some Critical Remarks on the Treatment of Morphological Structure in Transformational Generative Grammar', *Lingua*, 18, 352–83.

Dixon, R. (1972), *The Dyirbal Language of North Queensland*, Cambridge University Press.

Durand, M. (1936), *Le Genre Grammatical en Français parlé à Paris et dans la région Parisienne*, D'Arbey.

Elcock, W. D. (1960), *The Romance Languages*, Faber & Faber.

Emonds, J. (1976), *A Transformational Approach to English Syntax*, Academic Press.

Fillmore, C. (1972), 'On Generativity' in Peters (ed.) (1972), pp. 1–19.

Fillmore, C., and Langendoen, T. (1971), *Studies in Linguistic Semantics*, Holt, Rinehart & Winston.

Fodor, J. (1970), 'Three reasons for not deriving *kill* from *cause to die*', *Linguistic Inquiry*, 1, 429–38.

Fodor, J. (1975), *The Language of Thought*, T. Y. Crowell.

Fodor, J., Bever, T., and Garrett, M. (1974), *The Psychology of Language*, McGraw-Hill.

Fodor, J., Fodor, J. D., and Garrett, M. (1975), 'On the Psychological Unreality of Semantic Representations', *Linguistic Inquiry*, 6, 4.

Fodor, J., and Garrett, M. (1966), 'Some Reflections on Competence and Performance' in Lyons and Wales (eds.) (1966).

Fodor, J., and Katz, J. (eds.) (1964), *The Structure of Language*, Prentice-Hall.

Fodor, J. D. (1977), *Semantics: Theories of Meaning in Generative Grammar*, T. Y. Crowell.

Forster, K. (1974), 'Linguistic Structure and Sentence Production' in Cherry (ed.) (1974).

Fromkin, V. (1968), 'Speculations on Performance Models', *Journal of Linguistics*, 4, 47–68.

Fromkin, V. (ed.) (1973), *Speech Errors as Linguistic Evidence*, Mouton.

Gazdar, Gerald (1976), *Formal Pragmatics for Natural Language: Implicature, Presupposition and Logical Form*, unpublished Ph.D. thesis, University of Reading.

Gazdar, Gerald (forthcoming), *Pragmatics*, Academic Press.

Gimson, A. (1962), *An Introduction to the Pronunciation of English*, Edward Arnold.

Goodglass, H., and Blumstein, S. (eds.) (1973), *Psycholinguistics and Aphasia*, Baltimore.

Greenberg, J. (1963), 'Some Universals of Grammar with Particular Reference to the Order of Meaningful Elements' in Greenberg, J. (ed.), *Universals of Language*, M.I.T. Press.

Grice, H. P. (1975), 'Logic and Conversation' in Cole and Morgan (eds.) (1975).

Grinder, J., and Elgin, S. (1973), *A Guide to Transformational Grammar: History, Theory, Practice*, Holt, Rinehart & Winston.

Grosu, A. (1971), 'On Perceptual and Grammatical Constraints' in *Papers from the Seventh Regional Meeting*, Chicago Linguistic Society.

Hacking, I. (1975), *Why Does Language Matter to Philosophy?*, Cambridge University Press.

Halle, M. (1959), *The Sound Pattern of Russian*, Mouton.

Harman, G. (1973), review of Chomsky's *Language and Mind*, *Language*, 49, 453–64. Also in Harman, G. (ed.) (1974).

Harman, G. (ed.) (1974), *On Noam Chomsky: Critical Essays*, Anchor.

Harnish, R. M. (1977), 'Logical Form and Implicature' in Bever, Katz and Langendoen (eds.) (1976).

Hayes, J. R. (ed.) (1970), *Cognition and the Development of Language*, Wiley.

Hetzron, R. (1972), 'Phonology in Syntax', *Journal of Linguistics*, 8, 251–65.

Hockett, C. F. (1968), *The State of the Art*, Mouton.

Hoijer, H., *et al.* (1963), *Studies in the Athapaskan Languages*, University of California Publications in Linguistics, Vol. 29.

Hooper, J. (1976), *An Introduction to Natural Generative Phonology*, Academic Press.

Howard, P. (1963), 'A Preliminary Presentation of Slave Phonemes' in Hoijer *et al.* (1963), pp. 42–7.

Huddleston, R. (1976), *An Introduction to English Transformational Syntax*, Longman.

Hudson, R. (1976), 'Lexical Insertion in a Transformational Grammar', *Foundations of Language*, 14, 89–107.

Hurford, J. (1977), 'The Significance of Linguistic Generalisations', *Language*, 53, 574–620.

Hyman, L. (1975), *Phonology: Theory and Analysis*, Holt Rinehart & Winston.

Jackendoff, R. (1972), *Semantic Interpretation in Generative Grammar*, M.I.T. Press.

Jacobs, R. A. (1973), *Studies in Language*, Xerox College Publishing.

Jacobs, R., and Rosenbaum, P. (1970), *Readings in English Transformational Grammar*, Ginn & Co.

Jakobson, R. (1941), *Kindersprache, Aphasie und allgemeine Lautgesetze*, Uppsala, Almqvist & Wiksell. English translation A. Keiler (1968), *Child Language, Aphasia and Phonological Universals*, Mouton.

Jakobson, R., Fant, G., and Halle, M. (1951), *Preliminaries to Speech Analysis*, M.I.T. Press.

Jespersen, O. (1924), *The Philosophy of Grammar*, Allen & Unwin.

Joos, M. (1962), *The Five Clocks*, International Journal of American Linguistics, Vol. 28, No. 2, Part V.

Kaplan, R. (1972), 'ATNs as Psychological Models of Sentence Comprehension', *Artificial Intelligence*, 3, 77–100.

Katz, J. (1972), *Semantic Theory*, Harper & Row.

Katz, J., and Bever, T. (1976), 'The Fall and Rise of Empiricism' in Bever, Katz and Langendoen (eds.) (1977).

Kaufman, E. S. (1974), 'Navajo Spatial Enclitics: A Case for Unbounded Rightward Movement', *Linguistic Inquiry*, 5, 507–33.

Kavanagh, J., and Cutting, J. (eds.) (1975), *The Role of Speech in Language*, M.I.T. Press.

Keenan, E. (1976), 'Remarkable Subjects in Malagasy' in Li, C. (ed.), *Subject and Topic*, Academic Press.

Keenan, E., and Comrie, B. (1977), 'Noun Phrase Accessibility and Universal Grammar', *Linguistic Inquiry*, 8, 63–99.

Kempson, R. (1975), *Presupposition and the Delimitation of Semantics*, Cambridge University Press.

Kempson, R. (1977), *Semantic Theory*, Cambridge University Press.

Kenstowicz, M., and Kisseberth, C. (1977), *Topics in Phonological Theory*, Academic Press.

Keyser, S. J., and Postal, P. (1976), *Beginning English Grammar*, Harper & Row.

Kiefer, F. (ed.) (1969), *Studies in Syntax and Semantics*, D. Reidel.

Kimball, J. (1973), *The Formal Theory of Grammar*, Prentice-Hall.

King, H. (1970), 'On Blocking the Rules for Contraction in English', *Linguistic Inquiry*, 1, 134–6.

King, R. (1969), *Historical Linguistics and Generative Grammar*, Prentice-Hall.

Kiparsky, P. (1968), 'Linguistic Universals and Linguistic Change' in Bach and Harms (eds.) (1968).

Kuroda, S.-Y. (1969), 'Remarks on Selectional Restrictions and Presuppositions' in Kiefer (ed.) (1969).

Labov, W. (1972) (U.K. edition 1978), *Sociolinguistic Patterns*, Blackwell.

Ladefoged, P. (1971), *Preliminaries to Linguistic Phonetics*, University of Chicago Press.

Lakoff, G. (1969), 'Empiricism Without Facts', *Foundations of Language*, 5, review of Hockett (1968).

Lakoff, G. (1970), *Irregularity in Syntax*, Holt, Rinehart & Winston.

Lakoff, G. (1971a), 'Presuppositions and Relative Well-formedness' in Steinberg and Jakobovits (eds.) (1971).

Lakoff, G. (1971b), 'The Role of Deduction in Grammar' in Fillmore and Langendoen (eds.) (1971).

Lakoff, G. (1972), 'Linguistics and Natural Logic' in Davidson and Harman (eds.) (1972), pp. 545–665.

Lakoff, G. (1973), 'Fuzzy Grammar and the Competence-performance

Terminology Game' in *Papers from the Ninth Regional Meeting*, Chicago Linguistic Society.

Lakoff, G., and Thompson, H. (1975a), 'Introducing Cognitive Grammar' in *Proceedings of the First Annual Meeting of the Berkeley Linguistics Society*, pp. 295–313.

Lakoff, G., and Thompson, H. (1975b), 'Dative Questions in Cognitive Grammar' in *Papers from the Parasession on Functionalism*, Chicago Linguistics Society, pp. 337–50.

Langacker, R. (1972), *Fundamentals of Linguistic Analysis*, Harcourt, Brace, Jovanovich.

Langendoen, T., and Bever, T. (1973), 'Can a not unhappy person be called a not sad one?' in Anderson and Kiparsky (eds.) (1973).

Lasnik, H. (1976), 'Remarks on Coreference', *Linguistic Analysis*, 2, 1–22.

Lausberg, H. (1956), *Romanische Sprachwissenschaft*, 2 vols., Walter de Gruyter & Co.

Lemmon, E. J. (1966), 'Sentences, Statements and Propositions' in Williams, B., and Montefiore, A. (eds.) (1966).

Lenneberg, E. (1967), *Biological Foundations of Language*, Wiley.

Lewis, D. (1969), *Convention: a Philosophical Study*, Harvard University Press.

Locke, J. (1690), *An Essay Concerning Human Understanding*.

Luce, R., Bush, R., and Galanter, E. (eds.) (1963), *Handbook of Mathematical Psychology*, Vol. 2, Wiley.

Lyons, J. (1974), 'Linguistics' in *Encyclopaedia Britannica*, Vol. 10, pp. 992–1013.

Lyons, J. (1977), *Semantics*, 2 vols., Cambridge University Press.

Lyons, J., and Wales, R. (1966), *Psycholinguistic Papers*, Edinburgh University Press.

Marchand, H. (1969), *The Categories and Types of Present-day English Word-Formation* (2nd edn), München, Beck.

Matthews, P. (1974), *Morphology*, Cambridge University Press.

McCawley, J. (1968), 'The Role of Semantics in a Grammar' in Bach and Harms (eds.) (1968).

McCawley, J. (1970), 'English as a VSO Language', *Language*, 46, 286–99. Reprinted in Seuren (ed.) (1974).

McCawley, J. (1971), 'Prelexical Syntax' in O'Brien (ed.) (1971), pp. 19–33. Reprinted in Seuren (ed.) (1974).

McGregor, R. S. (1972), *Outline of Hindi Grammar*, Clarendon Press.

Meyerson, R., and Goodglass, H. (1972), 'Transformational Grammars of Three Agrammatic Patients', *Language and Speech*, 15.

Miller, G., and Chomsky, N. (1963), 'Finitary Models of Language Users' in Luce *et al.* (eds.) (1963).

Miller, G., and Johnson-Laird, P. (1976), *Language and Perception*, Cambridge University Press.

O'Brien, R. (ed.) (1971), *Report of the 22nd Annual Round Table Meeting on Linguistics and Language Studies*, Georgetown University Press, Washington.

O'Connor, J. D. (1973), *Phonetics*, Penguin.

Oh, C.-K., and Dinneen, D. (eds.) (1979), *Syntax and Semantics 11: Presuppositions*, Academic Press.

Partee, B. H. (1971), 'On the Requirement that Transformations Preserve Meaning' in Fillmore and Langendoen (eds.) (1971).

Peranteau, P., Levi, J., and Phares, G. (eds.) (1972), *The Chicago Which Hunt*, papers from the Relative Clause Festival, Chicago Linguistics Society. A paravolume to *Papers from the Eighth Regional Meeting*.

Perlmutter, D. (1971), *Deep and Surface Structure Constraints in Syntax*, Holt, Rinehart & Winston.

Peters, S. (ed.) (1972), *Goals of Linguistic Theory*, Prentice-Hall.

Peters, S., and Ritchie, R. W. (1969), 'A Note on the Universal Base Hypothesis', *Journal of Linguistics*, 5, 150–52.

Peters, S., and Ritchie, R. W. (1973), 'On the Generative Power of Transformational Grammars', *Information Sciences*, 6, 49–83.

Pike, K. (1954–60), *Language in Relation to a Unified Theory of the Structure of Human Behaviour*, Glendale.

Pinnow, H.-J. (1964), *Die Nordamerikanischen Indianersprachen*, Harrassowitz.

Postal, P. (1964), 'Underlying and Superficial Linguistic Structure', *Harvard Educational Review*, 34, 246–66.

Postal, P. (1971), *Cross-over Phenomena*, Holt, Rinehart & Winston.

Postal, P. (1972), 'The Best Theory' in Peters (ed.) (1972).

Postal, P. (1974), *On Raising*, M.I.T. Press.

Priestley, T. M. S. (1977), 'One Idiosyncratic Strategy in the Acquisition of Phonology', *Journal of Child Language*, 4, 45–66.

Pullum, G. (1977), 'Word Order Universals and Grammatical Relations' in Cole and Sadock (eds.) (1977).

Pullum, G., and Wilson, D. (1977), 'Autonomous Syntax and the Analysis of Auxiliaries', *Language*, 53, 741–88.

Pullum, G., and Zwicky, A. (forthcoming), *The Syntax-Phonology Interface*, Academic Press.

Quine, W. (1953), *From a Logical Point of View*, Harvard University Press.

Quine, W. (1960), *Word and Object*, M.I.T. Press.

Quine, W. (1972), 'Methodological Reflections on Current Linguistic Theory' in Davidson and Harman (eds.) (1972).

Quirk, R., Greenbaum, S., Leech, G., and Svartvik, J. (1972), *A Grammar of Contemporary English*, Longman.

Robins, R. (1971), *General Linguistics*, Longman.

Ross, J. R. (1967), *Constraints on Variables in Syntax*, Ph.D. thesis, M.I.T. Excerpts appear as Ross (1974) in Harman (ed.) (1974).

Ross, J. R. (1974), 'Excerpts from *Constraints on Variables in Syntax*' in Harman (ed.) (1974).

Ruwet, N. (1973), *An Introduction to Generative Grammar*, English translation by Norval S. H. Smith, North-Holland.

Ryle, G. (1949), *The Concept of Mind*, Hutchinson.

Sampson, G. (1974), 'Is there a universal phonetic alphabet?', *Language*, 50, 236–259.

Sampson, G. (1975), *The Form of Language*, Weidenfeld & Nicolson.

Schmerling, S. F. (1974), 'A Re-examination of Normal Stress', *Language*, 50, 66–73.

Searle, J. (1969), *Speech Acts*, Cambridge University Press.

Searle, J. (ed.) (1971), *The Philosophy of Language*, Oxford University Press.

Sebeok, T. (1977), *How Animals Communicate*, Indiana University Press.

Seuren, P. (ed.) (1974), *Semantic Syntax*, Oxford University Press.

Skinner, B. F. (1957), *Verbal Behavior*, Appleton Century Crofts.

Smith, N. V. (1969), 'The Nupe Verb', *African Language Studies*, 10, 90–160.

Smith, N. V. (1970), 'Bedik and Binarity', *African Language Review*, 9, 90–98.

Smith, N. V. (1971), 'Syntactic Universals and African Languages', unpublished mimeo, School of Oriental and African Studies.

Smith, N. V. (1973), *The Acquisition of Phonology*, Cambridge University Press.

Smith, N. V. (1978), 'Syntax for Psychologists' in Morton, J., and Marshall, J. (eds.), *Psycholinguistics Series*, Vol. 2, Elek.

Sperber, D. (1975), *Rethinking Symbolism*, Cambridge University Press.

Sperber, D., and Wilson, D. (forthcoming), *The Interpretation of Utterances: Semantics, Pragmatics and Rhetoric.*

Stampe, D. (1969), 'The Acquisition of Phonetic Representations' in Binnick *et al.* (eds.) (1969), pp. 443–54.

Steinberg, D., and Jakobovits, L. (eds.) (1971), *Semantics*, Cambridge University Press.

Stockwell, R. P. (1977), *Foundations of Syntactic Theory*, Prentice-Hall.

Straight, H. S. (1976), 'Comprehension versus Production in Linguistic Theory', *Foundations of Language*, 14, 525–40.

Trudgill, P. (1974a), *Sociolinguistics*, Penguin.

Trudgill, P. (1974b), *The Social Differentiation of English*, Cambridge University Press.

Vennemann, T. (1972), 'Rule Inversion', *Lingua*, 29, 209–42.

Weinreich, U., Labov, W., and Herzog, M. (1968), 'Empirical Foundations for a Theory of Language Change' in Lehmann, W., and Malkiel, Y. (eds.) (1968), *Directions for Historical Linguistics*, Texas University Press.

Wells, J. (1970), 'Local Accents in England and Wales', *Journal of Linguistics*, 6, 321–52.

Williams, B., and Montefiore, A. (eds.) (1966), *British Analytical Philosophy*, Routledge & Kegan Paul.

Wilson, D. (1975), *Presuppositions and Non-truth-conditional Semantics*, Academic Press.

Wilson, D., and Sperber, D. (1979), 'Ordered Entailments: An Alternative to Presuppositional Theories' in Oh, C.-K., and Dinneen, D. (eds.) (1979).

Zwicky, A. (1969), 'Phonological Constraints in Syntactic Description', *Papers in Linguistics*, 1, 411–63.

Index

P 121.S58
ledl,circ
Modern linguistics :

C.1

3 1862 004 384 802
University of Windsor Libraries

DATE DUE

MAR 0 5 1992
RETURNED

RETURNED
FEB 8 1993
RETURNED

RETURNED

JAN 3 0 2006
RETURNED

NOV 1 5 2006
RETURNED